Creating Learning Environments

The Behavioral Approach to Education

Therese M. Herman

Bard College
Montclair State College

Allyn and Bacon, Inc.
Boston, London, Sydney

Copyright © 1977 by Allyn and Bacon, Inc.
470 Atlantic Avenue, Boston, Massachusetts 02210.

Library of Congress Cataloging in Publication Data

Herman, Therese M   1940–
    Creating learning environments.

    Bibliography: p.
    Includes index.
    1. Educational psychology.   2. Behaviorism (Psychology) I. Title.
LB1051.H436   370.15   76–25070

ISBN 0–205–05591–5 (hardbound)
ISBN 0–205–05567–2 (paperbound)

TO PETER SISSONS

Contents

Preface

By applying the principles of conditioning to learning, behaviorists have become one of the strongest influences in contemporary Western education. This book takes a look at behaviorism, its hopes for education, and its applications in our schools today.

It is hoped that this book will help you become acquainted with behaviorist solutions to the problems of education. It is first of all, a practical book. In it, we look at strategies for solving pressing real-life and everyday problems in the classroom. In the first two chapters we examine the general principles of conditioning that underlie behaviorist educational psychology, where the theory has come from, and the kind of evidence it uses to back it up. In the remaining chapters, we explore how to apply these principles, using behaviorism to solve the problems that teachers face—choosing learning goals, planning lessons, testing, grading, dealing with special learners, and maintaining discipline. In each of these chapters are presented current behaviorist approaches to each particular educational problem, lists of step-by-step procedures for putting these strategies into practice in your own classroom, and an examination of the research that has been done to test just how good these strategies are.

Each chapter is designed as a practical demonstration of the learning principles of behaviorism that you are reading about. Therefore, each chapter:

- begins by letting you know its *behavioral goals* which tell you specifically what behaviors you can expect to have achieved at the successful completion of the chapter;
- tells you how your learning of the behavioral goals will be *evaluated* throughout the chapter;
- breaks material up into *small, progressive units of learning;*
- gives you the opportunity to receive frequent positive reinforcement and feedback in relation to your learning achievements by providing *progress checks* for each behavioral goal interspersed throughout the text.

A variety of different test formats have been used to acquaint you with those commonly used in education today. You will conveniently find the appropriate *answers to progress checks* in a special section on pages 265–274.

Ideally, the use of behaviorist principles should result in a tremendous increase in student and teacher enthusiasm, rapid gains in learning, a radical drop in discipline problems and boredom, and the emergence of workable answers for students' special needs whether they are related to cultural, social, economic, or physiological forces. Despite the fact that behaviorism is often successful, it can, at times, fail. Some people believe that these failures show a need for further refinements and improvements in the applications of behaviorism, though fundamentally it is still the most dynamic revolution to take place in our schools for centuries. Others are just as convinced that behaviorism will continue to fail as often as it succeeds, seeing it as stifling, regressive, and destructive. It is hoped that this book will provide you with the kind of information you need to evaluate behaviorism in education for yourself. To help you make your own critical and informed evaluation, each chapter presents the behaviorist position as well as some of the objections that have been raised against it—the reasons why some educators do not think the behaviorist approach is a very good one. The final decision is up to you, but by the time you have finished this book, it is my hope that you will ksow why you take the stand you do, and why you want one kind of education and not another for your students or your children.

To list everyone who has in some way contributed to this book would, I fear, require another book. I would like to thank especially my psychology chairman who made it possible for me to teach what I wrote, my students for their vigilant supervision of the quality of the progress checks included here, David McEttrick and Curt Whitesel of Allyn and Bacon for their initial and continued enthusiasm for the project, and most of all, my husband, Peter Sissons, without whom this book would not have been written at all.

T.   M.   H.

Creating Learning Environments

The Behavioral Approach to Education

A Scientific Psychology for Education: The Physics Model

1

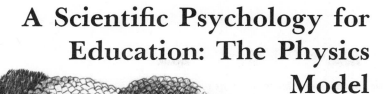

Chapter Objectives

We begin this book by looking at what makes behaviorism special—at some of the basic ideas and values that make it different from any other approach to educational psychology. You are shown how behaviorism models itself on physics and why behaviorists think their approach is more scientific than anyone else's. There are challengers who say that the physics model of behaviorism is based on a limited or erroneous world view and idea about man. Once you understand the basis of behaviorism you will be able to see why some people evaluate its educational methods so positively and why others fear that these methods could ultimately destroy fundamental human values.

The behavioral objectives of this chapter are to enable you to:

1. differentiate concepts that refer to observable factors acceptable in a behaviorist educational psychology from concepts which refer to factors which are not directly observable and therefore not acceptable to a behaviorist.

> *Progress Check:* 5-item quiz in which you are asked to underline explanations of school behavior that do not use observable factors.

2. separate causes of behavior that refer to causes within the person from causes observable within the environment.

> *Progress Check:* You are asked to identify as scientifically acceptable or unacceptable to behaviorism the cause of behavior assumed in five statements made in a hypothetical educational setting.

3. recognize statements accurately reflecting the behaviorist premise that human and animal behaviors are a result of conditioning.

> *Progress Check:* 5-item quiz in which your are asked to distinguish views held by behaviorists from those held by other nonbehaviorist psychologists.

THE WORLD VIEW OF BEHAVIORISM—WICKED OR WONDERFUL?

Behaviorists have long been accused of trying to replace the freedom and self-determination of the human spirit with robot-like characteristics, creating a 1984-world where scientific dictators apply the principles of conditioning on the masses. On the other hand, the behaviorists believe that they are helping to create a better world, where kindness replaces cruelty, sharing replaces selfishness, and learning replaces frustration. In this world productivity takes the place of destructiveness—peace replaces war. The behaviorists point to some of the things they have actually been able to accomplish:

- An eight-year-old girl who had consistently avoided going to school by throwing temper tantrums and becoming "sick" was cured of her schoolgoing phobia after four meetings with a therapist using the principles of behaviorism (Lazarus and Abramovitz 1962);
- An emotionally disturbed but normally intelligent eleven-year-old boy stopped kicking, screaming, using baby talk, and making incessant and irrelevant comments in class without once being punished by his teacher (Zimmerman and Zimmerman 1962);
- The retarded reading scores of over fifty children were improved significantly within weeks after teachers began to do nothing more than praise the students more often (Clark and Wallberg 1968);
- An institutionalized schizophrenic who had remained completely mute for 19 years began to speak after only ten behavior therapy sessions (Isaacs et al. 1960).

If it can be used to accomplish such obviously admirable results as these for education, why does behaviorism have opponents who still think it is so dehumanizing and destructive? The answer is twofold. The first reason is that behaviorist principles can be and sometimes are used (as are fire, nuclear energy, or sharp knives) to bring about both good and bad results. Some of the abuses are unquestionably grave. The second reason for opposing behaviorism is that it starts out with certain ideas about man and the world that some people believe are erroneous, dangerous, or degrading. We are going to examine some of these ideas and the way behaviorists are applying them in psychology and education. The evaluation of them, however, is up to you because, as we shall see now, they cannot actually be proved with scientific evidence.

Every scientific theory, even when it is backed up with evidence, has to start out with some basic ideas or assumptions that cannot be either scientifically proved or disproved. Science uses evidence to test its theories, but only *after* it has accepted some basic premises which are not proved. For instance, a crucial assumption that all scientists make is the belief that things exist outside of our own minds, that the world really exists and is not just the creation of our imaginations. It is an assumption that all of the world that we experience when we are awake is not just another dream like the ones we have when we sleep. There would not be any way to prove this, however, if someone were to argue that they did not exist. There just is not any experiment we could set up to prove that we were not dreaming. Since science cannot solve this dilemma, it does not try. All scientists just *assume* that the world is out there and that we are not just imagining it.

Physics: The Model for a Scientific Psychology of Education?

Behaviorists, like all psychologists, make certain assumptions about man and the world. However, unlike the assumption that the world is really out there, not all psychologists agree what these additional assumptions should be. At the very center of the controversy over behaviorism is a disagreement over the assumption that physics should be the model for studying and teaching human beings. The key question is whether man is constructed, operates, and can be studied in the same way as the material nonorganic universe.

The behaviorists believe that psychology, as a scientific study of people, should model itself on physics, the scientific study of matter. They reason that if psychology copies the ideas that physics adopted when it started to make such magnificent progress some five hundred years ago, that psychology too will make progress and develop into a strong, robust science of its own. This in turn will give us the kind of control over human beings that physicists are gaining over the material world. In the rest of this chapter we examine three ideas that behaviorists think psychology and education should adopt from physics. First, we look at the positions behaviorists ascribe to physics, and then at how they think these positions should be applied in psychology, and finally to education.

These basic ideas come up repeatedly throughout our discussion of behavior educational methods, and however you evaluate them should have a great influence on what you later decide about education, teaching, and learning. The behaviorists believe that until educators adopt these premises they will keep foundering with prescientific methods that cause so much current teaching to be inefficient. Other psychologists, however, do not adopt the physics model for studying humans in the same way and have developed different psychologies of education. You should be critical in your examination of these questions and the ways you think they should be answered since they relate to the foundations of the educational psychology you adopt.

THE MAN MOST RESPONSIBLE: BORRHUS FREDERICK SKINNER

B. F. Skinner is not the only man whose work is important to behaviorism's influence in education. He is not even the one who first started it all—that was Pavlov, a Russian, who discovered conditioning in dogs at the turn of the century, or Watson, an American, usually given credit for christening behaviorism with his book close to sixty years ago, or perhaps Pressey who designed a teaching machine in the 1920s. However, Skinner is responsible more than any other single individual for the widespread popularity of behaviorism today in schools, industry, prisons, mental hospitals, government, and private therapy practice. More than any other behaviorist, Skinner has been both praised and damned. He has been blamed for trying to design a scientifically controlled dictatorship, and he has also been voted the most important man in contemporary psychology for having the intellectual power and moral courage to point out the way to save mankind from the disaster of total annihilation.

Skinner was born in 1904 in Susquehanna, a railroad town in Pennsylvania. He describes his father as a lawyer who thought himself a failure, and his mother as "bright and beautiful" and one who created a warm home where he lived until he went to college. He had one younger brother who died as a teenager. Still influenced by the "Second Great Awakening," a religious revival that swept the area a century before, the Skinner family was strongly fundamentalist. When he was a small child, little Fred's grandmother opened the door of the kitchen's potbellied stove and warned him that the hot coals inside foreshadowed the hell that awaited all who did not repent. Later, his father took him through the county jail and solemnly promised a similar fate to him should he fall into evil ways.

When he was twelve, Skinner had what he calls his single mystical experience. He lost

his watch and, afraid to go home, he wandered around in anguish on his bicycle looking for it. Suddenly, in the midst of his pain, it was "revealed" to him that suffering was always matched eventually by equal happiness. After this insight into the supposed relativity of suffering and happiness he found the watch in a field, although he had "lost" it in town. He took it as a Sign. Despite the Sign, however, and the dire threats of eternal hellfire, within the year Skinner had become an aethiest, which he remains today.

Fred liked school and used to arrive at the small school house before his seven classmates, asking the custodian to let him sneak in early. He attended Hamilton College in New York where, though he graduated with the coveted Hawley Greek Prize, he was not quite a model student and was frequently involved in pranks and agitations over what he thought to be stupid requirements. After graduation, Skinner's first ambition was to become a writer, a goal given strong encouragement by the poet Robert Frost after Skinner had sent him some of his work. But within two years, including a span in Greenwich Village and a Parisian summer, Skinner pronounced himself a failure at this endeavor and decided to study psychology. He obtained his Ph.D. from Harvard in 1931, taught at the University of Minnesota, and served for three years as chairman of the psychology department in Indiana. During the Second World War he also participated in a secret government research project in which he used the principles of conditioning he had formulated to train pigeons to pilot missiles into the smokestacks of enemy naval destroyers. In 1948, he returned to Harvard University where he spent the major part of his career, and eventually retired as a distinguished professor emeritus.

All his life, Skinner seems to have been an

inveterate inventor. *Since childhood he has experimented with devices, contraptions, and machines to improve his world. When he was not allowed to smoke, he designed a gadget to blow hygienic smoke rings for him. When his mother set out to teach him to hang up his pajamas, he constructed a special hook in his closet connected by string and pully to a large sign, "Hang up your pajamas!" When the pajamas were off the hook, the sign dangled hugely in the middle of the door frame reminding him of his forgotten duty.*

Besides smoke-blowers and pajama hangers, Skinner (1967) writes that he "built roller skate scooters, steerable wagons, sleds, and rafts . . . seesaws, merry-go-rounds and slides . . . slingshots, bows and arrows, blowguns and water pistols from lengths of bamboo, and from a discarded water boiler a steam cannon with which to shoot plugs of potato and carrot over the houses of neighbors . . . tops, diabolos, model airplanes driven by twisted rubber bands, box kites and tin propellers which could be sent high into the air with a spool-and-string spinner." When he and a friend used to gather and sell elderberries, Skinner invented a flotation system to separate ripe and green berries, and he tried repeatedly, though unsuccessfully, to make a glider in which to fly.

Skinner has never stopped experimenting with designs to make the world a little bit easier to live in. When his second daughter was born, Skinner designed an Aircrib, which is rather like a large fish bowl, a small glass-enclosed, germ-free playpen in which the temperature and humidity can be controlled. Some have looked on this construction as a brilliant application of science to childrearing (it was made available on the commercial market for a brief time), but others thought it treated a baby too much like a laboratory animal. Whether or not you think an Aircrib is what every well-adjusted baby and liberated mother needs, it illustrates the concern for people that Skinner so actively tries to put into practice.

Within Skinner's professional work are the convictions that the world can be made a less painful place in which to live, that we must use science to find ways to reduce suffering, and that we can and must create an environment that is functional for people. Toward this end in 1948, he published Walden II, *a proposal written during the war for the ideal human community based on the conditioning principles he had studied. It is a utopian community where people live in harmony, rich in mutual rewards and peace. Although Skinner has never seen it, a community called Twin Oaks was set up in Virginia in the late 1960s based on the ideas of* Walden II *and is still in existence (Kinkade 1973).*

WHAT CAN BE STUDIED SCIENTIFICALLY?

This may sound like a simpleminded question until you realize that some of the answers are still sources of strong disagreement, especially among social scientists and educators. The behaviorists acknowledge the revolution that took place in physics when scientists stopped looking for inner states in inanimate objects. They now feel that a similar revolution should take place in psychology and education.

Physics: Studies Only What Can Be Observed

Aristotle explained that things fell to the ground because of the exuberance and joy they felt as they approached closer and closer to the earth, which was their true home. No one ever proved that Aristotle was wrong. No one ever proved that stones or apples or pennies don't feel joy as they fall to the ground. What scientists did do, though, was stop worrying about how stones or apples or pennies might feel, and began to concentrate on what they could actually see these objects doing. They began to concentrate only on what they could actually see, hear, touch, weigh, smell, count, or measure, or in other words, on what could be reliably observed.

Psychology: Should Study Only Behavior That Can Be Measured

Today, hardly a single adult in the Western world thinks inanimate objects have thoughts and feelings. On the other hand, the majority of us still think that humans are directed by inner thoughts and feelings. The behaviorists think this is a serious mistake. They argue that physics gave up the idea of an inner force inside objects as the cause of activity in the universe, and they believe that psychology should also give up this idea as it tries to understand the causes of human activity. There is no way to prove that people are not directed by their own thoughts and intentions anymore than it is possible, even today, to prove that stones and apples are not directed by their own intentions. We can explain and control the material universe so much better if we abandon that idea, however, and the behaviorists think the same is true of human beings. Like physics, then, psychology should study only what it can observe directly.

What can be directly observed in human beings are not inner states of other people but *behavior*. Any outside observer can agree that little Isabelle has just stamped her foot three times. However, they most probably will not agree whether she is *feeling* excited or angry or frustrated.

Behaviorists agree that people *have* thoughts and feelings and that these are important. The only one's thoughts or feelings you can observe directly, though, are your own, and sometimes (though not always) you can even count them. For example, it is possible to count how many times during the eight o'clock television program you thought of taking another piece of apple pie. But you cannot observe directly how often your girl friend in the seat next to you had this thought. You can only observe her behavior. Even if she were to tell you, you still would not know for sure if her private experiences were like yours. How often have people had to learn to their chagrin, for instance, that what one person experiences and means when he says "I love you" is not what another had in mind at all?

Because we cannot observe directly anyone's private experiences but our own, and because we cannot compare with much certainty private experiences of different people, the behaviorists do not believe that the private world of another person can be defined and studied scientifically. Psychology can study only behavior in others about which outsiders can agree, and not thoughts and feelings in others about which outsiders may not necessarily agree.

Education: Focuses On What Students Do

For the educator, concentrating on behavior means concentrating on things that students do and that others can actually see being done. This is not as easy as it sounds. It means redefining deeply ingrained and very noble concepts which are too vague to be used in their popular forms. Old psychological favorites such as: ego, intention, aggression, frustration, adjustment, guilt, Oedipal complex, wish, need, psyche, insight, hope, dignity, freedom, responsibility, and even love, and the educator's old standbys such as learning, readiness, test anxiety, and intelligence must all be either abandoned altogether or radically redefined in terms of behavior. The problem with every one of these concepts is that they refer to an inner state that simply cannot be measured because we cannot see inside another person's experience. How big is anxiety? Or, how deep is frustration? Whose guilt is greater? Or, who loves more? Behaviorists say such questions are unanswerable because all we ever know with certainty about another person is their behavior; we cannot see internal states.

If an educator is going to talk scientifically about a concept such as learning, for instance, she must really talk about behaviors that are labeled learning such as solving a problem, writing a paper, or getting a good exam grade. To explore scientifically how well-adjusted Marianne is to school a teacher must first define adjustment in behavioral terms. We can give a precise objective answer to how often Marianne plays with other children, how many letters of the alphabet she can recognize, or the number of times she smiled in school today, but we can't measure how Marianne might be *feeling* about school. In the same way, a teacher can reasonably ask how many times Johnny hit Sylvia, but she can't reasonably measure the size of Johnny's aggression if she defines it as something inside Johnny punching out at people. So too, it is with other forces that have so often been thought of as residing in the inaccessible regions of the mind or psyche of a student. We can see, study, and teach behavior scientifically. We cannot study hearts or minds or souls or psyches. However, the behaviorists say if we teach behavior all the rest will follow.

IS GOOD PHYSICS GOOD SCIENCE FOR PEOPLE?

A Behaviorist Point of View: Study Behavior, Not Mind

"We can follow the path taken by physics and biology by turning directly to the relation between behavior and the environment and neglecting supposed mediating states of mind. Physics did not advance by looking more closely at the jubilance of a falling body, or biology by looking at the nature of vital spirits, and we do not need to try to discover what personalities, states of mind, feelings, traits of character, plans, purposes, intentions, or other prerequisites of autonomous man really are in order to get on with a scientific analysis of behavior."

From chapter 1 in *Beyond Freedom and Dignity,* by B. F. Skinner.

Another Point of View: It Is Different If You Study People Instead of Stars

Not everyone agrees with Skinner about how psychology should resemble physics. Some psychologists say that stars and people, living and nonliving things, are too different from each other to be studied the same way. They say the idea that the inanimate universe is not controlled by thought and feelings is right for physicists but not for psychologists who are studying people. They argue that even if the universe does think and feel, there is no way for it to communicate with us. Psychologists are studying human beings who can communicate what they are thinking. Besides, they say, no one has ever actually seen an electron but we believe they actually exist *and scientists study them. Isn't it just as scientific to study feeling and thinking, which we never see, as it is to study the electron?*

Your Point of View

The position of the behaviorists as Skinner has outlined it is that people do, of course, feel and think, and that human beings are certainly different from stones and stars and other inanimate objects. Nonetheless, he argues that we cannot scientifically explore internal states of people (which often exist) anymore than we can explore the feelings of atoms (which probably don't exist). The psychologists who disagree with him think that it is possible to study scientifically inner states of humans because what people do and say most often reflects and is even caused by what they think and feel.

Do you agree with Skinner when he says that since we can only observe behavior that we should start spending more energy shaping how a person actually behaves? Do you think that a teacher, for instance, should worry more about how well her students compute the answers in a multiplication test, and worry less about their "understanding" it if they get the answers correct? Do you think it is important for teachers to be concerned with how their students feel about a subject? If a student gets A's in algebra, how important is it whether she hates math or likes it?

The question of whether or how thoughts and feelings can or cannot be studied by psychologists has been argued for years. We are talking about it here to acquaint you with the position most behaviorists take because it effects the kind of practical solutions to problems in educational psychology which they have developed. Psychologists who take a different view of the possibility of studying thinking or feeling are related to quite different educational practices. Before you draw a final conclusion yourself you should understand why the behaviorists do not think you can study someone else's private experiences, and perhaps why other psychologists take another view. Suggested readings on the subject are given at the end of the chapter, but meanwhile, here is a short quiz to see if you understand the behaviorist view so far.

Progress Check 1.1: Recognizing Observables

Directions: Below is an example of a typical problem that might face almost any teacher. The example is followed by a list of some explanations which you as a teacher might entertain as possible answers to why your pupil would rather carve up the desk than write on paper. Read each explanation and underline every word or set of words that from the behaviorist point of view do not refer to factors that are scientifically observable.

Problem: As a new third grade teacher, you watch your student, Alfred, meticulously carve his initials into the desk top and ask yourself why he approaches this task with such total and involved concentration when he always balks at writing on a conventional piece of paper, a feat he accomplishes only with extreme reluctance.

Possible Explanations:
1. Alfred is inherently destructive.
2. Alfred doesn't understand the value of property.
3. The desk carving produces a permanent and public mark of Alfred's presence in that desk to which Susan responded with a smile, while the writing on the paper receives a cursory grade assigned by the teacher privately and no comment at all from other students.
4. Alfred carves his initials as a means of self-expression; the initials reflect a deep inner need for love.
5. The boy who carves the most elegant initials is praised by the other boys, while boys who write papers are derided by the others.

If you think about it, you realize that certain answers to the question "Why did that happen?" are considered scientifically unacceptable. Answers such as "God made it happen," or "by magic," are not considered scientific, however right they may or may not be. Behaviorists believe that too many psychologists try to explain why people do things by using answers that are just as prescientific as "the witch doctors' magic did it." We will look at the kinds of answers behaviorists have identified as belonging to physics, and then at how they believe psychology and education can learn to use these same kinds of answers to explain and control human behavior.

WHERE DOES FREEDOM BEGIN?

Answer: In Man

"We hold these Truths to be self-evident, that all Men are created equal, that they are endowed by their Creator with certain un-alienable Rights, that among these are Life, Liberty, and the Pursuit of Happiness—"

Declaration of Independence

"The freedom that I am talking about is essentially an inner thing, something which exists in the living person . . . a freedom which he courageously uses to live his potentialities."

Carl Rogers in *Freedom to Learn*

"And God said, Let us put man in command of the fishes in the sea, and all that flies through the air, and the cattle, and the whole earth, and all the creeping things that move on earth."

Genesis I:26

A Different Answer: In the Environment

"The direction of the controlling relation is reversed: a person does not act upon the world, the world acts upon him. . . . Man's struggle for freedom is not due to a will to be free, but to certain behavioral process characteristic of the human organism.

B. F. Skinner in *Beyond Freedom and Dignity*

"A scientific analysis of behavior must, I believe, assume that a person's behavior is controlled by his genetic and environmental histories rather than by the person himself. . . . We cannot prove, of course, that human behavior as a whole is fully determined, but the proposition becomes more plausible as the facts accumulate."

B. F. Skinner in *About Behaviorism*

Your Answer

Because they have denied so explicitly that man is able to take direct responsibility for his own actions, the behaviorists have been attacked for destroying the foundations of our country and of our Judeo-Christian culture. The behaviorists claim to have the techniques to control not only what people do but what they think and feel as well, and as Skinner himself admits, "no part of the behavioristic position has raised more violent objections." *If you accept the behaviorist position, then you can't hold people responsible for what they do, you can't blame them either, or give them credit. People are not either intrinsically good or bad, and how they behave can be changed by changing the environment.*

On the other hand, others think that man interacts with the environment, not simply controlled by it, but controlling it as well. They disagree with the behaviorist for emphasizing only the environment's control over man, and not paying enough attention to what they think is man's special ability to understand and control himself and his environment. Man can make choices, they say. Intentions do direct what man does; we do more than react to the environment.

What is freedom? How responsible are we for what we do? Do you think the behaviorists degrade man by relocating the source of his control over himself in the environment? Do you agree that man is controlled by his environment just as surely as material objects are controlled by it? Or is man different? Do we need more courage to accept the responsibility of our own freedom, as Carl Rogers claims, or is it more courageous to accept ourselves as controlled by forces in our external world?

As a teacher, would you rather think of your students as controlled by their environment which it is your responsibility to control, or as free independent individuals to whom you can only offer guidance in their own search for self-development?

Physics: Matter Does Not Move Itself but Is Moved by External Forces

To explain as well as control the movement of matter the successful physicist could not develop a special language in order to carry on heart-to-heart conversations with it to find out why matter acts the way it does. Rather, the modern physicist assumes that matter is inert, that it does not move itself but is moved by forces outside it. This assumption of the physicist has been a very fruitful one and has given man a great deal of power over the physical universe.

Psychology: Man Does Not Direct Himself but Is Determined by His Environment

Behaviorists believe that psychology should emulate physics and make the same assumption about people as physicists make about matter. For them, man is completely controlled by external forces just as matter is controlled by external forces. Man is not free in the traditional sense. He cannot control himself by using his will power as we have so often been taught to try to do as children. Man is not directed by an internal force, either conscious (as the cognitive psychologists think) or unconscious (as the Freudians believe) anymore than a stone is. For the behaviorist, people are like sail boats moved by the wind or like balls of clay shaped by the potter (Skinner 1953).

People are sometimes quite amazed to hear that the behaviorists do not believe that people freely direct their own actions because their everyday experience is that they *do* make their own decisions and *are* responsible for their own behavior. Could this experience be just an illusion? We *experience* that the sun moves across the sky and sets in the west but we *know* that the sun really is still while the earth whirls around it. Is the experience of our own freedom the same kind of false illusion?

The idea that man is not free causes some people to be indignant and they call behaviorism an "empty box approach." The behaviorists look at the history of science to defend themselves. Some four centuries ago, Galileo presented Europe with the Copernican theory that the earth was not the center of the universe. People were outraged at a theory they saw as a threat to the basic dignity of man. They were so outraged that Galileo finally publicly recanted the theory under threat of torture and burning at the stake. The behaviorists, particularly in the person of the outspoken and explicit B. F. Skinner, have presented the twentieth century with the idea that man is not the center of his own personal universe either, and many people are just as outraged at this idea as they were at Galileo's. In the end, Copernican world view won out because it provided man with a greater control of the universe, and eventually even landed him on the moon. The behaviorists believe that the traditional ideas about man's freedom and responsibility for his own actions will eventually be replaced with their world view. They believe that, in the last analysis, controlling the environment will give man greater control over himself—a giant step forward even more incredible than walking on the moon.

Education: The Scientific Educator Changes Situations Instead of People

Shouting at a molecule will not affect it at all, but changing the environment around it will have a profound effect. If man, like the molecule, is controlled by his environment rather than by himself then the informed educator is going to learn how the environment controls students' behaviors. Rather than trying to change the understanding, motivation, or knowledge *inside* the students directly, the behaviorist teacher changes the environment that controls learning behavior. She concentrates on the situation her students are in and teaches by changing *situations,* not by trying to change *students.* The rest of this book examines the laws of environmental control formulated by the behaviorists, and the ways teachers can control the environments of their students in order to bring about the learning behaviors that they are supposed to. First, let us look at an analogy to see more clearly what the behaviorists mean when they say that changing situations is the way to change people.

Suppose there were a boulder at the top of a mountain, and below nestled a happy little village. If the boulder began to roll it could easily start an avalanche. Imagine that faced with imminent catastrophe, we called in an engineer to prevent the boulder from rolling. We should most certainly be flabbergasted and probably quite worried if the engineer walked to the top of the mountain and began a discussion with the stone, imploring it not to roll down the mountain, pointing out the great human misery it would cause, and appealing to its nobler instincts to cease this ignoble action.

What in fact would we expect from the engineer? We would expect him to change the conditions in the environment surrounding the stone in order to reduce the likelihood of the boulder's journey. Why, asks the behaviorists, do we think that human beings should be approached in a manner so entirely different? Let us take another example. Suppose that as a teacher you found the lock of your desk drawer repeatedly broken open and a copy of the exam being given to the class the next day removed. Since Harry's grades have just changed dramatically from *F*'s to *A*'s, you shrewdly guess who the lock-breaker is. There are several courses of action that may prevent the continued occurrence of burglaries. You may talk to Harry heart-to-heart, as did the engineer to the boulder, about fairness, honesty, and responsibility. However, *just* talking to people in order to change "their minds" or to bring about a "change of heart" that will consequently change behavior seems as useless and prescientific to the behaviorists as shouting at the molecule.

On the other hand, you may take out a cane and whip the errant boy. This is an example of punishment and we will see in the next chapter why the behaviorists claim that this often is a fairly inefficient way of controlling behavior. Finally, you may stop keeping the tests in the desk drawer, while at the same time adjust both the teaching methods and tests used with Harry so that he achieves consistent success when he takes the tests without the extra advantage of the previews provided by the break ins. (Methods that behaviorists suggest will help Harry achieve this kind of success are discussed in chapter 4.) This last course of action in the long run is apt to be the most effective means of permanently curtailing the break-ins, and it is an example of what the behaviorists mean when they claim that changing the environment is the best way to change what people do.

Does this mean that words never affect behavior? Of course not. All the time we see that they do. But words, the behaviorists say, effect behavior *only* when they are connected with changes in the environment. You can use words to control people in the same way you use words to control your dog. If you want to teach Rover to sit when you say "Sit," you reward him with a pat or a morsel of food when he sits after your command. Words are effective *only* to the extent that they are reliably connected with certain results in the environment, *not* because they change a person's mind. Just as you do not make Rover sit by "changing his mind" but by changing the environment when he obeys your command, so too, peoples' behaviors do not change because talking to them has changed their minds but because the talking is connected with changes in the environment.

Here is a short quiz to see not whether you agree with the behaviorist position but whether you understand it.

Progress Check 1.2: Differentiating Scientific Causes of Behavior

Directions: Below are five statements similar to ones frequently made by educators. Read each statement and place a *U* next to each statement that would be unsatisfactory to a behaviorist because it assumes a scientifically untestable cause of behavior. Place an *A* next to those statements which assume a scientifically testable cause of behavior and would therefore be acceptable as a behaviorist explanation. For further feedback, indicate briefly on the line below each statement the reason for your evaluation.

_____1. "Francine works in school because her parents always pay attention to the papers she brings home and praise her so often for what she has done."

Reason: _____

_____2. "I cannot influence your decision to study or not to study; you are free to choose to do what you wish."

Reason: _____

_____3. "Jonathan is not consciously trying to make trouble, but his unconscious hostility is difficult for him to handle."

Reason: _____

What Causes Are Scientific? How Is Behavior Controlled?   15

_____4. "To change Barbara's negative reactions to school I will listen to the yearning for self-expression buried inside her; when the real Barbara emerges she won't hate school anymore."

Reason: _____

_____5. "If you watch carefully, you will see that every time Harry throws a spitball somebody in the class snickers. He would probably stop it if the class stopped responding to him."

Reason: _____

HOW IS THE UNIVERSE CONSTRUCTED? HOW DOES LEARNING DEVELOP?

Since the Greeks, Western man has been looking for the building blocks of the material universe. Physics has identified the atom as the basic building block of the physical universe, and the behaviorists think they have found a starting point for psychology's study of behavior as well.

Physics: The World Is Composed of Atoms

One of the astonishing discoveries of the atomic age is that underlying the variety of our physical world—the sizes, shapes, heat and cold, colors, textures, densities, and weights—is a profound simplicity. The universe seems to be composed of only about a hundred different kinds of atoms that belong to only eight different families. The identification of the atom as the basic building block of matter and Mendeleev's formulation of the atomic chart was a great step toward our understanding and controlling of the physical world.

Psychology: Behavior Is Built-Up from Conditioning Units

The behaviorists believe they have identified the "atom" of behavior, that underlying simplicity of the seemingly endless variety of animal and human actions. This "atom" is conditioning, and it is the means by which all behavior is learned. From this point of view, behavior is built-up in the same way that physicists tell us the material world is built-up—atoms combine to make more complicated molecules which combine to make what we experience as different substances. Human behavior is built-up from innumerable conditionings until we have what we experience as a variety of different human and animal actions.

You will notice, particularly in chapter 4 where we study behaviorist methods of education, that more than any other theory behaviorism breaks material up into small units, small steps in which the student is conditioned to learn one-by-one until he reaches the final goal. The reason for this small unit approach is due, to the behaviorist belief that behavior is built-up of these small conditioned units like a house built of individual bricks, each put together one-by-one until the final building emerges. The teacher's role is to identify these "bricks of learning" and fit them together.

Many of behaviorism's ideas that conditioning is the basic element of human learning have been tested in laboratories, at first, with lower animals. Behaviorists talk so much about conditioning rats, pigeons, and rabbits that they have sometimes been dismissed by educators as "rat psychologists" having nothing to say to them. It is important, then, to see why behaviorists do not think they are wasting their time in observing animals to develop what they believe is a meaningful psychology of education for humans.

ANOTHER POINT OF VIEW: HUMAN AND OTHER ANIMAL BEHAVIOR ARE NOT ESSENTIALLY ALIKE

"A bird can count numbers, a baboon can compare shapes, a chimpanzee can grasp that a flame will not scorch after he has poured water on it. These are ideas: simple ideas, yet quite like human ideas. What keeps them so far short of the ideas of Shakespeare and Einstein? The animal cannot develop its ideas, it cannot carry them in the mind, put one idea beside another, do imaginary things with them."

J. Bronowski in *Insight*

"Man is the only one who is not locked into his environment."

J. Bronowski in *The Ascent of Man*

Behaviorist educational psychology is based on the belief that the fundamental law of learning operates throughout the phylogene-tic scale and that the behavior of lower animals and humans are alike in that they are both controlled by environmental contingencies. Bronowski argues that, although lower animals and humans are alike in important ways, they are also different in important ways. He believes that an essential difference is that because of superior brain capacities the human species can transcend its environment in a way that other animals cannot. Scientists who share Bronowski's point of view believe that behaviorism is one-sided because it concentrates on the similarities between humans and animals and does not take into real account the enormous influential differences.

Do you agree? Which view do you think comes closer to expressing man's condition? Can you see how the view one adopts in this matter can affect one's approach to education?

The educator is concerned with how people learn. The behaviorist is too, but the behaviorist has noticed a similarity between much animal and human learning. He believes that if he can understand how animals learn then he can understand more quickly how people learn. Human behavior is more complex and more sophisticated but still based on the same principles as all other animal behavior. A rat or pigeon is not identical to a human animal just as Con Edison's electricity-generating plant is not identical to a flashlight. The generating plant, however, although far more complicated operates on the same basic principles as the flashlight. Just as it is easier to understand the plant if you first understand the flashlight, so too, it may be easier to understand first the behavior of simpler animals in order to understand the more complex behavior of higher animals.

Most of us accept the idea that our physical bodies are similar to the bodies of other animals in many important ways. Few of us are indignant over studies of monkeys or rats or rabbits to develop cures for diseases affecting humans. We find it makes a lot of sense to do research with animals to increase our understanding about humans. The behaviorist claims that we can do the same between human and animal behavior as well. We behave with our bodies just as surely as we get sick with our bodies, and so, in relation to both our physical health and our behavior we may find informative parallels in lower animals.

The essential similarity, the "atom" of all behavior of all animals including the human animal, is that they—and we—learn through conditioning by our environments. The laws by which conditioning occurs are presented in the next chapter. Below is a short quiz to make sure you understand what has been said up to now.

Progress Check 1.3: Distinguishing Behavorist Views of Behavior

Directions: Place a check in the space provided in front of those statements which accurately reflect the behaviorist position as discussed in the preceding section of the text. For further feedback you may state the reason for your evaluation of each statement.

_____1. Man is essentially different from other animals in every important way because he can speak and think while other animals can only react.

Reason: _____

_____2. The study of lower animals can contribute almost nothing to the study of human psychology.

A Scientific Psychology for Education: The Physics Model

Reason: _____

_____3. Since man has a mind which controls his behavior, he is different from the lower ani-
mals whose behavior is controlled totally through conditioning.

Reason: _____

_____4. In order to understand human behavior we can gain much through understanding
the behavior of lower animals whose behavior is less complex than that of humans but controlled
by the same essential processes.

Reason: _____

_____5. Just as the physical universe is made of atoms, so too, human behavior is con-
structed of basic units which we call conditioning.

Reason: _____

SUMMARY

In this chapter we have looked at the world view of behaviorism and
examined how it has developed a psychology modeled after the hard sciences
—particularly after physics as it developed in the sixteenth century—and
how this model in turn effects the behaviorist approach to education. Behaviorism models itself on physics in three ways:

- First, behaviorists hold the view that since physicists do not study thought
  or feeling but only what can be observed in the material universe that, in
  order to be scientific, psychologists and educators should be concerned
  only with what can be observed in humans—behavior. Many psychological concepts should be redefined in terms of behavior, and educators
  should be primarily concerned with students' behavior that they can see
  rather than with inner states that, in others, cannot be directly studied
  scientifically.
- Secondly, physics assumes that matter does not direct itself but is controlled by forces outside it. Behaviorists believe that psychologists and
  educators should make a similar assumption in their study of human
  behavior and accept the view that human beings are not self-directed but
  controlled by forces in their environments. Thought, intention, or understanding do not *cause* behavior (an idea so often assumed by the man on
  the street), but are themselves controlled by the same environmental forces

that control behavior. The task of the educator is not to change people directly but to learn how to control their environments which in turn control them.

- Thirdly, just as physics identified the atom as the basis of the physical universe, the behaviorists believe they have identified conditioning as the basis of all learning in both lower animals and humans. Education, as the process of learning new behavior, takes place through continuous conditioning in which the teacher molds the students' new behaviors.

Key ideas such as these cannot be proven in the strict sense with scientific evidence, but it is necessary to make some assumptions in order to have any science at all. Not all psychologies are based on the same interpretation of physics as behaviorism, and do not necessarily accept the same assumptions as discussed here. They have, therefore, developed different psychologies of education from the behaviorist approach.

SUGGESTED READING

The topics covered in this chapter are discussed more fully in the philosophy of science. In this chapter we have presented the basic issues because every psychology is based on some philosophy of science and to understand behaviorism's impact on education it is important to be acquainted with its foundations as well as all its parts "above ground." If you find exploring these topics worthwhile, you would probably enjoy pursuing additional reading, or taking a course in the philosophy of science or the history and systems of psychology.

The following reading suggestions do not begin to cover the scope of material available but they point you toward some of the most important readings in which the foundations of behaviorism, particularly as they have been explicated by Skinner, are vigorously attacked and defended.

CARPENTER, FINLEY. *The Skinner Primer*. New York: Macmillan, The Free Press, 1974.

This book is definitely worth reading if the question of freedom and man's control of himself and his environment is a question that concerns you. It is easy to understand, and although Carpenter ultimately does not find Skinner's approach sufficiently complete, he presents his view fairly. See especially Part Two on problems of freedom and Part Three on psychological freedom and education.

Kolesnik, Walter B. *Humanism and/or Behaviorism in Education*. Boston: Allyn and Bacon, Inc., 1975.

Paperback. This is a short, clear, uncomplicated secondary source. For a look at the basic assumptions of behaviorism as compared to those of the humanists, see chapter 4, "Good People Don't Just Happen. They're Produced."

Rogers, Carl. *Freedom to Learn*. Columbus, Ohio: Charles E. Merrill Publishing Co., 1969.

Carl Rogers is often opposed to the behaviorist world view and articles by Skinner and Rogers are often placed side by side for comparisons. For a look at Roger's views, see chapter 13, "Freedom and Commitment."

Skinner, B. F. *About Behaviorism*. New York: Alfred A. Knopf, Inc., 1974.

This is the best, clearest, and most unambiguous book you can read on Skinner's basic assumptions about psychology as a science and the nature of man. Look particularly at chapters 1–4 and 12–14. Also available in paperback.

Skinner, B. F. *Beyond Freedom and Dignity*. New York: Alfred A. Knopf, Inc., 1971.

This is the book that has brought on Skinner's head the greatest laurels of praise and the strongest objections. Here he explicitly states that such concepts as freedom and dignity are not only outdated but positively harmful for the future of mankind as it struggles on the edge of sheer existence. A strongly recommended book in order to come to terms with whether you agree with Skinner or not. One cannot help but admire the scope of Skinner's attempt to make behaviorism relevant to the real world of man today. Also available in paperback.

Wann, T. W., ed. *Behaviorism and Phenomenology: Contrasting Bases for Modern Psychology*. Chicago: University of Chicago Press, 1964.

You probably will not want to read all of this book and if you are not philosophically inclined you may not like any of it. The articles by Skinner and Rogers present their cases clearly.

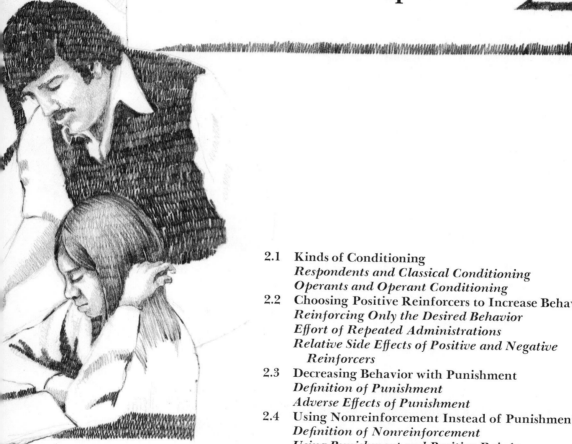

Using the Environment to Control Behavior: Basic Concepts

Chapter Objectives

We saw in the last chapter that the behaviorists believe that behavior is controlled by the environment. In this chapter we look at basic concepts which point to the particular aspects of the environment that behaviorists believe affect behavior, and the conditions under which it occurs.

Behaviorally, the goals of this chapter are to enable the student to:

1. *identify examples of the following:*
   unconditioned response
   conditioned response
   classical conditioning
   unconditioned stimulus
   positive reinforcer
   operant
   operant conditioning
   conditioned stimulus
   negative reinforcer

   Progress Check: In a 10-item quiz you are asked to recognize the above concepts in three different examples of conditioned behavior.

2. *compare the advantages of using positive instead of negative reinforcers.*

   Progress Check: In a 4-item sentence completion quiz you are asked to compare the advantages and disadvantages of increasing arithmetic behavior through use of positive or negative reinforcers.

3. *recognize statements concerning the effects of punishment which reflect behaviorist research findings.*

   Progress Check: In a 5-item true-false quiz, you are asked to distinguish between statements which accurately represent behaviorist principles of punishment and those which represent common fallacies with which many behaviorists disagree.

4. *predict the effects of environmental contingencies.*

   Progress Check: In a 12-item multiple-choice quiz you are asked to identify positive reinforcers, negative reinforcers, punishment, and non-reinforcers, and to predict their probable effects.

5. *differentiate the effects of reinforcement schedules.*

Progress Check: In a 4-item multiple-choice quiz you are asked to choose the most appropriate schedule in relation to four specified behavior changes.

---

6. recognize characteristics of cueing, discrimination, and generalization.

Progress Check: In a 10-item true-false quiz you are asked to analyze the kind of cues and their contingencies used in four vignettes of teacher-student behaviors.

KINDS OF CONDITIONING

The two basic processes you need to know about in order to understand behaviorism are classical and operant conditioning. The understanding of these concepts will allow you to understand why the behaviorists suggest the educational procedures that are discussed in the following chapters, as well as let you apply behaviorism yourself in making diagnoses and adjustments in the unique situations which you will face in your own classroom. This chapter is about these forms of conditioning—what they are, how they work, and how to use them. You will see that classical conditioning emphasizes the importance of controlling behavior by controlling the stimulus, or what happens *before* the behavior occurs, and that operant conditioning emphasizes the importance of controlling both the stimulus conditions before and the environmental contingencies *after* the behavior has been performed.

Respondents and Classical Conditioning

The phenomenon called classical conditioning was first demonstrated almost accidentally by the Russian, Ivan Pavlov, and his dogs. Pavlov considered himself a physiologist and neurologist, and originally he was trying to study the digestive processes. As he was carrying out his research (for which he won a Nobel Prize in 1904), he found that he was frequently unable to control the salivating of his dogs simply by either presenting or withholding food. Instead, after several sessions in the laboratory where the dogs were fed, Pavlov found that salivation began simply by bringing the dogs into the laboratory, without the slightest smell or sight of food at all. He then began to study the salivation process directly in order to bring it under his control so that he could get on with his study of digestion. As a result, he made a major contribution to psychology.

Pavlov found if he paired the dog's food often enough with any formerly neutral event such as the ringing of a tuning fork or bell, a light flash, or the sight of a white coat, eventually the dog would salivate to the ring or light or coat alone, without the additional presence of food. Pavlov published the results of what he had found (Pavlov 1927), and the process that he described eventually came to be known as classical conditioning.

Relevancy of Classical Conditioning to Human Behavior. Pavlov was not trying to develop a psychological theory. His research with dogs was picked up by John Watson, in the United States, and in applying it to humans a new psychology, christened Behaviorism, was born (Watson 1930). In a now famous experiment (Watson and Raynor 1920), Watson found that he could teach one-year-old Albert a fear response toward a white rat using the same techniques Pavlov had used to control the dogs' salivating. Watson reasoned that if he could control fear responses he could control all other human behaviors in the same way, and an enthusiastic application of his theory radically changed the child-rearing practices in the American 1930s. Feeding schedules were rigidly controlled and strict discipline became the byword for every enlightened household bent on producing model citizens and outstanding achievers.

Desipte the fact that classical conditioning has by now been amply demonstrated in almost every kind of animal and human species, evidence has also mounted that all human behavior is not controlled by this process, and the results in human terms of Watson's proposals were not quite all that he had so ardently promised. However, classical conditioning remains important to the educator today since techniques involving this process can be used with success in reversing inappropriate fear responses such as fear of heights, sex, crowds, tests, teachers, snakes, or darkness. Also, as we shall see, behaviorists still continue to believe, as did Watson, that it is possible to learn how to control the environment in order to produce the kind of human behavior that most benefits the individual and society.

What is Classical Conditioning? The key to understanding classical conditioning is *pairing*, which occurs in three stages. Let's go back and examine the case of Pavlov's salivating dogs, and then we will look at an example of classical conditioning of human behavior.

First Stage: Before Conditioning. Before any conditioning began, the dogs automatically began to salivate at the smell of food. In other words, before conditioning begins, there already exists a pairing between some environmental event (the smell of food) and an automatic response to it (salivating). In technical terms, the smell of food is called an unconditioned stimulus

(UCS) because without any conditioning it stimulates some behavior which, at this point, is known as a *respondent* or an *unconditioned response* (UCR). In abbreviated form, stage one pairing looks like this:

$$UCS \rightarrow UCR.$$

Second Stage: During Conditioning. During conditioning, Pavlov presented the dogs with food and rang a bell at the same time. The ringing of the bell is a conditioned stimulus (CS) because the dog will respond to it by salivating only when conditioning has occurred. The pairing during conditioning is between the CS and UCS and the entire process may be abbreviated like this:

$$UCS + CS \rightarrow UCR.$$

Third Stage: After Conditioning. When conditioning is complete, Pavlov found that the dogs salivated at the sound of the bell alone. At this point, the salivation is no longer called an unconditioned response but since it is given to the conditioned stimulus alone it is known as a conditioned response (CR). The new pairing is now between CS and CR and the process is:

$$CS \rightarrow CR.$$

Additional conditioning, or what is called higher-order conditioning, occurs when the CS (the bell) is paired with a second CS (a light flash) and the CR given to the first CS is transferred to the second CS as well.

Classical conditioning can explain the attentional response that almost all of us will invariably give to the sound of our own name. Research shows that though we may be snoring soundly through a roaring thunderstorm, we will respond to the mere whisper of our name. Classical conditioning is involved in producing this superresponsiveness when some stimulus which spontaneously attracts our attention occurs at the same time our name is spoken. As babies, warm milk, to which a baby will automatically give attention, probably often appears at the same time our mothers cooed our names. As we grow older, baby food is replaced with steak but the process of conditioning continues unabated, and we, like the dog responding to a bell that initially was paired with food, respond to our names repeatedly paired with some attention-getting event.

One of the important things to note about classical conditioning, because it differentiates classical from operant conditioning which we are going to discuss next, is that the controlling environmental events (the conditioned and unconditioned stimuli) occur *before* the response is given. Classical conditioning can explain some important human behaviors but a great deal of what people do does not seem to be automatically elicited by any specific environmental event which *preceded* it. To understand these other behaviors behaviorists look to operant conditioning.

Operants and Operant Conditioning

Behaviorists, like Watson, studying classical conditioning had concentrated on the importance of controlling behavior before a response was made. However, behaviorists like Edward Thorndike, studying what he called the Law of Effect (Thorndike 1911), and B. F. Skinner, studying operant or instrumental conditioning (Skinner 1938), emphasized the importance of what happens *after* behavior occurs. To predict whether behavior was going to occur again in the future, they began to look at the effects or consequences of that behavior in the past. When, for instance, a clever and hungry eight-year-old puts her hand inside the cookie jar and pulls out a fresh cookie the chances that she will engage in a similar behavior again—perhaps in a very short time —are quite high. On the other hand, if the cookie jar is empty, the chances that in a few minutes she will repeat that behavior are quite low. In either case, it is what occurs *after* she puts her hand into the jar that determines whether that behavior will be repeated.

Relevancy of Operant Conditioning to Human Behavior. The implications of the process of operant conditioning for controlling behavior are vast. In fact, most behaviorists today believe that almost all human behavior is controlled through operant conditioning. Skinner (1971) sees it as the means par excellence by which an individual adapts to the environment. Through this process, an individual's behavior changes so that he is apt to receive the maximum number of rewards from the environment, and he discontinues behavior which brings no rewards. Since behaviorists believe that operant conditioning plays such a crucial role in determining what man does, a great deal of time and energy has been spent studying the laws of this process.

How Operant Conditioning Works. An operant (as opposed to a respondent) is apparently spontaneously emitted behavior (rather than behavior, like a respondent, which is elicited by a stimulus). Operants include all behaviors which are not respondents, and the frequency with which an operant behavior occurs is a function of the consequences that follow it.

Another term for the consequences or effects of behavior is *environmental contingency.* The first extensive systematic research into their effects on behavior was done by Skinner (1953, 1958). Basically, there are three different kinds of contingencies and each effects behavior in a different way:

1. If behavior is followed by apparently favorable consequences, or by *reinforcers,* it will probably be *repeated;*
2. If behavior is followed by no apparent or indifferent consequences, or by *nonreinforcers,* it will tend to *disappear;*
3. And, if behavior is followed by negative consequences, or by *punishment,* it will tend to change so as to *avoid those consequences.*

All this may sound too simple to need learned psychologists to give a fancy name to something intelligent mothers and teachers have known for years, but behaviorism has made several startling and important contributions that implement—and correct—common sense. We will look at some of these contributions next. You will find that as a behaviorist educator you will use the principles of operant conditioning much more than those of classical conditioning. Therefore, the rest of this chapter is concerned with an elaboration of the ways in which you can use environmental contingencies and operant conditioning to increase, decrease, build up, maintain, create, and cue behavior.

Positive and Negative Reinforcers. As a teacher you will be concerned with increasing behaviors—playing, speaking, studying, and especially learning—behaviors in your students. The behaviorists believe they have found the key to making any behavior at all occur more often. Put quite simply, the key is this: *behavior followed by a reinforcer will tend to occur more often.* Your major role as a teacher, then, is to identify and use reinforcers to increase learning. If this is so, it is absolutely essential in order to be a good teacher that you know what a reinforcer is.

To define positive and negative reinforcers, let us first look at an example of two kinds of reinforcers and then explore the strict definitions.

EXAMPLE:
As the door slams behind him, Jeremiah lets out a sigh of relief as he sets out for school. He's leaving behind the cold, harsh two rooms where he lives under crowded conditions with his mother, three sisters, and two brothers. As he walks into the classroom, Miss Appleby, Jeremiah's second-grade teacher, greets him with a warm smile. "Good morning, Jeremiah. I was just beginning to worry that you weren't going to be here for the morning song. You know how much better it sounds when you play the drums." Jeremiah smiles back, hangs up his coat, and proudly takes down his drum from the shelf.

In this example, the positive reinforcer is the welcome given by Miss

Appleby to Jeremiah after his arrival at school on time.   The negative reinforcer is the removal of the harsh realities of Jeremiah's home following his
behavior of leaving for school on time.   Strictly speaking, a reinforcer, either
positive or negative, is any event that follows a behavior and that increases
the likelihood of that behavior's repetition.   Although one may assume that it
is experienced as something pleasant, the strict definition of reinforcer does
not specify that a reinforcer is accompanied by any subjective feelings at all,

DOES CONDITIONING REALLY CONTROL HUMAN BEHAVIOR?

*Since there is so much research in which hu-
man behavior is changed by applying the
principles of conditioning, why isn't everyone
convinced that the behaviorists are right when
they say that conditioning controls what we
do? Isn't this proof? How can an intelligent,
informed, unbiased person not agree with the
behaviorist conclusions? Few people deny that
behavior has been changed or question the
research results using conditioning methods
to control behavior. They do differ, however,
in their interpretation of why the results occur. That is, there are different explanations
for why behavior changes.*

THE BEHAVIORIST INTERPRETATION

*Behavior of almost every variety has been
changed because it has been conditioned according to the operations of classical or operant conditioning. Behavior is changed through
conditioning by manipulating the contingencies in the environment to bring about the
desired behavioral results.*

A COGNITIVE INTERPRETATION

*Behavior changes as a result of the activity of
the higher mental processes. Put into any sit-*
*uation, the person tries to "figure out" what
is happening and what he has to do to get the
results from the environment that he chooses.
Behavior is a result of what a person thinks
the environment is, and what he wants to get
from it. Behavior changes as a result of a
change in a person's awareness of the possibilities in the environment.*

YOUR INTERPRETATION

*What is your opinion? Do you believe that a
person's understanding of his environment is
the cause of what he does? Or do you think
that the person's environment is the cause of
what he both thinks and does? As a teacher,
if you agree with the cognitive interpretation,
you may tend to present problems to your
students and use verbal interactions to develop their "understanding" and awareness,
and their ability to "figure out" the environment. If you accept the behaviorist interpretation, you may concentrate more on changing the environment itself using verbal
interaction to cue students' behavior.*

pleasant or otherwise. If it increases the probability of the behavior it follows, it is a reinforcer.

Behaviorists are not sure why reinforcers are reinforcing or how they work (Hilgard and Bower 1966). Therefore, they cannot identify a reinforcer for certain *before* behavior occurs and is effected, only afterwards. If you recognize this as a circular definition, you are right to wonder how the behaviorists can logically say that they can predict behavior when in fact it has already occurred before they can identify the events controlling it. In practice, however, behaviorists have not found this logical fallacy as inhibiting as one would expect, and reinforcers have been successfully used to control almost every conceivable kind of behavior.

Despite their names, both varieties of reinforcers, positive and negative, increase the probability of a response. A positive reinforcer is any (apparently positively-experienced) event which begins or is added to the situation after the behavior has occurred and increases the probability of that behavior occurring again. A negative reinforcer is any (apparently noxious or negatively-experienced) event which is taken away after the behavior has occurred and increases probability of that behavior's repetition. Since the stopping of something noxious or painful is usually a pleasant experience, negative reinforcers, like positive ones, are probably experienced as pleasant. Do not be confused by their names. Negative and positive reinforcers both increase the likelihood of a behavior occurring again, and they often do so in a very powerful way.

If you think about it, you will see that behavior followed by a negative reinforcer is *escape behavior*. It permits the individual to get away from some situation, and if that situation is noxious, painful, or terrible enough the behavior that allows the individual to escape from it will be very strong indeed. That is, if a man suffering from cancer can escape the pain it causes by taking a shot of morphine, the next time the pain begins, he is likely to want another shot. Or if running away from home enables a child to escape from yelling and screaming and humiliation, he is apt to try to run away again should he be brought back to that same home and humiliation.

Closely allied to escape behavior is *avoidance behavior* which is very often learned after escape behavior and permits the individual not only to escape a noxious situation but to avoid it altogether. Escape and avoidance behavior in relation to really noxious situations are two of the most permanent kinds of behaviors currently identified by behaviorist research.

However, despite the fact that positive and negative reinforcers both increase the likelihood of behavior, they are not equally effective for the teacher who is trying to control behavior. Why this is so will be discussed following this test to assure you that you understand the concepts covered so far.

Progress Check 2.1: Identifying Conditioning Concepts

Directions: Read the three examples of behaviors described below, and correctly complete each statement in the spaces provided following each example, choosing your answers from the following list:

unconditioned response	operant	classical conditioning
operant conditioning	positive reinforcer	negative reinforcer
unconditioned stimulus	conditioned stimulus	conditioned response

Example A: Linda was a new third grader in PS 172. The first time she went toward her desk in her new class she let out a cry of surprised pain and tears sprang to her eyes as a rubber band shot against her leg. This happened again after the morning recess and again after lunch. The next morning there was no rubber band, but as Linda approached her desk she was fearful and there was a hint of tears in her frightened eyes.

In Example A, at first, Linda's tears were a(n) _____. Through a process
                                                                  (1)

of _____, her fearful tears were transferred from the rubber band shot at her leg,
        (2)

which had served as a(n) _____, to walking toward her desk which had become a(n)
                                (3)

_____.
     (4)

Example B: Pat used to throw his coat over a nearby desk until the day when, because no desk was immediately available, he put the coat on a hook. His teacher, Mrs. Pell, profusely praised him that day and several days following and called him a gentleman. From then on, he always hung his coat up in Mrs. Pell's classroom.

In Example B, Pat's coat-hanging behavior was effected through a process of _____.
                                                                                (5)

This behavior is called a(n) _____, and Mrs. Pell's praise acted an a(n) _____.
                                   (6)   **(7)**

Example C: Philip was a conscientious worker but he was having a difficult time doing the multiplication problems given to him by Mr. Bard, his beloved fourth-grade teacher. When most of the children had finished and gone out to recess Philip didn't like staying behind. Mr. Bard stopped at Philip's desk and praised him generously for the problems he had done correctly. Then pointing to an incorrect answer he said, "You may go outside when you get this one right as well." Philip corrected his answer and left the stuffy classroom with a shout of joy.

In Example C, Mr. Bard's praise of Philip was meant to serve as a(n) _____

(8)

in a process of _____. while letting Philip escape from the classroom to join

(9)

the others on the playground was meant to serve as a(n) _____.

(10)

CHOOSING POSITIVE REINFORCERS TO INCREASE BEHAVIOR

Although research has established that both positive and negative reinforcers increase behavior, both are not equally useful. Positive reinforcers provide greater opportunities to control the exact desired response. The use of positive reinforcers makes it possible to reinforce *only* the particular response one wishes to strengthen. By contrast, when using negative reinforcers *any* response that will end the unpleasant stimulus, even temporarily, is reinforced.

For example, suppose a teacher observes Johnny engaged in a stimulating activity that unfortunately involves racing around the classroom at speeds which she estimates to be about fifty miles per hour, and which she insightfully perceives to be incompatible with learning the arithmetic lesson for the day. What is she to do? The teacher's goal may be to control Johnny's behavior in such a way that he will sit at his desk for a period of at least fifteen minutes at a time and give full attention to the arithmetic lesson before him. The teacher may set up a program using positive reinforcers, such as public praise, reinforcing Johnny every time he displays behavior that is in the direction of the ultimate goal. On the other hand, the teacher may engage in a program of negative reinforcement, a common though poor strategy. Here, instead of publicly praising Johnny every time he engages in the desired behavior, the teacher decides to publicly humiliate him by making Johnny stand in the waste basket until he does what she wants him to, at which time she reinforces the desired behavior by letting him out of the basket. The strategy is that the cessation of humiliation should increase the probability of Johnny's engaging in study behavior, but you probably know what usually goes wrong with this kind of program.

Reinforcing Only the Desired Behavior

The problem with a negative reinforcement approach is that there are a variety of other behaviors aside from arithmetic behavior which will get

Johnny out of the basket but that will not get him any closer to his arithmetic. He may, for instance, leave school, arrive late for school, get himself sent to the principal where he can wait in the quiet of the hall for half an hour, take extra and extended trips to the lavatory, or start a total uproar in the classroom. Since all of these behaviors would get Johnny out of the basket they would be just as reinforcing as doing his school work would have been, and they would therefore tend to occur again.

Effort of Repeated Administrations

A second problem with a program using negative reinforcers is that it usually requires a great deal more effort than a program using positive reinforcers. Again, let us take the example of Running Johnny. Humiliating Johnny, running after him, hitting him, and yelling at him will all require a great deal of energy on the part of the teacher, particularly if she is also trying to continue the impossible task of teaching her well-behaved students the arithmetic. Should the teacher finally get Johnny seated and working she can negatively reinforce this behavior only once while his good behavior continues. On the other hand, positive reinforcers can be administered periodically while the arithmetic lesson is proceeding and as often as the teacher wishes.

Relative Side Effects of Positive and Negative Reinforcers

Positive reinforcers rarely have the undesirable and destructive side effects often accompanying the behavior changes of the person being negatively reinforced. These side effects include anger, discouragement, lack of cooperation, hostility, and even desire for revenge. These side effects are similar to those often found in relation to the use of punishment as well.

All in all, then, positive reinforcers have four advantages over negative ones:

1. Positive reinforcers can be used *to strengthen that behavior and only that behavior* which is desired. This cannot be done so easily with negative reinforcers.
2. A program using positive reinforcers is generally *easier to administer* and *less time-consuming* than one using negative reinforcers.
3. Positive reinforcers can be *administered repeatedly* while the desired behavior is occurring, while negative reinforcers can be administered only

once at the initial onset of the behavior and cannot be repeated until the desired behavior has stopped and then started again.

4. Positive reinforcers *rarely have the undesirable side effects* which so often accompany the use of negative reinforcers.

Now, if you are able to state some of the advantages of using positive instead of negative reinforcers the following quiz will provide positive reinforcement in the form of correct answers.

Progress Check 2.2: Comparing the Usefulness of Positive and Negative Reinforcers

Directions: Read the descriptions below of the two teachers attempting to increase arithmetic-learning behavior through the use of reinforcers. On the lines provided, indicate at least two advantages of Mrs. Bertram's use of positive reinforcers and two disadvantages of Mrs. Abrams' use of negative reinforcers to accomplish their teaching goals. Can you hypothesize some of the possible results—intended or unintended—of each program?

Descriptions:

(1.) When Mrs. Abrams' pupils came into their third-grade classroom Monday morning, attached to the front of each of their desks were two very large red S's. Mrs. Abrams told them, "These S's on your desks stand for Slow and Stupid. Now if you don't want everyone to know that you are slow and stupid, you can get the S's taken off your desks. Everyone who finishes ten addition problems correctly gets to have one S taken away; when you have finished twenty problems correctly you may have the other S taken away. So everyone work as hard as you can so nobody in this class can be called slow or stupid."

(2) When Mrs. Bertram's pupils came into their third-grade classroom Monday morning, lined up across the entire bulletin board was a huge array of very large red S's. "These S's, Mrs. Bertram told them, stand for Smart, Special, and Super. Everytime you finish ten addition problems correctly you can take one of the S's for your desk. Everytime you do ten more problems you can take another S for your desk. So everyone work as hard as you can so that we can see that everyone in this class is smart, and maybe even super special smart."

1. Two advantages of using positive reinforcers are that positive reinforcers _____

_____ and _____.

2. Two disadvantages of using negative reinforcers could be that negative reinforcers _____

_____ and _____.

DECREASING BEHAVIOR WITH PUNISHMENT

Besides increasing desired behavior, teachers also occasionally need to decrease undesired behavior. Although it is almost always preferable to emphasize the positive whenever possible, it is sometimes necessary to attempt directly to decrease the occurrence of some behavior. There are two ways to do this. One way is through punishment, the other with nonreinforcement. They are not equally effective and do not have identical results. In fact, research has indicated that some of our most deeply ingrained ideas about child-rearing, teaching, and about social control in general—including practices to which most of us have been subjected in greater or lesser degrees—ought to be changed. Let's see why.

Definition of Punishment

Punishments as identified by behaviorists are generally the same as those identified by most of us most of the time. It is usually a punishment when a student is told to stand in the corner with his face to the wall, or a person is made to pay a twenty-five dollar fine after parking the car by the fire hydrant. Although in a strict behaviorist definition punishment is defined only in terms of its effects on behavior, in the practical arena punishment usually appears to be an aversive or unpleasant event impinging on the individual involved following certain behavior. Thus, it may be either the addition of a noxious stimulant, or the taking away of a pleasant one. It may be pain caused by being hit or shocked; it may be embarrassment, rejection, disapproval, reprimands, or loneliness. It may be a bad grade, missing recess, standing in the hall, or being placed conspicuously in the front seat under the close supervision of the teacher.

Behaviorists' extraordinary contribution to our understanding of the role of punishment is the evidence that it is often a highly inefficient way of controlling behavior. This is so despite the fact that it is probably the most commonly accepted means in our society of attempting to do so. Many of us in our individual lives, and certainly in our institutional and societal norms, demonstrate an erroneous view of the effects of punishment. Punishment, or the threat of it, is one of the primary means by which government attempts to insure obedience to its laws and a similar situation exists in many of our schools.

However, punishment, unfortunately, often merely *suppresses* behavior temporarily without really eliminating it, and it returns at its full strength when the threat is removed. To use punishment effectively, then, the threat must be continuously present. Thus, societies using punishment most effectively to control behavior are police states. Teachers who use it as their primary means of controlling discipline often cannot leave their students alone without bedlam breaking out, and halls and lavatories must be patrolled. The problem student who is kept in line by threats of being sent to the principal, of receiving ridicule, or getting a low grade, or suspended from school rarely becomes a model student because as soon as the threat of these unsavory events is removed even temporarily his apparently studious behavior disappears.

If the use of punishment, according to research evidence thus far, is generally such an ineffective way of controlling behavior and involves so much extra effort, why is it so often used? The reason is probably that most people do not know how to control behavior in any other way. Besides, intuitively, it seems to make sense. No one, it seems reasonable to say, wants to be whipped or deprived of dessert, or sent to the principal, put in prison, or given a parking ticket, and therefore people will act to avoid these things. Punishment does affect behavior; its effects are not always totally negative, and behaviorists believe that there is a place for its judicious use. Their argument is simply that punishment is too often inappropriately or overly used. To understand when punishment should or should not be used we will look first at some of the effects of punishment, and then explore how it may most effectively be used when it's use is necessary.

Adverse Effects of Punishment

If very severe punishment is administered or threatened a behavior may be suppressed for a very long time, even permanently (Solomon 1964). Does this mean that severe punishment is better than mild punishment? Does this mean that the government should not abolish capital punishment but should actually increase its use? Should our schools return to a policy of physical beatings and parents to the strategy of locking misbehaving children in dark closets? No, say the behaviorists, because use of punishment shares two major problems with negative reinforcers.

Unforeseen Side Effects. First of all, punishment, especially severe punishment, often has unforeseen and undesirable side effects. Your own self-observation in the face of punishment at some time or other may help you understand the behaviorist research findings that punishment often leads to responses of fear, anger, aggression, uncooperation, and the desire to escape. You may remember some particularly hated teacher who although he controlled the class by strict disciplinary measures did not have disorder in the classroom and consequently was severely disliked. Unfortunately, an additional result is that students often dislike the subject taught by such a teacher. Most of us know at least one person who learned to hate math because the method used in teaching was the "Get the right answer or get him" method.

When punishment is constantly used to control behavior a person often develops generally aggressive behavior not only against his punisher and what he represents but even against other people who are in the same situation as the person being punished. What sometimes seems to be senseless aggression against people who have done no harm to the aggressor at all is clearly understood by the behaviorist as a possible result of well-meaning parents', teachers', and other authorities' excessive use of punishment. Therefore, we find that children who are hit often by their parents frequently are those who hit other children the most.

Emphasize the Negative. A second problem with using punishment to control behavior is that while punishment may weaken the undesired behavior (and as we have said, it often does not), it does not strengthen the desired behavior and may very well strengthen some other undesirable behavior. It almost always leads to some kind of escape behavior. Actually, this is usually what the punisher has in mind, but the escape behavior performed by the escapee is very often not the escape behavior the punisher intended. Instead of settling down and learning his arithmetic, the errant student may escape punishment by dropping out of school. A teacher may inhibit Johnny's propensity to go around socking girls in the class by sock-

---

MANY BEHAVIORISTS INSIST THAT PUNISHMENT IS USUALLY NOT THE BEST WAY TO CONTROL BEHAVIOR

"Our present culture is in trouble because of its prodigious use of punitive control. Our international stance sets the pattern: when a nation displeases us, we bomb it, and we refuse to relinquish the power to do so in order to move toward an effective world government. Order in the streets is now treated almost entirely as a matter of police power. Children are still severely beaten in some of our schools."

From the Forward by B. F. Skinner in *Walden Two Experiment* by K. Kinkade

Have you ever seen punishment produce results which interfered with a student's learning or further progress in school? Have you ever seen punishment increase *the behavior problem the teacher was trying to control? Can you offer any alternatives for controlling behavior that you think might have been more effective? Could positive reinforcement have been used in the place of or along with the punishment to avoid negative results?*

---

ing Johnny himself but she has not strengthened Johnny's tendency to accomplish some academic work as she had hoped. She may even inadvertently have encouraged Johnny's propensity to engage in some other disruptive behavior in the boys' room. Behavior which has been learned to escape punishment is some of the longest lasting, resistent to change behavior that psychologists know of.

Fortunately, there is an alternative to punishment in order to decrease undesired behavior. With the hope that it is a positively reinforcing and not a punishing task, you can test yourself to see whether you are able to recognize the principles of punishment that have just been discussed by taking the following progress check.

Progress Check 2.3: Recognizing Behaviorist Principles of Punishment

Directions: Place a check beside those statements which accurately reflect the behaviorist position in regard to punishment presented in the text. For additional feedback, indicate on the line provided the reasons for your evaluation of each statement.

_____1. When punishment is constant or severe it usually has very little effect on behavior.

Reason: _____

_____2. When threat of punishment is removed behavior often reasserts itself in full strength.

Reason: _____

_____3. Behavior which permits an individual to escape from punishment is often very long lasting.

Reason: _____

_____4. Punishment often has undesired or unforeseen side effects.

Reason: _____

_____5. Despite some disadvantages, punishment is an almost indispensable tool for strengthening most kinds of behavior.

Reason: _____

USING NONREINFORCEMENT INSTEAD OF PUNISHMENT

It is often possible to end behavior permanently without resorting to punishment. This can be done by using nonreinforcement. When behavior is followed by neither reinforcement nor punishment it is nonreinforced and the behavior will gradually decrease. It is deconditioned, or extinguished. Through this reversal process called *extinction,* behavior is deadened just as a flame is extinguished. It will not flare up again once extinction is complete unless there are new reinforcements used to recondition it again.

Definition of Nonreinforcement

If the behavior being extinguished is followed by neither reinforcement nor punishment, what then is it followed by? What specifically is nonreinforcement? Nonreinforcement is either a neutral or indifferent event, or it is a nonevent coming as close to no change as can be arranged. Remember the cookie jar? If it is empty the first three times I lift the lid after coming home starved from school I probably will stop engaging in this nonreinforced behavior.

Note that finding an empty cookie jar, which leads to nonreinforced behavior, is generally apt to lead to much longer-lasting extinction than is punishment. Compare, for instance, the potential effects of finding an empty cookie jar (nonreinforcement) with the effects of finding a cookie jar jammed full of freshly baked goodies. As I prowl toward the jar, my mother forcibly inhibits my progress, saying that those cookies are for dessert, that they'll ruin my appetite, and that under no circumstances am I to have one. Now imagine that my mother leaves the house for half an hour (that is, threat of punishment is removed). There is at least a strong possibility that I may engage in the forbidden behavior to lift out just one cookie that will hardly be missed, isn't there? Whereas when my behavior was nonreinforced by the empty cookie jar, my tendency to open the jar when my mother had gone out was no stronger than it was when she was in the kitchen.

Strange as it may seem, then, and sometimes initially difficult as it may be to convince ourselves of its usefulness, nonreinforcing behavior is often more effective than punishment. However, it is not *always* advisable to use nonreinforcement instead of punishment. This is so in the face of behavior that for some reason must be stopped immediately and in the case of behavior which is intrinsically reinforcing.

Using Punishment and Positive Reinforcers Together

Although it might be ultimately effective, it is sometimes not advisable to wait for the effects of nonreinforcement to extinguish behavior. Children playing with knives or fires are obvious examples. There may be certain behavior in the classroom, as well, which a teacher may find so disruptive or potentially harmful that it must be stopped immediately. Punishment or its threat, then, may be necessary as a temporary stopgap. In addition, there are some behaviors which carry their own reinforcers so that just doing them is terribly rewarding. Some examples might be executing a perfect jackknife dive, listening to a Mozart concerto on a cool spring evening, possibly mainlining heroine, or getting repeatedly drunk on alcohol. In cases such as these, it is usually not possible to stop reinforcing the behavior because the reinforcement is intrinsic to the behavior. In such cases punishment may be a necessary adjunct.

However, punishment should *never* be used alone in order to control behavior. Punishment may provide the time while undesired behavior is temporarily suppressed to reinforce other incompatible and more positive behavior so that when the effects of punishment "wear off" the other reinforced behavior is already taking its place. This is so whether the reason for using punishment was the necessity of stopping dangerous behavior immediately or to counteract the effects of intrinsically rewarding behavior. The positive use of punishment is discussed again in chapter 6 on behavior modification techniques.

Advantages of Using Nonreinforcers Instead of Punishment

It is sometimes necessary to use punishment but nonreinforcement has several advantages over the use of punishment. A program of nonreinforcement will extinguish behavior permanently and after behavior is extinguished no further conditioning to maintain extinction is necessary. Punishment, on the other hand, often must remain generally constant to maintan its effectiveness, and when the threat is removed the behavior may reappear in full bloom. Nonreinforcing undesired behavior is usually much less effort than punishing it as well, and this can be an important asset to the busy teacher. Lastly, nonreinforcement is not accompanied by the undesirable side effects which so often accompany the use of punishment and which often interfere with learning.

Identifying and using appropriate nonreinforcers and punishments in education is discussed more fully in chapter 6. Meanwhile, here is a short quiz to see if you can predict the effects of the four contingencies we have been talking about.

Progress Check 2.4: Predicting the Effects of Positive and Negative Reinforcers, Punishment, and Nonreinforcement

Directions: In the following examples, behavior is being changed through operant conditioning. In the spaces provided, indicate whether behavior is being controlled through use of:

a) positive reinforcer
b) negative reinforcer
c) punishment
d) nonreinforcement,

and whether therefore it should:

1) occur more often
2) occur less often
3) temporarily disappear
4) remain unchanged in rate of occurrence.

Example A: A pigeon lifts its left foot. A food pellet arrives and is immediately consumed by the pigeon. These events are repeated several times. The food pellet probably acts as a

_____, and left-foot raising should _____.
        (1)   **(2)**

Example B: A third grader bites her fingernail. The teacher immediately slaps her hand. This

event is repeated several times. Being slapped probably acts as _____ and fin-
                                                    (3)

gernail biting will probably _____.
                          (4)

Example C: A monkey is playing with a box. He turns it upsidedown, bangs it on the floor, and pushes the lid from underneath. Nothing happens until the last of these behavior when the box springs open revealing a banana inside which the monkey immediately consumes. The banana

probably acts as a _____, and the monkey's behavior of pushing the lid of
                                    (5)

the box from underneath in the future will probably _____. His behavior of bang-
                                                                  (6)

ing the box on the floor was followed by _____ and will probably _____.
                                          (7)   **(8)**

Example D: Little three-year-old Oscar starts crying loudly and pulling at his mother's coat demanding a piece of candy. "Oscar, stop crying! Here!" responds his mother in exasperation

and hands him the candy. Candy probably served as a _____ for Oscar's coat-
(9)

pulling and candy-demanding behavior and it should probably _____. The
(10)

termination of Oscar's crying probably acted as a _____ for Oscar's mother,
(11)

and her candy-bestowing behavior in the future will probably _____.
(12)

CONTROLLING BEHAVIOR WITH THE RIGHT REINFORCEMENT SCHEDULE

So far we have studied the contingencies a teacher can arrange following behavior to increase or decrease its occurrence. Usually these contingencies must follow behavior more than once before they will be effective. The question we are going to discuss now is *how often* should these contingencies follow behavior? Every time it occurs? Or only sometimes? On the whole, evidence indicates that partial reinforcement leads to longer-lasting behavior once it is firmly established than does continuous reinforcement in which every incident of behavior is reinforced. This may be a relief since in the "real world" in which we exist as parents or teachers, constantly reinforcing the desired behavior of our children or students may be exhausting if not downright impossible if we are to get anything else done.

There are different reinforcement schedules, or relationships, between the number of times a behavior occurs and the number of times it is actually reinforced. Each schedule effects the building-up and maintenance of behavior differently (Ferster and Skinner 1957). We will look at the differences between interval and ration, fixed and variable or random, and between frequent and infrequent reinforcement schedules.

Interval and Ratio Schedules

Interval schedules refer to periods of time, ratio schedules to the number of times a behavior occurs. Monthly salary checks are given on an interval schedule. The teacher who puts a gold star beside Johnny's name on the bulletin board after every ten minutes during which he has been either at

THE RESULTS OF DIFFERENT REINFORCEMENT SCHEDULES

REINFORCEMENT SCHEDULE	REINFORCES BEHAVIOR	RESULTING IN	FOR EXAMPLE
frequent	often, even everytime it occurs	rapid build up of behavior but rapid decrease when reinforcement ceases	student's writing ability rapidly increases with teacher A who praises it frequently but drops off in teacher B's class in the absence of praise
infrequent	relatively infrequently; occasionally	slow build up of behavior but may maintain established behavior at high levels	occasional praise following punctual behavior to maintain punctuality
fixed interval	after regular and specific intervals of time	rapid increases in behavior just before reinforcer is due, then rapid decrease until just before next reinforcer	"cramming" just before tests with little study behavior after test until just before next test
fixed ratio	after behavior occurs specific number of times	behavior either rapidly increase to maximum or extinguishes	student promised a reward for every 10 problems done correctly may soon work at A levels, or after failing to achieve rewards, give up altogether
random interval	after varying intervals of time	relatively slow build up but can maintain behavior at high and steady levels with few reinforcements	a man will go on fishing and fishing even when his catches are few and far between
random ratio	after varying occurrences of behavior	relatively slow build up but can maintain behavior at high and steady levels with few reinforcements	gambling behavior once established is usually difficult to extinguish even when losses far exceed gains

study or quietly engaged in social play without hitting or yelling at his peers is also using reinforcement on an interval schedule.

On the other hand, the baby who receives a spoonful of applesauce as a reinforcement after every four spoonfuls of spinach is on a ratio schedule. Similarly, a pieceworker in a factory who gets paid for every twenty-five pieces of work is on a ratio schedule. So is Johnny who gets an *A* for every ten problems he does correctly in his arithmetic book, no matter how long it takes him.

On an interval schedule, an individual is reinforced after definite *intervals of time* if the specified behavior has occurred at least once and incompatible behavior has not been exhibited. The intervals of time selected may be long or short or they may vary, leading to either relatively frequent or infrequent reinforcements. On a ratio schedule, reinforcement is delivered after a specified *number of occurrences* of the specified behavior instead of after a specific time period. The number of occurrences likewise may be large or small or they may vary.

Fixed and Random Schedules

All schedules are either ratio or interval schedules, and they are also either fixed or random. Fixed schedules are regular; random schedules vary.

On a *fixed schedule* an individual is reinforced after a specified and unvarying interval of time or occurrences of behavior. Johnny knows, for instance, that he will earn an *A* after he has done ten problems correctly. The policeman knows he will receive his pay-check every two weeks. Johnny is on a fixed radio schedule; the policeman is on a fixed interval schedule. One special kind of fixed schedule is called *continuous* and it is the kind of schedule in operation when every instance of a specified behavior is reinforced.

A monkey receiving a banana after the first, third, fourth, ninth, eleventh, and twentieth time he puts a ball into a box is on a random ratio schedule and may in addition become very sick of bananas. The pupil who receives a smile from the teacher once in a while for his good behavior is being reinforced on a random schedule. The parent who occasionally comments with approval on his child's exemplary report card is reinforcing on a random schedule.

Random schedules are the opposite of fixed or regular schedules and are called random because reinforcements are delivered after varying numbers of intervals or occurrences of behavior. Instead of steadily or consistently reinforcing behavior random schedules do so *randomly*.

Effects of Different Schedules

Different reinforcement schedules effect behavior differently, and depending on what your goal is you will select a different schedule.

Behavior which has been reinforced on a fixed interval schedule tends to be moderate but persistent although quite variable, increasing quite rapidly just before the reinforcement arrives and tapering off until just before the next reinforcement is due. The perennial pattern of the student who works into the wee hours of the morning cramming the books just before a test in order to receive the reinforcement of a good grade, and whose activities in this area then tend to decelerate until just before the next exam is showing the typical effects of a fixed interval schedule. If the teacher should wish to increase the spurts of study behavior he may increase the number of exams during a semester since if intervals are shortened, behavior rate increases. If intervals are lengthened, behavior rates decrease.

Behavior conditioned on a *fixed ratio schedule* is highly variable. Like the little girl with the curl, when a fixed ratio schedule is good it is very very good, but when it is bad, it is horrid. A fixed ratio schedule can be a very effective way of getting high rates of work from highly skilled workmen who receive a high number of reinforcements, and in school, it is often effective for good students. On the other hand, if for some reason, a person does not or cannot perform the specified behavior at a high rate, the number of reinforcements will drop off. This decrease in reinforcements may lead to a further decline in performance, which in turn will lead to an even further decrease in reinforcement creating a vicious circle in which productive behavior may cease appearing altogether, to be replaced very often with high levels of anxiety, frustration, or apparent apathy. Obviously, the use of such reinforcement schedules with students who do not do a great deal of school work to begin with is apt to be dysfunctional.

Random scheduling is what occurs most often in our daily lives, and although it builds up behavior relatively slowly, its effects are extremely stable. Behavior which has been reinforced on a random schedule is extremely resistant to extinction and so will last a long time in the absence of any reinforcements at all. Pigeons reinforced on a random schedule with pellets of food for pecking at a bar have been observed pecking at the bar thousands of times without any further reinforcement at all. Skinner says that persistent human behavior which seems to reflect determination or will power or stubbornness really is not due to any sterling characteristics within the person but is really the result of behavior previously reinforced on a random schedule. Random reinforcement schedules may, of course, deliver reinforcements relatively frequently or infrequently.

As you become more sensitive to the exact needs of students in your class you can acquire facility in changing these schedules to bring about the behavior changes you desire. In the beginning, you may find the following helpful as a practical rule of thumb.

Fixed interval schedules with short intervals or fixed ratio schedules leading to very frequent and consistent reinforcement, even continuous reinforcement, are the most effective schedules to build-up or strengthen weak behavior, behavior that does not initially occur very often. It is usually the best kind of schedule to use at the beginning of conditioning. Random schedules with irregular and less frequent reinforcements are the most effective in maintaining behavior at a high and stable rate, and it should be used after a desired behavior is already occurring at a sufficiently high rate and you want to support the already-established habit.

If you want to see how well you have understood what has been said so far about schedules of reinforcement take the following short quiz.

Progress Check 2.5:   Differentiating Reinforcement Schedules

Direction: In the following examples, behavior is being changed through use of positive reinforcers. Place a check in front of the reinforcement schedule which, according to the principles just presented in the text, best completes the statement at the end of each example.

Example A: By feeding it a tasty fly every time it did so, Jackie had taught her pet turtle to put its head out of its shell whenever its shell was tapped twice by Jackie's fingernail. To maintain this behavior, Jackie needs to continue to present the fly as a reinforcer at least on a

_____ frequent fixed interval schedule.

_____ infrequent random ratio schedule.

_____ infrequent fixed ratio schedule.

_____ infrequent fixed interval schedule.

Example B: Only rarely does Jonathan make his bed. To increase the likelihood of Jonathan's bed-making behavior, his mother should reward him initially on a:

_____ frequent fixed ratio schedule.

_____ infrequent fixed ratio schedule.

_____ random interval schedule.

_____ random ratio schedule.

Example C: Mr. Pembleton takes his sixth grade class of boys on a hike every Friday afternoon if everyone has done at least 80 percent of the assigned math problems correctly that week. He has noticed that math behavior accelerates rapidly on Thursdays and Fridays, not a surprising result since he is using a

_____ fixed interval schedule.

_____ random interval schedule.

_____ random ratio schedule.

_____ continuous reinforcement schedule.

Example D: Bernadette and Cathy are trying to increase the number of smiles which Miss Egan bestows on the freshman class during her history lectures. They have set up a program whereby they reinforce Miss Egan with studious looks of concentrated interested and notetaking after every third smile. Miss Egan is being reinforced on a

_____ continuous reinforcement schedule.

_____ infrequent random interval schedule.

_____ frequent fixed ratio schedule.

_____ frequent fixed interval schedule.

CREATING NEW BEHAVIORS

Suppose a teacher has selected an armament of positive reinforcers, which he is eagerly waiting to dispense to his worthy students on a continuous schedule of reinforcement, and the behaviors of studying and learning never appear in his students. How can he reinforce behavior that never occurs?

Shaping

Shaping is the alternative to sitting idly by waiting for the behavior to appear miraculously. It is the process of reinforcing *successive approximations* to the goal behavior. If Sally never reads during study hour a teacher who has set up the goal of increasing Sally's attention span to twenty minutes cannot begin by reinforcing Sally every time she sits in studious concentration for at least twenty minutes. The whole term may go by during which the teacher will not have had the opportunity to bestow a single reinforcer.

Instead, the teacher observes Sally's *baseline* behavior—how long does she sit at her desk now before any conditioning begins? Having ascertained that Sally seems to sit quietly for periods ranging from thirty to ninety seconds the teacher may decide to reinforce Sally for this behavior when it lasts for at least a minute. Gradually this time period is lengthened and Sally is reinforced only after she has sat quietly for two or five minutes. Then the teacher may make reinforcement contingent on Sally's actually opening a book for a short period, and so on until Sally has reached the ultimate goal.

When you cannot reinforce the behavior that you ultimately want, start out by reinforcing whatever relevant smaller unit of behavior that does appear, gradually building-up toward the larger unit of behavior. Since much of education is concerned with teaching students new behaviors, shaping is built into most behaviorist instructional methods. The teacher or parent who finds himself able to give reinforcement only rarely is either using an ineffective reinforcer or is concentrating on a unit of behavior which is not occurring with sufficient frequency and should use shaping techniques.

Cueing Behaviors Before They Occur

One of the most helpful tools the teacher has in helping to shape and control behavior is cueing. *Cues* are an indication that some consequence will follow on certain behavior in a particular situation. In some way, verbal or nonverbal, cues communicate "if—then" information. If certain behavior occurs, then certain consequences—reinforcement, punishment, or nonreinforcement—will follow. A teacher who promises his class that everyone who gets at least a *B* in the biology exam tomorrow will not have to take the final exam is cueing his students that reinforcement is going to follow certain behavior. Deliberate cues are very often verbal but they may be as subtle as the raising of an eyebrow, the flick of a wrist, a threatening step forward, or an encouraging smile.

There are two particularly important sets of cues which are related to processes called generalization and discrimination.

Generalization: When It Is the Same. Generalization is the tendency of an individual to repeat behavior learned in one situation in a variety of similar situations. The young man who has learned that carrying heavy bundles for his mother is apt to be reinforced is generalizing if he also carries heavy bundles for his wife or girl friend as well. Teachers hope that a student reinforced for handing in math assignments on time will be apt to hand in English assignments on time as well. In fact, the entire school system is based on the hope that behavior learned in the classroom will be generalized to the student's life outside the classroom many years after school is over.

Generalization occurs when cues say, in effect, to the individual, "This situation is *like* some other; behavior in this situation will result in the same consequences that result in that other situation." Cues leading to generalization, then, can be used as a powerful teaching device. Teachers and parents often find that students can easily be taught apparently new behaviors if it is possible to point out how these new behaviors are like behaviors already used successfully in other situations. "You already know how to write an essay," says the teacher beginning a class in composition. "It is just like writing a paragraph with a beginning that expresses the main idea, a middle that develops the idea, and an ending that finishes it." Or the teacher may tell the first-grader learning to write, "You already know how to make the letter *l*, and you already know how to make the letter *o*. The letter *b* is just the same except you put them very close together so they are touching."

What each of these teachers is doing is cueing behavior by indicating to the student that the behavior which was reinforced by success in previous situations will be reinforced by success in the new learning situation as well. This process, unfortunately, will not work for the benefit of students who may generalize failure instead of success. "Going to work is very much like going to school," says the teacher trying to encourage a frightened student starting out on his first paid job. But if the student has failed more than he has succeeded at school these cues about the similarity of school and job may be much more frightening than helpful, particularly if the student has come to accept this teacher's cues as reliable. In situations such as these the teacher wants to help the student to *discriminate* rather than to generalize.

Discrimination: When It Is Different. Discrimination is based on the response to cues which indicate how situations are *different* rather than the same. It is the process by which an individual learns that certain contingencies which follow behavior under one set of circumstances will *not* follow in other circumstances. Discrimination has occurred when a young man learns that kissing his mother as she steps off the plane at the airport will be followed by rewarding hugs and smiles but that engaging in this same behavior toward the stranger next to his mother will not bring about the same consequences. It has occurred when a student learns that an essay is *different* from a paragraph because it is longer. It has happened when the young student learns that writing the letter *b* is different from writing the letters *l* and *o* because they are "so close together that they are touching."

Cueing Behavior Does Not Cause Behavior. Using cues to control and shape behavior, particularly by directing the processes of generalization and discrimination in which students learn how things are the same or different, is one of the most frequently utilized and powerful teaching devices teachers have available to them. Unfortunately, the use of cues can be almost totally ineffective if teachers expect cues to produce behavior by themselves.

It is a common mistake to attempt to cue behavior in the expectation that cues will produce behavior independently of reinforcement. However, cueing behavior *does not in itself make behavior happen.* Cues simply indicate the increased probability of reinforcement or punishment under certain conditions if the individual behaves in a certain way. So if that reinforcement or punishment does not follow that behavior—if the cues were not correct—then they will shortly become ineffective in controlling behavior. Cues cannot operate effectively without the help of the four environmental contingencies—positive and negative reinforcement, non-reinforcement, and punishment—that we have already discussed.

Almost everyone exposed to contemporary education has observed at least once in their educational lives the spectacle of a teacher whose cues for silence are utterly ignored, and some of us have on occasion been that teacher. Why does this happen? The diagnosis of the behaviorist is that in the past the teacher failed to back up her cues with consequences. The teacher threatens that anyone who talks during class must stay in the class-room during recess but when recess comes everyone is allowed to go outside. The teacher is trying to be nice but instead she is ineffective. Or, the teacher has promised that everyone who is quiet during reading period may work on his art project for an extra half hour but when art period comes, the teacher is too disorganized to keep his promise.

Because cueing behavior is effective only when the individual has learned that these cues are consistently reliable indicators of consequences following behavior, it is very important for educators to make sure that they follow through on their promises and threats, and should not make them if they cannot or will not keep them. It is a very old precept that people should keep their word. Behaviorists provide a new rationale for doing so. If a person wants to be able to cue behavior effectively, if a teacher wants his students to believe him, then he must have kept his promises consistently enough in the past so that students rely on him as an accurate indicator of future reinforcement, punishment, and nonreinforcement.

Progress Check 2.6: Analyzing Cues

Directions: Indicate whether the statements following each vignette below accurately reflect statements made in the text. Mark accurate statements with a *T,* inaccurate ones with an *F.*

Vignette A: Mr. Perles announced to his sophomore history class, "Just because you are allowed to hand in your papers late in Mr. Allen's class and still get a good grade doesn't mean you can be tardy in my class and still get away with a good grade, because you can't."

_____1. Mr. Perles is cueing his class that they should generalize between Mr. Allen's and his class.

_____2. According to Mr. Perle's cues, tardy behavior in his class will not be reinforced.

_____3. According to Mr. Perles, punishment will follow tardy behavior in Mr. Allen's class.

Vignette B: It was a sorry sight to see Mrs. Appleby repeat again and again to her jabbering and exicted students that they should sit down and be silent. She even threatened to bring the principle in to deal with them, but even though the class was not quiet she didn't call the principal anyway.

_____4. Mrs. Appleby's cues to the class were ineffective because she was trying to use nonreinforcement instead of positive reinforcement.

_____5. Mrs. Appleby would probably be able to cue her class more effectively if the cues more reliably indicated the contingencies that actually would follow the students' behavior.

Vignette C: Mrs. Garcia was horrified when she heard Lucy, who had taught herself Spanish from a book, pronounce manana as if it rhymed with banana. "No!" said Mrs. Garcia, "the words are different. They do not rhyme. All the *a's* should sound like the *a's* in mama."

_____6. Initially, Lucy had inappropriately discriminated between the *a* sounds in banana and manana.

_____7. Mrs. Garcia was trying to teach Lucy to generalize between the *a* in ma and manana.

Vignette D: It was rest period, and Miss Richards told all the kindergarteners that if they were very quiet "like in the movies" that they would all have popcorn afterwards.

_____8. Since Miss Richards' cues indicated the similarities between the movies and rest period, she was hoping to teach the children to generalize between them.

_____9. The reinforcement that Miss Richards' cues promised would follow quiet behavior during rest period was going to the movies.

_____10. According to the behaviorists, Miss Richards' cues would probably be less effective among her pupils who did not like popcorn than among those who did.

SUMMARY

This chapter has covered the essential concepts on which contemporary behaviorism is built:

Classical conditioning controls respondent behavior. In the first stage of conditioning the *respondent* is also known as the *unconditioned response* because it can be elicited automatically without training by a specific environmental stimulus known as the *unconditioned stimulus* (UCS). In the second stage, the UCS is paired with a neutral stimulus or *conditioned stimulus* (CS). This pairing is repeated until stage three when the respondent (now known as the *conditioned response*) can be elicited by the presence of the CS alone in the absence of the UCS.

Operant conditioning controls operant behavior. It is the way that the frequency of behavior is controlled by its consequences or by the environmental event following it. These environmental contingencies are:

1. *positive reinforcers* (probably pleasant events) which increase the behavior they follow when they are added to a situation;
2. *negative reinforcers* (probably pleasant events insomuch as they involve the removal of unpleasant events) which increase the behavior they follow when they are taken away from a situation;
3. *nonreinforcers* (probably neutral or nonevents) which decrease the behavior it follows;
4. *punishment* whose effects are variable and may be either the addition of a noxious stimulus or the subtraction of an apparently pleasant one.

These contingencies may be delivered on varying schedules. Behavior is most quickly built-up when consequences follow behavior *frequently and regularly*. Behavior is maintained most economically on a relatively *infrequent and random* schedule.

Shaping is the process of gradual approximations to achieve the final goal behavior. This is accomplished by reinforcing increasingly larger segments of behavior in the direction of the goal behavior until the full behavior is performed.

Behavior can be *cued* before it occurs. Cueing does not cause behavior to happen and is effective only to the extent that the cues are reliable indicators of environmental contingencies which will follow a particular behavior if it occurs under certain circumstances. Cues may indicate that in certain situations particular behavior will be followed by the same contingencies as in other *similar* situations, in which case they increase the probability of *generalization,* or they may indicate that a certain situation is *different* from other situations in which case they increase the probability of *discrimination*.

SUGGESTED READING

For a simple introduction to behaviorism, one of the best places to go for a clear presentation of the basic fundamentals is the section on behaviorism is an introductory psychology text.

BREWER, WILLIAM F. "There Is No Convincing Evidence for Conditioning in Adult Humans." In *Cognition and Symbolic Processes,* edited by Walter B. Weimer and David S. Palermo. New York: John Wiley & Sons, Inc., 1974.

This is an excellent, simple presentation by a cognitive psychologist of why he believes the conditioning interpretation is wrong, and why he thinks his cognitive interpretation is better.

FERSTER, C. B., AND PERROTT, M. C. *Behavior Principles,* New York: Meredith, 1968.

Tougher reading but an excellent elaboration with extensive research of the principles of behaviorism discussed in this chapter.

HILGARD, ERNEST R., AND BOWER, GORDON H. *Theories of Learning,* 3d ed. New York: Appleton-Century-Crofts, 1966.

This book is for the student who wishes to examine the development of a variety of behaviorist and other learning theories in greater detail, and who wishes to be acquainted with other theorists whose ideas have influenced contemporary educational thinking.

KELLER, FRED S. *Reinforcement Theory.* New York: Random House, 1969.

This is another simple but comprehensive presentation of behaviorism's basic concepts by a man who has spent considerable time applying these concepts to education.

KINKADE, KATHLEEN. *A Walden Two Experiment.* New York: William Morrow, 1973.

This is a report of a real community applying the principles of *Walden Two.*

SKINNER, B. F., AND HOLLAND, JAMES G. *The Analysis of Behavior: A Program for Self-Instruction.* New York: McGraw-Hill, 1961.

This book covers all the essential concepts presented in this chapter. Written as a linear programmed instruction, it teaches in the way that Skinner thinks is the best application of these principles themselves to human learning.

SKINNER, B. F. *Walden Two.* New York: Macmillan, 1948.

This is Skinner's blueprint for Utopia based on principles of operant conditioning. It's a classic, and if you haven't read it, and want to take behaviorism seriously, you should.

JOURNALS

Current research on the application of behaviorist principles is also published in journals. If you want to keep abreast of what is happening in this field, both within and outside education, two of your primary continuing sources are these:

Journal of Applied Behavior Analysis
Journal of Behavioral Research and Therapy

Where Are You Going, Teach?: Behavioral Objectives

3

Chapter Objectives

In this chapter we begin to apply the basic concepts of behaviorism covered in the last two chapters to the particular needs of education, specifically to the development of goals of teaching, both long-term and short-term. First we look at survival as the ultimate purpose of education, and then examine behavioral goals for day-to-day teaching, including steps for designing goals for your own classroom use. Finally we discuss some of the arguments and research in favor of and in objection to using behavioral goals.

The behavioral goals of this chapter are to enable you to:

1. distinguish behaviorist long-range goals for education.

> *Progress Check:* You are asked to pick out behaviorist goals among six suggested goals reflecting either behaviorist or nonbehaviorist values.

2. differentiate behaviorist definitions of thinking, learning, and problem-solving from non-Behaviorist or common-sense definitions.

> *Progress Check:* A 4-item multiple-choice quiz asks you to choose phrases which best complete sentences representing the behaviorist positions.

3. identify ascending levels of learning behaviors used in many behavioral objectives.

> *Progress Check:* A 14-item fill-in quiz asks you to list and define in your own words Bloom's taxonomy and Gagne's hierarchy of learning.

4. design your own behavioral objectives.

> *Progress Check:* You are asked to identify and evaluate in each of five objectives the three components essential to a complete behavioral objective.

5. *demonstrate an acquaintance with the arguments in favor of and against using behavioral objectives.*

Progress Check: In a sentence completion format you are asked to state at least three possible advantages of using behavioral objectives and three possible objections to their use.

THE ULTIMATE GOAL: SURVIVAL

Although most teachers in their day-to-day activities in the classroom are necessarily more concerned with whether Johnny has learned his multiplication tables yet than with the great questions of human existence, every educational system is based on some underlying values of society. A society that believes that man is fulfilled only by living for others, for instance, may set up an educational system like the one in China today that stresses the importance of cooperation and sharing. Capitalist societies like our own, on the other hand, tend to emphasize competitive behavior and the accomplishments of the individual more than the accomplishment of the whole group. Our educational system reflects these values in our grading and selection practices. In societies where the roles of men and women are sharply delineated, the educations given to boys and girls are dramatically different. In a society such as ours where the differences between sexes are more subtly expressed, the differences in educational practices are less apparent as well.

Education, then, is an expression of society. It is the means by which society teaches its children to assume the roles that it values in order to become the kind of adults that it needs, living what its individual members believe represents a meaningful or successful life. Many of the differences of opinion about educational practices go back to differences in these fundamental values about man, his fulfillment, and his relationship with his fellow man.

Behaviorism, like every other educational theory, is based on certain priorities and values. From a behaviorist point of view, the ultimate value in life is survival (Skinner 1971). The final norm by which we can judge the value of any behavior is its contribution to the survival either of the individual or of the human species as a whole. It is the greatest of all reinforcements. The ultimate goal of education, then, is to develop survival behaviors. There are three kinds, leading to three educational subgoals of increasing values to survival. We will look at each one and examine its implications for education.

Increasing Personal Freedom in Life and Career

The behaviorist concept of freedom is not the traditional one of independence from external control. Over the centuries, when men have struggled for such independence or for what they *called* freedom they have really been struggling to free themselves from control exercised by *threat of punishment*. They have not freed themselves from control itself because everyone is controlled by his environment. The difference is that the apparently "free" man has been able to replace aversive controls with positive ones. The free man, for instance, goes to work because it is followed by the positive reinforcement of a good salary, social prestige, or his ability to support his family; the "unfree" man goes to work because he will starve if he doesn't.

The school can increase personal freedom first by substituting punishing controls with positive ones. Instead of using threat of failure, for instance, the school can substitute the achievement of success—in place of ridicule, praise. We will see, in the next chapter, how behaviorists have attempted to do this with programmed instruction.

Besides changing its own methods of control from punishment to reward, the school contributes to personal freedom by providing students themselves with the behavioral skills which enable them to control their own lives with positive reinforcement. The primary and most important way the school can do this is by preparing each student with job skills. In this sense, behaviorism is quite pragmatic. In evaluating curriculum development the first concern is whether there are jobs for people with the behaviors these courses would provide. The important consideration is not so much whether students would enjoy these courses or whether they would feel that they are having good learning experiences, but the extent to which the courses might contribute to the students' potential job opportunities. The person with employment skills that society needs is freer in the behaviorist sense than the person who has few such skills.

This emphasis on the practical contribution that education should make to work abilities does not mean that the behaviorists are all sheer vocationalists obsessed with monitoring the job market to insure that schools are churning out just the right proportion of engineers, law-reforcement agents, lawyers, teachers, doctors, and typists, however. Skinner, among others, discusses the importance of developing behaviors which will prepare students to live and work in a changing evolving society with behavioral skills that are flexible, and points out that "learning how to learn" is often a more important skill than the learning of a single saleable skill itself.

The second set of survival behaviors, and so the second subgoal of education, is behavior undertaken for the good of others. These behaviors may appear at first to be unselfish in the sense that they are done at the sacrifice of personal reinforcers, but in reality, personal reinforcers are replaced by less obvious but equally powerful reinforcers such as admiration, praise, or status.

Education should deliberately reinforce behavior done for the good of others, and reinforcers for such behavior should be stronger than the reinforcers that accompany behavior accomplished solely for the good of the individual himself. The practical application of this principle would result in a great reduction of the cutthroat competition that pervades most of our educational system, replacing it with the cooperative behavior necessary to solve some of humanity's most urgent and pressing problems.

"The world," says Skinner (Kinkade 1973), "must do something about its food supplies, its educational system, its sanitation and health, its 'interpersonal' relations, its cultural activities. . . ." Because mankind must learn cooperation in order to solve such problems that threaten our very survival, an educational system that teaches its children to succeed by "beating out" everybody else is actually destructive—destructive in a rational, scientific, ultimately measurable sense—of the survival of the human race. It is counterproductive, doing more harm than good. Competitive behavior, many behaviorists believe, has resulted in a world where too few have too much, and too many have much too little. It has led to a world of mistrust, fear, lies, and thievery, while people struggle either to get what someone else has, or to hold onto what someone else is trying to take from them.

At present, our educational system, our entertainments, our sports and leisure time, and our job market all are strongly marked by competitive incentives. The behaviorists would change this. Although in the past, competition has provided strong motivation for some great accomplishments, the situation now one of global interdependence so that we cannot solve our greatest problems until we learn to cooperate. We cannot make the best possible use of the world's energy resources, we cannot preserve our environment, prevent war, distribute world food supplies to prevent mass starvations, or adequately dispose of our wastes without cooperating on an international scale. To put this cooperative principle into practice in the educational system, behaviorists use what they call criterion-referenced grading in which everyone is able to succeed, instead of norm-referenced grading in which only a few can come out on top and others must fail. This is discussed further in chapter 5.

IS COMPETITION GOOD FOR US?

Yes

Traditionally, we have taught our children to compete. The foundations of the whole American capitalist way of life is based on competition and if we eliminate it, we eliminate one of our greatest sources of strength. If people do not have to compete for what they get, they will give up trying at all. Competition is the biggest reason why America has accomplished so much. According to Darwin's law of evolution, competition for survival is how the human species developed and it is what will continue to keep us strong and vibrant; it will keep us from becoming sluggish and lazy. If we eliminate competition, we may reduce some of our problems, but at the same time we will eliminate what is best in our culture as well. We may no longer have people who fail but we will also no longer have people who try, who know how to struggle against all odds to stand out from the crowd, people who achieve something brilliant, something special, something which will make a major contribution to mankind. We will no longer have people who know how to fight to live, and that's one talent mankind can't afford to loose.

No

Competition is no longer the survival-producing incentive that it used to be. If the human species is going to continue to evolve it must learn cooperation now instead of competition. We must learn to share with each other, to help each other if we are not going to make our lives together on this planet intolerable or even absolutely impossible. The massive competition to develop increasingly destructive nuclear weapons, for instance, is the kind of behavior which may lead to the extinction, not the evolution, of the human species.

In education, competition may work well in motivating some students in the short run but it teaches them behaviors at the same time which are ultimately destructive for mankind. Besides, competition often discourages students and convinces them that they are failures so that they never produce the best work of which they are capable.

What Do You Think?

Is too much competition used to motivate the students in our schools? Should teachers use less competitive methods to motivate learning? Would it be better to praise a student for helping someone else learn the lesson rather than for learning the lesson himself first and fastest? Would it be better to have an honor role of students who are most helpful to others instead of one for students who earn the best grades for themselves? As you are preparing students to live in the world as it is today, and as you help to shape it for tomorrow, do you think it is more important that they leave your classroom with the strengths that come from competition, or with the abilities that come from cooperation?

Designing a Culture for the Human Community

The greatest challenge facing man today is the design and building of a working culture—the construction of a society in which men can continue to live with a minimum of suffering and in socially constructive ways. The final and most important goal for education is to contribute to the building of this culture in which man can survive.

Man must learn how to cooperate, but a readiness to help each other is not enough. We need to design solutions to our problems. We need to study our situation and draw up workable plans, programs in which mutual reinforcements will ensure that population, nuclear power, and natural resources are well-used and equally distributed in a satisfying and mutually enriching way. Our problems are grave and great, and it is education which must produce men and women capable of devising solutions to them. One such design in which every individual has an important contribution to make to the community, and in which all feel a sense of responsibility is Skinner's *Walden II,* but the design is for only a small community. China, Israel, Britain, the United Nations, and the United States are each examples of different plans designed to maximize both the contributions and rewards of each individual within the community. Each of these plans poses us with different problems and possibilities, and we need much more study and many more solutions for our worldwide problems.

The ultimate and highest goal of education, then, is to produce men and women who can contribute to the design of culture, and so increase the probability that the human species can continue to live as a community on the face of the earth. Here is a short quiz to see if you know what the behaviorists hope to do.

Progress Check 3.1:   Distinguishing Behaviorist Goals of Education

Directions: Below are six statements proposing long-range educational goals. Some of them represent behaviorist goals of survival behaviors; others do not. Place a check beside those goals which do represent a behaviorist orientation. For further feedback, indicate in your own words on the line provided why you evaluate each statement the way you do.

_____1. The final goal of education is the creation of better human beings capable of spiritual transcendence.

Reason: _____

_____2. The individual must be trained for a role in society which is both rewarding to him and a contribution to the good of society.

Reason: _____

_____3. The chief goal of the ideal educational system would be the discovery of identity.

Reason: _____

_____4. The goal of education is to teach people how to achieve for themselves the positive benefits of life in our society, and then to share these benefits with others.

Reason: _____

_____5. Education has failed to reach its most elementary goal if students are not equipped in the end to get a job.

Reason: _____

_____6. The goal of education is to refreshen consciousness so that we are continually aware of the beauty and wonder of life.

Reason: _____

STATING LEARNING GOALS AS BEHAVIORAL OBJECTIVES

The ultimate goal of education is to teach students behaviors that will positively contribute to their personal survival and to the survival of the whole human community. How can teachers begin to achieve these goals in the process of daily school life? How are these ultimate goals to be put into practice by teachers formulating short-term goals from day to day or year to year? Since learning *is* behavior, and since the behaviorists emphasize that all we can observe about another person is his behavior, they believe that teachers should state their learning goals in terms of behavior rather than in terms of the internal state within the student which may accompany learning behavior.

Learning goals stated in terms of behavior are called *behavioral* or *performance-based*. When they are designed as specific goals of instruction, they are most often referred to as *objectives* rather than goals, however. In essence, behavioral objectives or goals state what it is that the student should be able to do as a result of instruction—how he will behave in specific circumstances. They do not specify how or what the student may be thinking or feeling. It is not always easy to learn to state objectives behaviorally but the application of almost every other behaviorist principle in education depends on this first essential step. The teacher who cannot or does not state goals behaviorally cannot possibly be utilizing behaviorism in any real sense. The rest of this chapter examines things you need to know to use and formulate behavioral goals. We will look at thinking, learning, and creativity first, and examine how these important educational processes (which have traditionally been thought of as being primarily mental functions) are defined by the behaviorists as observable behaviors.

To Think Is To Do

When we say that someone is "thinking about something" what we really mean is that someone is *behaving in relation to something*. The behaving may be covert but it is behaving nonetheless and "not a fancied inner process" (Skinner 1974). For example, if you were to describe Franklin Roosevelt as someone who "thought politically," what you would really mean is that Roosevelt acted, responded, or behaved in relation to political events as opposed to musical events or engineering events. We say that Roosevelt *thought* politically but what we really mean is that he *acted* politically. Similarly, the teacher who describes Ralph as a student with a gift of "thinking mathematically" is really saying that Ralph behaves in a particularly effective way when he is presented with an environmental situation in which numbers are involved. Thinking musically, socially, or historically can be translated as behaving in relation to music, social needs, or historical events.

Learning Is the Change to More Effective Behavior

Learning for the behaviorist is a relatively permanent increase in reinforced behavior in relation to particular situations or environments. In other words, learning is a change from behavior that is either nonreinforced or punished to behavior that is reinforced. Again, let us look at the little mathematician, Ralph, about whom his teacher may proudly tell his parents, "He has learned to add." What the teacher means is that when Ralph is faced with a series of figures such as $3 + 4 = \underline{\hspace{1cm}}$ he now writes 7 instead of 9 or 1 or nothing at all. Ralph's behavior in this situation has changed from erroneous scribbles to behavior which is reinforced by a smile from the teacher, a gold star, and a shining A on his report card. Cathy has "learned to play the piano" when her behavior at the piano is reinforced by recognizable sounds instead of random cacophony. Bob has "learned to read" when his behavior in relation to a book is reinforced by the information it contains.

IS THINKING ALL IN THE MIND?

Thinking is behaving. The mistake is in allocating the behavior to the mind. . . . All these forms of knowing depend on a previous exposure to contingencies of reinforcement.

B. F. Skinner in *About Behaviorism*

There are many gifts that are unique in man; but at the centre of them all, the root from which all knowledge grows, lies the ability to draw conclusions from what we see to what we do not see, to move our minds through space and time and to recognize ourselves in the past on the steps to the present.

J. Bronowski in *The Ascent of Man*

Two great scientists disagree. Bronowski says that man is unique because he possesses a mind with the power to imagine and think. Skinner says that mind is not even a concept that we can talk about scientifically, that we should talk about thinking behavior and see how it is controlled by the environment, not by the "mind." As a teacher, you will be concerned with thinking either as an inner process and a product of the mind, or as a behavioral process and product of the environment. Which do you think best describes man? Which do you think best fits your definition of science? Which do you think will be most helpful to you as a teacher?

Creativity Is Rearranging the Environment

Problem solving and creativity are particular kinds of behaviors that, like all other thinking behavior, can be learned. Problem solving is the behavior of *changing a situation so that reinforced behavior is possible* (Skinner 1968). It is not always possible to engage in behavior that will be reinforced without changing the situation first, so that the problem is to change the situation so that reinforced behavior can occur.

For example, a child who wants a cookie kept in the jar on the top shelf must first change the situation in such a way that the behavior of getting the jar open is possible since jar opening is the behavior that is finally going to be reinforced by possession of the contraband cookie. In this case, the problem can be solved by rearranging the kitchen furniture in such a way that the stool is directly in front of the shelf where the cookie jar has been placed in its exalted position. Once he has done this, the reinforced behavior of getting the cookie jar open is possible and the problem has been solved.

Appropriate behaviors to solve different kinds of problems include clarifying a situation, isolating parts of it, rearranging, grouping, organizing, reorganizing, or adding to it. People can and should be specifically trained to engage in these behaviors to increase their problem-solving abilities.

Here is another short quiz so that you can see if you have learned what the behaviorists mean by learning.

Progress Check 3.2:   Recognizing Behaviorist Learning Definitions

Directions: Circle the letter next to the phrase which, according to the text, most accurately completes each statement.

1. From a behaviorist perspective, learning
    a. is the ability to think out loud.
    b. refers to a relatively permanent change of behavior which leads to reinforcement more frequently than the behavior which preceded it.
    c. is possible only in children who have reached a certain stage.
    d. is controlled by the person's mind.

2. Behaviorists believe that problem solving
    a. cannot be taught.
    b. is not controlled by environmental contingencies.
    c. can and should be taught.
    d. unlike thinking, is not a scientific concept.

3. According to the behaviorist, thinking is
    a. an inner process with which scientists cannot be concerned.
    b. a set of observable, controllable, and ultimately predictable behaviors.
    c. not subject to the laws of operant conditioning.
    d. erratic behavior.

4. Changing a situation so that reinforced behavior is possible is a behaviorist definition of
    a. behavioral objectives.
    b. problem solving.
    c. content learning.
    d. jar opening.

LEVELS OF LEARNING GOALS

Goals in education are not haphazardly piled up on top of each other with no particular order or sequence. Learning is a developmental process which becomes more complex as it grows, and builds on what has already been learned. Learning goals, then, should reflect this development. Two theorists who have addressed themselves to analyzing the development of learning are Benjamin Bloom and Robert Gagne. Both have constructed guidelines which you can use in developing an ordered and integrated series of learning goals. We will look at the work of these two men, and then examine in detail the steps for you to take in designing your own behavioral goals.

Bloom's Taxonomy

Benjamin Bloom's taxonomy (Bloom 1956) is a hierarchy of six levels of learning which has proved extraordinarily helpful to many educators in constructing performance-based objectives. Although in its original form, the taxonomy did not always state goals behaviorally, it easily lends itself to behavioral statements. Taxonomies actually have been developed for the cognitive, affective, and psychomotor domains but we will examine here only Bloom's cognitive domain.

Level One: Knowledge. Knowledge is reflected in a student's ability to perceive or remember facts or information. Behaviorally, knowledge is manifested when the student is able to *label, recognize, list,* or *recall* material. For example, the first step in learning to read is the ability to recognize letters. Objective tests to see whether the learner has memorized certain facts are testing for knowledge on this level. "How much are eight times six?" "Who can recite the Pledge of Allegiance?" or "What is the capital of Ohio?" are questions testing knowledge behaviors.

Level Two: Comprehension. Comprehension is a higher form of learning than knowledge because it requires not only that a student memorize but also understand information. Understanding is seen in behaviors in which the student is able to *summarize, paraphrase, restate, explain, interpret, illustrate, demonstrate* or *convert* information he has learned. Testing for comprehension on an objective test is more difficult because one can often not be sure that the student hasn't really simply memorized the information on the knowledge level. The short essay question in which the student paraphrases specific ideas is an ideal way of testing for this level of learning. Examples of comprehension questions are "State in your own words the key elements of the Monroe Doctrine," or "In your own words, give a brief summary of the causes of cancer as the author of the text delineates them."

Many teachers, unfortunately, do not use learning goals above Level Two. If students can demonstrate that they have memorized material and that they understand what they have memorized, some teachers assume that students are able to use these learnings effectively. This can result in education that is unstimulating, and which students find boring or irrelevant. One solution to this problem is to set up and use learning goals included in the next four levels which demand a higher-level utilization of material than simply comprehending it.

Level Three: Application. When the student is able to use information and concepts in *new* situations about which he has not been specifically taught he has reached the application level. It is reflected in behavior of *modifying, using, relating, applying, changing,* or *extending* information or principles in new circumstances. Some of the behavioral verbs already suggested for levels one and two may be appropriate here if they are being manifested in new situations which the teacher has not already explicitly covered.

Essay questions can be used to elicit application learnings. "In terms of the principles we have studied using the psychology of color, discuss the use of the color red in the movie, *The Red Desert*" or "Apply Marxian principles to a discussion of two economic forces which help to maintain aparteid in South Africa" are two examples of questions requiring high-level application. Application can also be exhibited in a whole array of simulated or real-life situations, limited only by the imaginative possibilities envisioned by the teacher. For example, children who have learned to add and subtract can be given the opportunity to apply this learning in a buying and selling situation, or in using and balancing a check book. Trips to museums, parks, urban centers, zoos, or production centers can all be planned to stimulate application and other higher level learning behaviors as well.

Level Four: Analysis. Analysis rests on the student's understanding of the organization or structure of the material he has learned. He is able not only to relate to individual facts as required by level two comprehension, but because he understands the organization of the material, he is able to distinguish between elements that are important and those that are irrelevant, between facts and inferences. He is able to pick out key ideas and distinguish them from perhaps interesting but less central concepts. Analysis is reflected behaviorally in the student's ability to *distinguish, differentiate, discriminate, describe differences between, select parts of, divide, diagram,* or *outline* material.

Any assignment requiring critical examination of an argument, a problem, or structure requires analysis. "Analyze the arguments put forward by the author to substantiate a need for population control," for example. A fruitful way to stimulate analytical behaviors is to require students either in essay or debate to compare and contrast opposing viewpoints in relation to a critical issue. "Compare the economic and environmental problems noted by the author of the text of developing solar energy sources with the problems of developing nuclear sources of energy for mass use within the next fifty years," or "Analyze the concept of childhood reflected in this twelfth century painting with that reflected in this eighteenth century painting" are two examples.

Level Five: Synthesis. Unlike analysis, synthesis requires that the student not only understand the organization of material but is able himself to produce or create organization of a myriad of discrete elements or facts. Any production in which the student creates a new concept, theory, a new composition or work which is different from anything he has been explicitly taught belongs in this category. It reflects not simply his ability to understand, apply, and analyze the work or thought of others but actually to create his own individual contribution. It is reflected in behaviors of *organizing,* or *reorganizing, designing, arranging,* or *rearranging, classifying, planning, combining, composing, putting together,* or *relating.* Any assignment asking the student to develop or organize material or arguments himself into a coherent pattern requires synthesis. An original play, art work, or story belongs in this category as well.

Level Six: Evaluation. Evaluation is the process in which the student is able to judge the logic, usefulness, validity, or accuracy of concepts, policies, construction, or arguments. The criteria by which a judgment is made may be selected by the evaluator himself or may be made in terms of some externally imposed constraint. A learner can evaluate when he can *criticize* or *support, appraise, justify, evaluate,* or *judge.* Examples of evaluation questions or assignments are: "Appraise the design of the Washington Bridge for its strength in sustaining the two-way flow of traffic of at least one hundred cars in each direction;" "In view of your standards for effective governmental control of the economy, evaluate the recent congressional decision to lower corporate taxes;" or, "Evaluate, in terms of your own criteria of educational goals, the contribution made by each of the three theoretical schools discussed in this book."

A Developmental View. If you take an overall view of these six levels, you will see that each higher level presupposes the student's ability to carry on the lower levels. Each level, in other words, reflects a greater development of learning than the lower levels. For this reason, Bloom's hierarchy can be particularly useful when teachers are dealing with great differences in learning abilities among students. Slower students can be given assign-

USING BEHAVIORAL VERBS IN BLOOM'S TAXONOMY

LEVEL OF LEARNING	EXPRESSED IN BEHAVIORS SUCH AS
1. Knowledge	*to label, recognize, list, recall, restate*
2. Comprehension	*to summarize, paraphrase, restate, explain, interpret, illustrate, demonstrate, convert, translate, transform, transmit, formulate*
3. Application	*to modify, use, relate, apply, change, extend, generalize, predict, revise, estimate, extrapolate*
4. Analysis	*to distinguish, differentiate, discriminate, describe differences between, select parts of, divide, diagram, separate, deduce, relate*
5. Synthesis	*to organize, reorganize, outline, design, arrange, rearrange, classify, categorize, plan, combine, compose, put together, propose, originate*
6. Evaluation	*to compare, contrast, criticize, support, appraise, justify, evaluate, judge, validate, verify, question*

ments on the lower levels while students who progress more quickly can continue to learn the same material on higher levels.

To illustrate how the same material can be continuously developed on higher and higher levels, let us look at two sets of goals in different learning areas, and see how goals may be spiralled according to the ascending achievements of the student.

EXAMPLE 1

LEARNING AREA: Nineteenth Century Painting

LEARNING GOALS:

1. Knowledge: Students will be able to select ten nineteenth century paintings in a selection of twenty-five assorted paintings of various periods.
   Or: Students will be able to recall three differentiating characteristics of nineteenth century painting.

2. Comprehension: Students will be able to explain in their own words at least three differentiating characteristics of nineteenth century painting.

Levels of Learning Goals   71

3. Application: Students will be able to demonstrate how two nineteenth century paintings which have not previously been discussed in class possess at least three differentiating characteristics of painting of this period.

4. Analysis: Students will be able to compare and contrast nineteenth century paintings with one produced in the fourteenth, and one produced in the twentieth century.

5. Synthesis: Student will produce his own painting, illustrating at least three characteristics possessed by nineteenth century painting.

6. Evaluation: Students will be able to evaluate the degree to which a painting of a fellow student is marked by characteristics of nineteenth century painting.

EXAMPLE 2

LEARNING AREA: Structure of Government

LEARNING GOALS:

1. Knowledge: Students will be able to recognize the principal responsibilities of the president, senate, house of representatives, and the court in the United States government.

2. Comprehension: Students will be able to explain in their own words the principle duties of the executive, legislative, and judicial branches of the federal government.

3. Application: When given a series of various duties or responsibilities not explicitly discussed in class, the student will be able to assign them to the appropriate branch of government.

4. Analysis: Students will be able to diagram the various branches of the federal government, indicating the various responsibilities of each.

Or on a higher level of analysis: Students will be able to compare and contrast the United States form of democratic government with the parliamentary form of democracy in present-day England.

5. Synthesis: The student will be able to design an alternative form of government in which the legislative, judicial, and executive duties of government are carried out in a manner different from that stated by the United States Constitution.

6. Evaluation: The student will evaluate the effectiveness of the present form of United States federal government in terms of its capacity to provide the essentials of food, clothing, housing, medical care, and employment for the maximum number of citizens.

If you examine these sets of goals, you can see that students cannot possibly accomplish the higher goals without possessing the skills required by the lower goals. Another theorist who accepts this developmental view of learning is Robert Gagne.

Gagne's Hierarchy

Robert Gagne is not strictly a behaviorist. His approach is called "Information Theory," and he is really a neobehaviorist insofar as he believes that active internal processes of direct scientific value take place and can be validly inferred through the observation of behavior. He does agree with the behaviorist view that learning takes place primarily through the process of repeated reinforcements, and that what is eventually a complex behavioral repertoire is built-up initially of very small elements.

Gagne (1970) has developed a hierarchy in which basic elements of learning are gradually united and composed into eight ascending levels of increasingly complex behavior. Each type of learning is distinguished chiefly by the conditions under which it occurs. Gagne's view of learning might be compared to the construction of a protein. A protein is made out of atoms, and then of molecules of carbon, hydrogen, and oxygen. These molecules then combine to make the essential amino acids which then eventually combine to make up the large protein. For Gagne, human learning starts out with *signal* and *stimulus-response* learnings which generally correspond to classical and operant motor responses. These two first kinds of language are like the atoms of the protein. These "atoms" then combine with each other to produce the third type of learning which is *chaining* or associative learning in which the individual learns to connect two previously learned stimulus-response units. The fourth learning is *verbal association* and refers to learning to construct verbal chains or sentences, first short, and then longer ones.

Learning type five is *discrimination* in which the individual learns to discriminate first simple stimuli from each other, and then even complex chains of stimuli from each other. The child who has learned to say "daddy" only to daddy and not to the mailman or grocer has learned simple discrimination; the biologist who is able to distinguish between two strains of virus has learned more complex discrimination. The sixth type of learning, *concept learning,* is possible only when a sufficient, complex neural process exists to represent mental images. Concept learning involves abstract thinking and the ability to classify in terms of shape, color, material, texture, use, position, or other characteristics.

Rule learning, the next type of learning, is possible only after concept learning. In the strict sense, it is *not* mere memorization of a string of words, but rests essentially on an understanding of the basic idea involved in the rule. The last and highest type of learning is *problem solving.* Problem solving is like rule learning but instead of learning rules made by someone else, problem solving is the process of thinking out new rules for oneself.

Some behaviorists are not concerned with a hierarchy of learning. They tend to believe that anyone can learn anything if material is broken up into sufficiently small units which are followed by proper contingencies. However, Gagne believes that it is not possible to plunge into the middle if the student has not already learned the first, more simple steps. When a pupil is having trouble learning, the teacher should move down lower on the hierarchy and see what elements are missing so that the student has the blocks to build the next level toward which he is struggling.

If you have understood Bloom's taxonomy and Gagne's hierarchy, the following quiz will be easy.

Progress Check 3.3: Identifying Levels of Learning

Part I. Directions: Name and define in your own words the six levels of Bloom's taxonomy and the eight levels of Gagne's hierarchy.

Bloom's taxonomy:

Level: Defined as:

One: _____   _____;

Two: _____   _____;

Three: _____   _____;

Four: _____   _____;

Five: _____   _____;

Six: _____   _____;

Gagne's Learning Hierarchy:

Learning Type: Defined as:

One: _____   _____ ;

Two: _____   _____ ;

Three: _____   _____ ;

Four: _____   _____ ;

Five: _____   _____ ;

Six: _____   _____ ;

Seven: _____   _____ ;

Eight: _____   _____ ;

Part II. The following are offered for a higher evaluation of your learning of the material:
1. Design a series of behavioral objectives in a field which you might teach using Bloom's or Gagne's hierarchies.
2. Evaluate the potential usefulness to you as a teacher of using Gagne's hierarchy or Bloom's taxonomy in guiding your educational goals.

DESIGNING YOUR OWN INSTRUCTIONAL OBJECTIVES

In designing a course of studies you will design a series of learning goals, starting out with simple basic knowledge or learning, and progressing to complex learning behaviors. Either Bloom's taxonomy or Gagne's hierarchy will be useful guides to you in spiralling your goals in a logical and coherent way so that each goal is built on the previous one. It is necessary to develop a complete behavioral goal, that is, to follow each of the following three steps, for each level of learning.

A complete behavioral goal, one which can guide you in teaching, evaluating, and communicating to others what is to be learned, is sometimes called an *instructional objective* and contains a statement of 1) the behaviors to be learned and work to be produced by the student; 2) the conditions under which learning is to be tested; and, 3) the criterion of success, or the level at which you will be satisfied that the student has successfully achieved the learning goal (Mager 1962). Each component corresponds to a step in the design of your instructional goal.

Step 1: Identify Learning Behaviors and Their Products. What do you want your students to be able to *do*, and what do you want them to *produce?* The answer to this question is the first component of your behavioral objective. You may want your student to add numbers, write a history essay, read a second grade book, paint a picture, build a table, or deliver a speech. Whatever it is, it should be *observable*. The first part of the objectives stated at the beginning of each chapter of this text are examples of this first step.

Learning behaviors should be specified by *action verbs*. Action verbs refer to activities of the students which literally can be seen or heard rather than to internal processes referred to by traditional educational verbs as to learn, appreciate, understand, think about, or comprehend. The preceding section on Bloom's taxonomy and Gagne's hierarchy has already suggested many action verbs and there are hundreds more. The object of the action verb is the product of the student's behavior which, like the behavior itself, can be observed. Products that cannot be seen should not be used. For instance, neither the behavior nor the object of goals such as "to understand the concept," or "to appreciate the value," or "to think about the implications" can be observed. On the other hand, both the action and the product can be observed in goals such as "to name the first five presidents of the United States," or "to play the Danube Waltz on the piano," or "given a one hour essay exam, evaluate the effect the use of unleaded gasoline has had on the pollution problem."

This first component of the instructional goal which identifies learning behaviors and their products is sometimes called an *informational objective* because it is usually all that is necessary when you are communicating in a general way to a parent or another educator what a student has or should have learned. If a behavioral goal is to be a fully adequate goal in guiding the design of your instruction it must include two additional components as well.

Step 2: Specify Testing Conditions. After identifying the behaviors to be learned, you then should specify in detail how you are going to evaluate the learning of your students. The specification of testing conditions should include information about the kind of test that you are going to give (for example, a multiple choice test, an essay exam, or an oral quiz) and the number of items or length of the text (for example, ten items or five hundred words). The description of the progress checks included with each objective at the beginning of each chapter in this text are specifying testing conditions.

A teacher evaluating the multiplication tables may state that this behavior will be tested in "a ten item test consisting of single-digit multiplication problems using the same form but different digits than those used in practice problems in unit 12." A teacher evaluating the student's knowledge of the three key causes of the American Revolution may state the testing conditions as "a ten item multiple-choice test covering the three ideas presented in the fourth chapter of the student's text." The testing conditions in which learning behavior is to be evaluated need not be a test in the traditional sense but may include oral presentations, creations, essays, or any other behavioral manifestation which the teacher thinks is suitable to the performance of the particular goal.

Step 3: Determine the Success Level. Lastly, you must decide what level of accomplishment is necessary for you to consider the behavior successfully acquired by the student. As you well know, students do not all receive grades of either 100 percent or zero. Most students fall somewhere in between. The success criterion included in the instructional objective states at what point the teacher considers the goal to have been reached, or in other words, specifies what a passing grade will be. Will the goal be accomplished if a student answers eight out of ten items correctly? Or only if he answers all ten correctly? Or ninety out of a hundred? Whatever it is, the level or criterion you decide on should be stated in this first step, not *after* the students have all taken the test and you see how they do. Criterion levels are not specified with the objectives in this text because it is assumed that you should answer every item correctly. In other words, the criterion level is 100 percent.

Recently, there has been evidence indicating that teachers who begin with a relatively low criterion which gradually increases over the school year or semester get better overall learning results from their students than teachers who set one criterion and stick to the same level of success all year. Carlson and Minke (1975) found college classes that used ascending criteria beginning with a passing grade of 60 percent which gradually increased to a passing grade of 90 percent at the end of the semester averaged better grades than classes using a fixed criterion of 80 percent as a passing grade the whole term.

Once you have completed these three steps, you have a complete instructional objective that can guide you in designing your lesson plan and in grading. Instruction and grading are topics of the next two chapters, and you will be able to see how closely related they are to your original behavioral goal. Here is a short quiz that will enable you to see if you can recognize a correctly-stated instructional objective.

Progress Check 3.4:   Evaluating Instructional Objectives

Directions: Circle the letter of the phrase which most accurately completes each of the statements following each instructional objective.

Objective A: The student will be able to write the names of at least four of the five major composers of the eighteenth century listed in chapter 4 of the text when asked to do so in a sentence-completion exam.

1.   The first component or informational objective in Objective A:
   a.   uses an action verb.
   b.   is contained in the words "when asked to do so in a sentence-completion exam."
   c.   is missing.
   d.   is inaccurately stated.
2.   The success level in Objective A is specified
   a.   in the words "will be able to write the names of major composers."
   b.   inaccurately.
   c.   in the words "in a sentence-completion exam."
   d.   in the words "four out of five."

Objective B: Students will develop a clear understanding of long-division problems and will receive a grade of at least 75 percent on the final

3.   In Objective B, the first or informational component is stated:
   a.   in the words "on the final."
   b.   by the success level of 75 percent.
   c.   in nonbehavioral terms.
   d.   accurately and completely.
4.   The second component or testing condition in Objective B is:
   a.   incomplete.
   b.   "a grade of at least 75 percent."
   c.   well stated.

Objective C: Students will acquire a detailed comprehension of the molecular structure of a simple protein by reading chapter 10 in *Biology for Everyone.*

5.   The informational component in Objective C is:
   a.   stated in behavioral terms.
   b.   missing.
   c.   inaccurately stated.
   d.   "by reading chapter 10 in *Biology for Everyone.*"
6.   The testing component in Objective C is
   a.   inaccurate.
   b.   missing.
   c.   incomplete.
   d.   contained in the words "comprehension of the molecular structure of a simple protein."

Objective D: The student will be able to thread correctly an electric Singer sewing machine within a period of two minutes after being seated before an unthreaded machine with a full spool and bobbin.

7. Instructional Objective D:
   a. contains only one component of a correctly stated objective.
   b. contains only the first two components of a complete objective.
   c. does not state how the learning will be tested.
   d. sets the criterion as "within two minutes."

ARE BEHAVIORAL GOALS A HELP OR HINDRANCE?

For those who accept the behaviorist view that psychology can make progress only when it concentrates on observables, the use of behavioral goals is absolutely essential to the improvement of teaching in our schools. Others, either psychologists who are not convinced that the behaviorist definitions of such concepts as learning are adequate, or educators who fear that the effects of using behavioral goals are not what the behaviorists intend, question whether they are an advance for education at all. Research evidence is mixed (DuChastel and Merrill 1973; Duell 1974), sometimes indicating that using behavioral objectives seems to improve learning, but just as often that it does not. We will look at some of the arguments on both sides, but the final evaluation is up to you.

Pros in Favor of Behavioral Objectives

"I believe that those who discourage educators from precisely explicating their instructional objectives are often permitting, if not promoting, the same kind of unclear thinking that has led in part to the generally abysmal quality of instruction in this country" (Popham 1968). Educators such as Popham believe that despite the lack of unequivocal research supporting the benefits of behavioral objectives they are of major importance in improving the level of teaching. They believe that research has not included all the benefits of using them and that the benefits of greater clarity, improved teaching, clearer communication, and more precise measurement make behavioral goals an indispensable asset.

Clarity. One of the best reasons for using behavioral objectives, according to the behaviorists, is the increased clarity they provide and the corresponding advantages that result when teachers and students both know exactly what a teacher is going to teach and what exactly it is that a student is supposed to learn. This kind of clarity prevents teachers from hiding shoddy thinking behind a screen of fine-sounding but ultimately quite vague ideas. It prevents them from delivering promises that stir the heart and sound strong and beautiful but in actual fact are trivial, meaningless, boring little exercises.

Imagine, for instance, that a music professor, instead of announcing that the goal of his course was to give the student "a deeper appreciation of the magnificence of Beethoven's Nine Symphonies" stated his goals in terms of what the student could do at the end of the course. Would the student be able to complete a matching test between lists such as "Eroica, Choral, Pastoral" and "III, VI, and IX"? Or would he be able to recognize themes developed throughout a symphony, and distinguish them from other themes? Would he simply be able to report that he "felt good" after listening to one of the symphonies without knowing necessarily that it was Beethoven rather than Mozart? When a teacher has specified exactly which of these goals he is actually trying to achieve, students will know what to expect.

Better Teaching. One of the effects of clarifying a teacher's goals is that it should increase the probability that these goals are actually achieved. The reasoning is that when a teacher has specified exactly what goals he is trying to achieve, his course plans will be clarified as well, leading to more effective teaching and to more learning on the part of the students.

In support of this position, Popham (1971) found that nonteachers did as well in teaching as experienced teachers of comparable IQ and general educational level when behavioral objectives and other behaviorist methods were used. The claim, however, that behavioral goals lead to better teaching is one of the most disputed aspects of this subject, and even their most ardent supporters admit that research does not always clearly indicate the superior results of using them. One of the important questions under dispute is whether goals can be stated just as clearly in nonbehavioral terms (as many nonBehaviorists believe) leading to teaching just as effective as teaching guided by behaviorally stated goals.

Research exploring the use of taxonomies such as Bloom's, applied either from a behaviorist or nonbehaviorist perspective is equivocal as well, indicating that such hierarchies may not necessarily and automatically contribute as significantly to improved education as one might expect. Although it is not always easy to know exactly which category certain student behaviors might fit into, there is general agreement that "low-level thinking" requiring little more than the basic understanding and memorization of facts, and "high-level thinking" in which the student applies, interprets, and actually manipulates the material are valid and useful distinctions. In addition, research in actual classrooms indicates that Bloom's original accusation that educators spend most of their time teaching and evaluating knowledge "out of all proportion to its usefulness and its relevance for the development of the individual" (Bloom 1956) seems to be accurate.

Research also indicates that teachers can be trained to use higher-level categories in their teaching, and that when they do so students' behavior also is often on a higher level (Dunkin and Biddle 1974). However, Rogers and Davis (1970) found no relationship between student behavior and the level of questions used by the teacher, and Ragosta et al. (1971) actually found a *negative* relationship. This study found that the more teachers used lower-level categories of questions, the more pupil, higher-level behaviors increased. This research does not indicate that taxonomies are destructive of productive teaching, but it does suggest that using any educational method is probably not uniformly or necessarily always positive.

Improved Communication. A third argument for using behavioral goals is the claim that they enable teachers to communicate more accurately to other teachers, to other schools, to parents, and to students themselves. Teachers are often called on to tell others what a student has learned, but this communication is often unclear and sometimes even inaccurate and destructive.

Let us take a simple everyday example. A teacher writes at the bottom of Sandra's report card that she "understands fractions." What does this particular teacher mean when she says "understands"? Can Sandra do ten out of fifteen fourth grade fraction problems correctly in an hour? Can she cut a pie into the correct number of equal pieces for eight people? Has she helped other students learn their fraction problems? All these behaviors may be described as reflecting understanding but Sandra may or may not be able to do any of them. If the teacher had specified what Sandra had learned in terms of what she could do, that is, in terms of her behavior, we would know the answer to these questions.

Teachers need to know what a student has learned; parents have a right to know what their children have learned; students are motivated by feedback about what they have learned; employers ask for information about what a prospective employee has learned. In almost every aspect of his life, a student is intimately affected by the communication given by the educational system concerning what he has learned. It is crucially important to him that this communication be accurate and fair. The behaviorists position is that the only way this can be accomplished is to communicate what a student has learned in behavioral terms which can be objectively measured against unbiased standard criteria.

Precise Measurement. Another claim for behavioral goals is that their accomplishments can be measured quite precisely while such concepts as understanding, or learning, or other mental concepts in their untranslated forms cannot. Accurate measurement of learning goals is a great advantage in education since it makes it possible to know when and how much progress has been made, or when no progress has been made at all. Accurate measurement replaces a dependence on such feelings as "I worked hard so I *must* have learned a lot," or "This student showed a lot of enthusiasm so I'll give her a good grade."

When learning is reported on bases such as these, it is not possible for students or teachers to make valid judgements about the important processes which are supposedly occurring in the classroom. How can we know, for instance, whether students might learn just as much if they were permitted to sit in the library all day, or to play in the streets instead of coming to class? How can we conclude that one teaching method, one textbook, one class, one teacher, one school, one anything is better than any other in promoting learning? We can't. We may have hunches, opinions, attitudes toward questions such as these but we cannot know the answers with any assurance until we can measure learning, and compare learning under one set of conditions with learning under another.

THE VOTE ON BEHAVIORAL GOALS

ALL THOSE IN FAVOR

- *Clearer communication!*
- *Fewer high-flying empty promises!*
- *Learning without trivia!*
- *Better research into learning!*
- *Better teaching!*
- *More learning!*

ALL THOSE OPPOSED

- *Too static and rigid for a dynamic society!*
- *Learning limited to narrow objectives!*
- *Real learning doesn't develop from small pieces at first!*
- *Some learning doesn't show up in behavior for years!*

- *Clarity is not quality!*
- *Ignore values and feelings!*

YOUR BALLOT

- *Research results are mixed; what do you think?*
- *Are fuzzy nonperformance-based objectives one of the causes of educational disaster?*
- *Or do behavioral goals contribute to dry, barren, uninspired education?*
- *Do you think behavioral goals would improve or stifle your own learning? your teaching?*

Perhaps it is important to note first that educators who object to using behavioral goals are rarely objecting to formulating goals as such, but are questioning the necessity or even the advantages of using *behavioral* goals. They fear that in practice if not in theory behavioral goals lack flexibility and suggest that they fail to take into account values, feelings, or aspects of learning that do not manifest themselves behaviorally.

Too Limiting. There is some research that indicates that students given limited and specific goals do better in relation to them than students not given such objectives. At the same time, students given these specific objectives have done *worse* than students given no objectives on items not specifically included in the goals given to the students (Rothkopf and Bisbicos 1967). This probably isn't surprising. How often do students interrogate a teacher about exactly what is going to be on the test? Opponents of behavioral goals suggest that spelling things out in terms of goal behaviors encourages teachers to teach and students to learn for the test but fails to broaden learning abilities in general.

By narrowing the focus of teacher and student to a single manifestation of learning, opponents point out that using behavioral goals can actually lower the aspirations of what the teacher tries to accomplish and what the students are motivated to learn. Behavioral goals, they fear, increase preoccupation with test grades that reflect a narrow span of learning instead of encouraging students and teachers to find varied ways of validating and expressing their learning. Take the example of Sandra who might "understand" math. Proponents of behavioral goals argued that to understand math might mean many different kinds of behaviors and behavioral objectives made it clear just what behaviors Sandra may exhibit. Adversaries say this proves their point—that understanding *can* be exhibited in a variety of different behaviors and that behavioral objectives zeroes in on just one of them.

Teachers then become very narrow in their definitions of learning, and students who may for motivational, cultural, or creative reasons exhibit high levels of comprehension in some way which has not already been prespecified by the teacher are penalized. A grade school teacher once described her own behavior in early grade school. When she was given arithmetic problems she did the first three problems on each page. Then having ascertained that she understood how to do them, became bored with the prospect of working through ten or fifteen more problems of the same variety and so randomly filled in any kind of answer to the rest of the problems. She received quite low grades in math all through grade school, but she was able to help her twin brother with his math, and when it came to calculating such personally important arithmetic problems such as how far she could stretch her allowance her arithmetic skills were quite adequately advanced.

All students are not motivated to accomplish the behaviors the teacher may have set up, even though learning may actually be taking place. Since students' needs and motivations are so varied, some educators fear that if teachers try to teach a set of prespecified behaviors, they will not notice alternative behaviors that demonstrate that learning is occurring. So the question is whether behavioral objectives are too constricting, whether it is better for a teacher to be open to different expressions of learning without predetermining how learning should be expressed.

Lack Flexibility.   People who fear that behavioral objectives are too narrow usually fear as well that they lack the flexibility necessary for a changing society. "The things for which we can clearly use a training methodology designed to bring people to performance criterion apparently are limited to static knowledge," Cronbach (1971) argues; "basically these skills constitute education for a static society." In *Technology of Teaching*, Skinner admits that his methods thus far have been most useful in situations in industry or technical schools where the goal of teaching is the acquisition of specific concrete skills. So the question is whether behavioral goals will help create students who know very well the few things specifically taught them in school—whether it be typing or math, carpentry or chemistry, history or algebra—but who at the same time are not able to relate to new situations, to gain the new knowledge required by a society that continues to change at an ever increasing rate. When a society is in flux, when much of what students are taught can be out of date within ten years of graduation, are behavioral goals too rigid?

Not Based On the Real Learning Process.   Behavioral objectives are based on the assumption that learning brings about observable changes in behavior. Some educators are disturbed though by behavioral goals because learning is not always immediately manifested in observable behavior. Research in latent learning has demonstrated that people can learn all sorts of things that do not show up in behavior until some time later, sometimes even years later.

These educators are particularly worried that if teachers emphasize only behavioral goals they will not try to instill those kinds of learnings which cannot be observed easily in the classroom or demonstrated on a test but are nonetheless of crucial significance. They fear that behavioral objectives are not apt to include such goals as responsibility, commitment, enthusiasm, values, or moral principles either because they are too hard to measure or because they may not be manifested in behavior for many years to come. These educators are asking whether behavioral goals can really include some of the most important goals of education.

Other objections come from the cognitive theorists who argue that human learning is not the result of a chopped up process in which bits of information are learned one by one. They believe that a series of specific behavioral goals makes sense only to someone who already knows what is being learned, but that it is not the best way to go about learning something in the first place because the individual begins by looking at the overall structure of what he is learning first and then fits the parts into the whole. As one educator (Stake 1970) explained: "Analysis does not necessarily aid performance. A designer of 'paint by numbers' kits might point, as I believe information theorist Claude Shannon has, that any painting is essentially a collection of areas of discernibly different solid colors. It does not follow that painting by numbers is the best way to paint a Mona Lisa."

This difference of opinion about how learning occurs is related to a long-standing debate in education sometimes called the "Whole versus Part Learning Controversy." Behaviorist teaching methods tend to reflect a belief that the student will learn part by part until he has learned the whole, while the cognitive methods tend to reflect a belief that a student learns better by having an overview of the whole before she begins to understand the individual parts and how they are related to each other. Chapter 4 gives many illustrations of various approaches to individualized instruction which reflect a part-first rather than whole-first approach. This approach is a result of the behaviorist conviction that learning is a result of a multiplicity of individually reinforced behaviors, but since the cognitive psychologists do not believe that that is how we learn, they believe that beginning with a highly detailed list of behavioral goals to be taught one by one is the wrong approach to setting up goals.

More Nonsense. Some behaviorists have argued that using behavioral objectives will inevitably reduce the trivia that so often pervades our classrooms by exposing it—by making it so patently clear to anyone with a modicum of common sense that what a teacher is pursuing is obviously ridiculous uselessness that it will be dropped from the curriculum (Popham 1968). The opponents of behavioral goals suggest that this happy possibility is not what actually occurs. Unfortunately the ridiculous trivia is not as obvious as anyone with that modicum of common sense would think, they say. Teachers go blithely on teaching nonsense but because they are using behavioral goals, the nonsense is given an aura of scientific respectability and so is even less apt to be recognized for the riduculous trivia it is. In fact Ebel (1971) argues that all the designers of behavioral goals tell you is how to make clear goals, but they don't tell you at all how to make good quality goals.

Your Own Evaluation

The scope of the arguments for and against behavioral objectives as we have them is somewhat limited by the necessity of discussing other contributions of behaviorism to education. Using behavioral objectives is still a subject of controversy, however, and all the pros and cons presented here have been elaborated, refuted, amended, supplemented, supported, and opposed by various psychologists and educators, and it is quite possible to argue that vital arguments and counter arguments have been unfairly omitted.

Your own judgement of the validity of behavioral objectives will depend on your basic assumptions about the nature of the science of psychology and the process of learning, on your evaluation of the arguments on either side, and perhaps later on, on an analysis of your own teaching experiences. Several readings are suggested at the end of this chapter that discuss the subject further, and you are strongly encouraged to supplement your understanding of the issues touched on here by reading and thinking about them.

This, nor any other book cannot make a final judgement for you, but you can take the following quiz to see whether you remember some of the principal issues involved.

Progress Check 3.5: Recalling Possible Benefits and Problems of Behavioral Goals

Directions: Complete the two sentences below stating three possible advantages and three possible disadvantages of specifying goals in behavioral terms. To clarify your own position, you may write in the spaces provided a short evaluation, as you see it now, of each point.

A. Three possible advantages of using behavioral objectives are:

1. _____

(Evaluation: _____

_____):

2. _____

(Evaluation: _____

_____):

3. _____

(Evaluation: _____

_____).

B. Three possible disadvantages of using behavioral objectives are:

1. _____

(Evaluation: _____

_____);

2. _____

(Evaluation: _____

_____);

3. _____

(Evaluation: _____

_____).

SUMMARY

The ultimate goal for all education is survival. Survival behaviors are of three increasingly valuable kinds, and constitute three goals for education. The first is behavior to increase personal freedom in life and careers, to which education contributes by using positive instead of punishing controls, and by adequate and relevant career education. The second is behavior undertaken for the common good to which education can contribute by encouraging cooperative instead of competitive behavior. The highest goal of education is to contribute to the third kind of survival behavior which is to design a culture in which the human community can solve its imminent and increasingly urgent problems.

Learning and thinking, as the particular goals of education, can be defined in terms of specific and observable behaviors. Behavioral goals specifying behaviors to be acquired, and the conditions under which learning will be tested, should be used by all teachers employing behaviorist methods. Bloom's taxonomy and Gagne's learning hierarchy can be used to develop learning behavior goals. Behaviorists believe that behavioral objectives results in greater clarity, which makes better communication and the objective measurement of learning possible but other educators object that behavioral goals are too restrictive and will ultimately choke off important nonbehavioral aspects of learning.

SUGGESTED READING

BLOOM, BENJAMIN, ED. *Taxonomy of Educational Objectives: Cognitive Domain.* New York: David McKay, Co., Inc., 1956.

For a more detailed look at the basics of Bloom's taxonomy discussed here, including many examples of text items for each category.

GAGNE, ROBERT M. *The Conditions of Learning,* 2d ed. New York: Holt, Rinehart and Winston, 1970.

In this book Gagne explains in detail the learning hierarchy discussed in this chapter and implications for education in terms of motivation, development, and instruction. If you like his approach, see also *Principles of Instructional Design* by Gagne and Briggs, also published by Holt, Rinehart and Winston, 1974, and *Essentials of Learning for Instruction,* a short paperback published by Dryden Press, 1974, which makes a brief presentation of Gagne's position.

KIBLER, R. J.; CEGALA, D. J.; MILES, D. T.; AND BARKER, L. L. *Objectives for Instruction and Evaluation.* Boston: Allyn and Bacon, Inc., 1974.

This is an excellent, detailed little paperback giving you a lot of practice in designing behavioral objectives, and relating them to other educational procedures including lesson plans and evaluation. It goes into much greater detail than we have in this text, and also has an appendix which lists a number of sources where behavioral objectives for various subject areas may be both withdrawn and contributed.

MAGER, R. F. *Preparing Instructional Objectives.* Palo Alto, Calif.: Fearon Publishers, 1962.

For those who prefer to go to original sources. This is the classic on behavioral objectives, and it's programmed.

SKINNER, B. F. *Beyond Freedom and Dignity*. New York: Alfred A. Knopf, Inc., 1971.

This book was already listed for suggested reading after chapter 1, but if you are interested in Skinner's presentation of three levels of survival behaviors, see chapter 8, "The Design of a Culture."

SKINNER, B. F. *The Technology of Teaching*. New York: Appleton-Century-Crofts, 1968.

Do take a look at this book. Skinner discusses many educational issues, including behavioral definitions of thinking, learning, and problem solving.

For a look at some of the pros and cons of behavioral goals, see

ATKIN, J. M. "Some Evaluation Problems in a Course Content Improvement Project." Journal of Research in Science Teaching, 1 (1963), pp. 129–132.

EBEL, ROBERT L. "Criterion-Referenced Measurements: Limitations." *School Review* 79 (2) February 1971, pp. 282–288.

POPHAM, W. J. "Probing the Validity of Arguments Against Behavioral Goals." *Current Research on Instruction,* Prentice-Hall, 1969.

Designing Learning Environments: Instructional Methods

4

Chapter Objectives

In the previous chapters we saw that the behaviorists believe that, through the principles of conditioning, the environment controls what we do. In this chapter, we examine various instructional methods designed by behaviorists during the last twenty years as learning environments with reinforcement and nonreinforcement contingencies to increase the student's learning behaviors. Then we look at steps you can take to apply behaviorist principles to your own instructional planning and the design of a learning environment in your own classroom.

The behavioral goals of this chapter are to enable you to:

1. *distinguish the characteristics of the following behaviorist instructional methods:*

   linear programmed instruction
   branching programs
   mathetics
   learner-controlled instruction
   the personalized system of instruction
   computer-assisted instruction

   Progress Check: You are asked to complete sentences by filling in seventeen names or major characteristics of the individualized instructional methods discussed in the text.

   ---

2. *demonstrate a familiarity with several proposed advantages and disadvantages of programmed instruction.*

   Progress Check: You are asked to evaluate as correct or incorrect fourteen statements in which relative advantages or disadvantages of programmed instruction are asserted.

   ---

3. *recognize the five steps in the design of a behaviorist instructional plan.*

   Progress Check: First, you are asked to state in sequence the five steps suggested by the text in designing your own instruction. Secondly, your are asked to designate to which step each of twelve separate characteristics belongs.

Learning takes place everywhere all the time. It is often a haphazard affair, just as much a matter of luck as of deliberate planning if an individual leaves the kitchen, pool hall, movie house, local bar, or the street with learning that is beneficial. However, the place where learning should not be haphazard is in school. Behaviorists have studied conditions under which learning occurs and they believe that long years of continuous and repeated research and experimentation no wallow them to specify quite accurately conditions which most effectively control it. In applying what they have learned they have developed a series of instructional methods.

Depending on which aspect of the method a particular author wants to emphasize, behaviorist instructional methods have been variously known as self-study, self- or auto-instruction, individualized, personalized, performance-based, competency-based, contingency-managed, and criterion-referenced instruction. They have been developed to teach large numbers of students in a way that is feasible and efficient from a behaviorist point of view, and there are currently literally hundreds of different teaching machines and devices for such instruction including books, machines, movies, television and computer programs in which the student may be asked to read, write, listen, type, or respond orally or in writing to screens, pictures, and blanks.

All of these programs are based on the principles of operant conditioning and on the assumption that learning is acquired through repeated reinforcement of behavior. They all define learning in *behavioral terms,* and almost all shape the student's behavior through a *gradual progression* toward the goal. They provide for *constant and immediate feedback, liberal positive reinforcement*, and *self-pacing* insures that no student must fail just because he learns less quickly than others.

Whatever the form of the program, the responsibility for teaching lies primarily with the program, not with the student. The age-old excuse that some students are too lazy, stupid, or unmotivated is just not acceptable for the behaviorists who argue that it is the conditions for learning that must be criticized or blamed, not the student. Students' learning is a result of environmental contingencies and it is up to educators to arrange the environment suitably to produce learning. That is what each of the following instructional methods tries to do.

Linear Programmed Instruction

Using the largely ignored pioneer work of Sidney Pressey some twenty-five years before, Skinner (1954) developed linear programmed instruction after he visited his daughter's school and was somewhat appalled at the quality of some of the teaching he saw there. In his opinion, students had far too few opportunities to exhibit learning behaviors which, in any case, were much too infreqeuntly reinforced, and then often only after too great a delay and in a disorganized manner not planned to lead to the optimal acquisition of learning behaviors. Linear programming was designed to eliminate all of these critical flaws. Here is an example of a short program:

PROGRAM

OBJECTIVES: You have successfully completed this program when you are able to identify the following:

> The King of Pattalan
> The Chief Adviser and Friend of the King
> Man's Best Friend in Pattalan

DIRECTIONS: Following is a 4-frame program. Each frame has a blank which you should fill in with the correct answer. Use a piece of paper to cover the correct answer given at the bottom of each frame until you have filled in the blank with what you believe to be the correct answer. Then compare your answer with that provided. Do not proceed to any frame until you have given the answers in all the preceding frames.

1. *Pattalan* is the name of the country in which all of six-year-old Peter's friends lived. An inhabitant of Pattalan was called a Pattalanian. By the end of Peter's sixth year, a total of seventeen

_____ lived in Pattalan.

Pattalanians

2. Since Peter constructed Pattalan single-handedly, the King of Pattalan

was, of course, _____ himself.

Peter

3. King Peter's chief adviser and constant companion was his canine friend Maximillian Noel Snitch Snossis, referred to, except on formal occasions,

as "Max." Although he often engaged in rowdy behavior, _____ possessed royal blood just as Peter did.

Max

4. As a result of his friendship with Max, Peter decreed to all of his sub-

jects: "A _____ is a man's best friend."

dog

Scientifically Constructed. Skinner believed that linear programmed instruction was the best possible answer to educational needs. It is constructed to include all the important characteristics which research has proved essential in learning as the behaviorists have defined and studied it.

The student's learning is defined in *observable terms,* and the program is set up in such a way as to demand a constant and *overt active response* from the student. The material is broken up into *small progressing units,* shaping the student's behavior until it reaches the final goal, and at each step the student is required to construct an answer to which he receives *immediate feedback,* telling him whether his answer is right or wrong. This makes it possible at any given time for both student and teacher to see exactly where the student stands, how much he has learned, and how much further he has to go to reach the goal.

Prompts. Although nonreinforcement insures that the student will not go through the entire lesson practicing in a mistake which later must just as laboriously be practiced out, linear programs are constructed so that students will make a minimum number of mistakes to begin with. This is done by using prompts—cues or hints to the student to increase the probability that he will give the right answer rather than the wrong one or no answer at all. Gradually the prompts are withdrawn or "vanished" and the student is able to make the complete response with no outside help at all.

Prompts come in many forms. *Partial prompts* give part of the right answer to the student (A tulip is a fl__ __ __ r). There are *picture prompts* (A ◯ is called an octagon because it has _____ sides): prompts that *rhyme* (It's a gnu, one of the strangest animals in the _____); *context setting prompts* (A forest is full of trees; the elm and birch are both _____ that grow there); and, prompts using *synonyms or antonyms* (Scientifically speaking, black which contains no colors or light at all is the opposite of _____ which contains all the colors of the light spectrum). These prompts are used in other programs as well, and may be usefully adopted by the teacher for his own use.

Positive Reinforcement, Self-Pacing, and Built-In Success. Feedback to the student that the answer he has just given is correct is meant to serve as positive reinforcement, and so strengthen the response just given. Feedback from the program is continuous, inexhaustible, and automatic, meant to work with peak efficiency in shaping the learner's behavior. Because feedback is given after each frame, it is administered on a schedule of continuous reinforcement—a schedule which we have seen is very efficient for initially building up behavior. Later, random and less frequent reinforcement in and outside the classroom should maintain learning.

Feedback provided by even the most conscientious teacher in the traditional classroom rarely has all these advantages, usually drying up when the majority of the class has reached a level of acceptable performance. As a result, students who need to proceed slower are abandoned at the bottom of the class, while students who proceed quickest are often bored. Because each student works at his own program, linear programming permits each student to learn at his own individually suited pace without disturbing the pace of others. Thus, programmed instruction should insure that nobody *has* to fail. Anyone who successfully completes the program has earned an *A* whether it has taken him a short or a long time to reach the goal.

Skinner (1968) believed that because everyone can pass with a high grade, the destructive competition and often debilitating anxiety that exists among students in so many of our classrooms fighting for a limited number of available high grades is alleviated. He also wrote that simply manipulating a teaching machine is so intrinsically rewarding that it will keep most children working at it for an adequate length of time each day (although, unfortunately, many teachers working with actual children do not agree with Skinner's optimistic prediction).

Linear programs comes in book and machine form. Machines were very popular in the 1960s, at a time when many educators thought they were the first wave of an educational revolution. The machine has the advantage of keeping the correct answer out of the sight of the learner until he has constructed his own answer, while the book form depends on the student's voluntary cooperation of not looking at the answer until he has written his own, a cooperation some students agree is not always forthcoming. The initial enthusiasm for teaching machines has been greatly tempered in the reality of a classroom full of alive, pulsating students however, and except where computerized programs are available, almost all linear programs are used today in book not machine form.

Branching Programs

A major modification of linear programming was introduced by N. A. Crowder (1963) in the form of *branching programs*. Branching programs are based on the assumption that if a student gives the wrong answer there is some problem, some gap in the learner's understanding which should be remedied. It is also sometimes called *intrinsic programming* because it is shaped by the needs of the individual using it.

Branching programs can be used in either book form or presented by a machine or computer. The book, introduced by Crowder in the form of a "scrambled book" involves elaborate turning of pages and even of turning

IS PROGRAMMED INSTRUCTION JUST AN EFFICIENT WAY TO LEARN DEAD FACTS?

"This [behaviorist] approach assumes that our knowledge of the world is a fixed and orderly body of facts and conclusions. It implies a concept of reality wrapped up in separate little packages and tied with string, stacked neatly on the shelves of a vast warehouse. But . . . reality is . . . a process, flow, a great running together, a barely intelligible, absurd, endless poem, a brilliant light at the entrance to our cave. . . . There are many, I know, who do not experience any distastes in living among and through machines, just as there are many who feel perfectly at home with plastic furniture, synthetic flavored food, and tranquilized affect; and to such as these, of course, these remarks will have little relevance, except as an opportunity for an ascription of questionable motives. Such is the temper of our times! Nevertheless, I find the thought of millions of children spending hours each day with millions of machines in millions of separate cubicles an appalling prospect."

H. T. Fitzgerald (1962)

On the one hand, there are educators who are more delighted and excited by the behaviorist programs for learning than by any other alternative ever presented to them. For them, Behaviorism is clear; it is specific, testable, organized, and effective. Behaviorism is light and fresh air in an otherwise confused and muddled educational system.

On the other hand, there are also some educators like Fitzgerald who are horrified by what they believe to be the stifling, neat, efficient, prepackaged and artificial knowledge transmitted through programmed instruction. For them, knowledge is exciting because it cannot be bundled up into sets of right answers like merchandise coming off the assembly line but is a changing, dynamic property of living human beings. For them, learning from people and learning from programs are drastically different. They see individualized instruction, with its unit-by-unit approach accomplished privately by each student learning separately from other students, not as a dream to improve education but as a nightmare destroying all that may be delicate and human or precious about it.

With whom do you agree?

---

of the book around into what would usually be considered the upside-down position. This may be considered a novelty or a nuisance depending on your point of view. A machine branching program, of course, can be programmed to switch automatically to the appropriate branch and eliminates the awkwardness of the book form.

The following is a short branching program:

PROGRAM

OBJECTIVE: On the successful completion of this program, you should be able to identify the means of reading this text in order to receive the highest possible grade with the least possible effort.

DIRECTIONS: Read each frame as many times as necessary to understand it clearly. Then select what you think is the best answer for the question asked and follow the directions corresponding to your answer. *Do not* read the frames in the order they occur but go directly to the fame indicated next to the answer your choose.

1. There are many reasons why someone may possess this textbook. To the student, the primary reason is most often to use it in order to obtain information deemed necessary to pass a final exam. The means of accomplishing this acquisition of knowledge is an art most successfully developed among certain members of the student community.

If you were looking for advice concerning reading this text as an aid to passing the final exam to be given at the termination of this course, would you consult:
a. your doctor (go to frame 4).
b. your astrologer (go to frame 7).
c. a selected student (go to frame 3).

2. You have chosen an incorrect answer. Probably you have not read the frame carefully. Note that February follows the exam for which you are preparing. Reread carefully the frame which you have just completed, and select your answer again.

3. You are correct. Students usually are in a better position than doctors or astrologers to give you advice concerning exams at school. Contrary to popular practice, the best way to read a book for an exam is not the night before the exam in question. The successful student will tell you that, optimally, a textbook should be opened initially about three months before the proposed exam.

If you are taking an educational psychology exam in January, this text should be initially opened by you no later than:
a. October (go to frame 6).
b. February (go to frame 2).
c. December (go to frame 8).

4. Your answer is incorrect. Although doctors are sometimes very knowledgeable, available research indicates that they are not usually experts in educational psychology texts. Go back and read frame one again, selecting another answer.

5. Your answer is incorrect. Either you have not read the frame carefully in which case you should read it again, or you should not be reading this text at all, in which case you should stop here.

6. Good, you are correct. The optimal time to open the book initially is several months before the exam, that is about October. The important question now is how to read the book once you have opened it. The successful student who likes to do other things besides read textbooks will

tell you that special attention to the following items will shorten the time spent reading and increase exam grades:

anything underlined

anything written in very black print

anything written in large letters or italicized

anything also mentioned by the teacher in class

chapter headings

introductory and summary paragraphs.

When studying for an exam, the most efficient and quickest method of reading a text is to pay particular attention to:

a. the pictures (go to frame 5).

b. key ideas (go to frame 10).

c. every word (go to frame 9).

7. This is an informed answer since astrologers are often consulted to answer questions which few others are able or willing to answer. However, astrologers as a group are not experts in textbook reading, and your answer in incorrect. Reread frame one and select another answer.

8. The answer you have chosen typifies the student known as a "crammer." Your grade will depend on the amount of material, the kind of material, and the development of your cramming skills. If your goal is to receive a consistently high grade, you should start reading the book at least three months before the exam, simply reviewing the material immediately before the test. Note the sequence of months includes the following: September, October, November, December, January, February, March, April, May.

Three months before January is:

a. October (go to frame 6).

b. September (go to frame 5).

c. June (go to frame 5).

9. Your answer is that of many students and you may or may not receive an average or better grade. If your goal is to receive a high grade an to reduce the time necessary for study, you should rturn to frame 6, choosing your answer after careful consideration.

10. Correct. You have now successfuly completed this program. It is suggested that you review the program objectives to see whether they have been achieved to your satisfaction.

Resembles Linear Programs. Like linear programs, branching programs define learning in *observable terms*, present material in relatively *small and graduated units* to which the student must *actively respond*; they provide *immediate* and *continuous feedback*, permit *self-pacing*, and maintain motivation through *positive reinforcement*.

Special Characteristics.   The branching program also differs from a linear program.   First of all, for reasons that nobody really knows, frames in branching programs tend to be *longer* than frames in linear programs.   Secondly, in order to send the student to the remedial help he specifically requires, each frame includes a *multiple-choice question* but does not ask the student to construct an answer as does the linear program.   The relative advantages and disadvantages of constructed versus multiple choice answers have been hotly debated but research indicates tht the differences in effect on learning are often minimal (Krumboltz 1964).   Branching programs also provide an explanation after each answer indicating why it is right or wrong.   The advantage of this procedure when the student has chosen the wrong answer is that it points out the reason his thinking is faulty.   The student who has chosen the correct answer either through pure guesswork or with somewhat fuzzy reasoning will also gain by reading the explanation accompanying the correct responses.

Branching programs often incorporate *"skip techniques"* as well, which allow the student to skip over sections of the programs which he may already know.   They thus provide several considerations for individual differences not allowed for by linear programs, making it possible for the learner not only to proceed through the material at his own pace but also to cover anly the amount of material necessary for him.

WHERE IT HAS REALLY BEEN TRIED

The idea that teachers can completely substitute traditional approaches to teaching with a full-scale implementation of programmed instruction is in practice not as popular a notion as it has been in the past, and programmed instruction is seen now to be useful only as one but not the only means of necessary instruction. What is taking the place of the idea that teachers should begin individually to use programmed instruction are large-scale implementations for individualized instruction involving a reorganization of the educational set up throughout the whole school. Three major plans based on behaviorist principles have been put into practice in the United States since the late 1960s.

All the plans operate with the aid of a computer as a record-keeper, scorer, and often adjunct diagnostician making recommendations

for further student learning projects. They all include the use of behavioral goals, make an assessment of the student's initial learning levels before making recommendations for teaching-learning exercises, and provide frequent feedback evaluation to guide and motivate further learning.

INDIVIDUALLY-PRESCRIBED INSTRUCTION (IPI)

IPI was planned and set up by the University of Pittsburgh (Cooley and Glaser 1969). After the student's initial learning levels or entry behaviors are measured, the teacher prescribes the appropriate unit for each student to work with. After the student has completed the unit—usually working alone—he is given a test on the material he has learned. The test is scored immediately by the teacher who evalu-

ates the results and prescribes either a unit covering new material or another unit in which the student can get the practice he still needs on the material he has already been studying.

IPI is used for half the school day for reading, arithmetic, and science. The school is a graded one but students can move on to the material appropriate for the next grade level if he has achieved all the goals for a subject in his own grade. Research (Scanlon et al. 1970) shows that IPI students did better academically than students in two other control schools not using the IPI system but they also had lower self-concepts than students in the control school (Myers 1972).

PROGRAM FOR LEARNING IN ACCORDANCE WITH NEEDS (PLAN)

Like IPI, PLAN assesses initial learning levels and prescribes appropriate learning units to each individual. It tries to respond to individual learning styles by including teacher-learning lessons not only in programmed form but also in lectures, films, and books. It is used in language, social studies, science, and career guidance, which is an integral part of the PLAN project. As part of the career guidance, the student is given information about any occupation of his choosing and is encouraged, within the format of the available behavioral objection, to manage his own instructional plan in relation to his self-chosen career plans.

Research (Flanagan 1971) shows the teachers and students are enthusiastic about using PLAN but there is no research yet telling us whether PLAN students are learning more than students in control schools not using it.

INDIVIDUALLY GUIDED EDUCATION (IGE)

IGE was first set up in seven schools in Wisconsin and the midwest and is the most radical departure from traditional schooling of the three plans. Each school has several units, each of which has a teacher-leader, a staff of an additional two or three teachers, paraprofessional teacher aids, a secretary, and often teacher interns (Cooper 1972). The whole school has a principal, a school committee, learning consultants, and teacher representatives from the units.

The school is ungraded so that there are groups of students of various ages learning together with the consequent advantages of this approach for both younger and older students, and an emphasis on the importance of individual learning styles of students is reflected in the variety of ways available to respond to individual student needs. Amount of one-to-one instruction, kind of teaching materials, group size, and both teacher and student activity are adjusted to the needs of the individual student (Klausmier et al. 1968). Cooperation is considered a key factor in a successful educational endeavor so team teaching is common and decisions about what units are to be studied are made cooperatively by teacher, student, central committee for the school, and sometimes with input from the district committee.

Mathetics

Although linear and branching programs account for the major thrust of behaviorism's impact in educational instruction, several other suggestions for learning are also being taken seriously. One of them has been offered by T. F. Gilbert (1962) who calls his system "mathetics," from the Greek word meaning to learn.

The principles of mathetics are often used today in foreign language courses. Rather than beginning at the logical point with the basics of nouns and verb endings, tenses and participles, the course begins by teaching students phrases and sentences that make it possible for them to engage in short dialogues in their new language. The accomplishment of actually understanding and speaking in another language is so reinforcing that the students are encouraged to continue their study. Speed-reading courses also employ some principles of mathetics by offering introductory mini-lessons during which the student is able (at least temporarily) to increase reading speeds by as much as 75–150 words a minute. Such an increase can be tremendously motivating and given such fantastic results, encourages students to take the rest of the course.

Gilbert was once a student of Skinner's, and his methods closely follow operant principles. However, mathetics is different from linear programming in two significant ways—by a rather novel approach to organization known as "backward chaining," and by its choice of positive reinforcement.

Backward Chaining. Gilbert began to develop his theories about human learning after observing that the learning of other animals is sometimes very sophisticated. He noticed that his dog could easily be taught to eat food from a dish. Quite soon, however, Rover began to show delight at the mere appearance of an empty dish, having learned that it would soon lead to supper. With increased experience, Rover wagged his tail at the mere sight of the can opener, and if he were very hungry, it was impossible even to walk in the direction of the kitchen without bringing forth a yelp of anticipatory joy. And so on.

The dog had learned a chain of events which eventually led to supper. The chain became longer and longer as the dog learned more and more events which were connected to the final supper. Gilbert reasoned that, although the dog learned this chain very quickly, if he had tried to teach Rover the same series of behaviors going in the opposite direction that it would have been far more difficult and time-consuming. In other words, it was much easier to teach these behaviors as they led *backwards* from the final goal, rather than teaching them forwards, as it were, leading to the goal.

Gilbert decided that if this principle of learning applied to Rover, then it applied equally well to his students who, being brighter, could learn even more complicated chains than Rover.

Mastery Performance. For students trying to get an education, Gilbert reasoned that the parallel to the can of Rover's food was mastery performance—the ability to perform like masters in the field. They come to class because they want to be pros. It is this final goal that makes education really relevant and what the student finds most reinforcing.

The positive reinforcement used by Gilbert is the attainment of the final goal of the course—mastery performance in the area being studied. As often and as completely as possible, mathetics gives the student the opportunity to achieve the final goal, and material is gradually lengthened leading *back*, not *up*, to it. (Here you will be able to see how mathetics differs from linear and branching programs which use feedback that the answer the student has just given is correct as the positive reinforcement to maintain interest in continued learning.)

The first step for the teacher using mathetics is to identify the goal of mastery performance which the student can accomplish and find rewarding. If possible, the teacher finds a way for the student to actually achieve some segment of the final goal. In the case of a foreign language course, we have seen that the opportunity to actually speak and understand others speaking commonly-useful phrases and sentences can be used. A typing class may begin by giving enough practice for students to type their own names with sufficient speed to be reinforcing. Diving classes may begin with a modified dive begun from a low-crouch position at the side of the pool. Statistics classes might begin with the last step (instead of the first) leading to the final answer of a complicated statistical analysis. A history class might begin by teaching students at least to recite the major historical events during the period covered in the course. If actual student performance is not feasible, the teacher may give a demonstration of mastery performance. A course in educational psychology, for instance, instead of beginning with the theoretical ideas underlying teaching methods, might begin by actually giving students a demonstration of various instructional methods.

After demonstrating the final mastery performance that the student will have at his full command by the end of the course of instruction, the teacher gives a rather broad overview of the course, indicating the pattern through which the various subgoals of the course are eventually linked to the final goal. Each individual exercise is then set up, moving the student one step further from the goal and requiring him to complete the "chain" leading to the goal himself. As the chain gradually lengthens, the student remains motivated since he is constantly reaching the end of the chain and experiencing the sense of achievement that comes with reaching that final goal.

The biggest problem with a mathetics approach arises when the student is not motivated to achieve the final goal the teacher may have set up. Mastery performance of reading, arithmetic, history, algebra, sewing, carpentry, language, cooking, or even sports will be to no avail for the teacher of the student who is not interested in doing any of these things, and who does not find their achievement reinforcing.

Learner-Controlled Instruction

Learner-controlled instruction (Mager and McCann 1961) also uses mastery performance as the major reinforcer of learning. Mager and McCann, however, propose a program that calls for much greater determination by the student himself of the steps to be taken to reach that final goal. Learner-controlled instruction begins, as does mathetics, with a demonstration or participation in mastery performance. However, instead of then guiding the student through the progression of steps gradually leading to a path between the goal and the learner's original position, the teacher simply tells the student to ask for any information or explanations which he may need to enable him to reach that goal. The teacher's role is to provide the information asked for. Some educators suggest that the problem of students' possible lack of interest in achieving a goal can be alleviated by having students participate in the actual formulation of the performance goals as well as in the means of achieving them.

This type of instruction is a very demanding one for the teacher, requiring him to be ready to answer a large variety of questions, many of which he possibly has never thought of before. Of all the instructional programs presented thus far, this method probably requires the most thorough knowledge of material, since the instructor does not have the option of presenting a lecture full of everything he knows and carefully deleting any mention of what he doesn't know.

Besides being difficult for the instructor, learner-controlled instruction is equally demanding for the student, and assumes that the student is in the best—or even adequate—position to know how to get from where he is to the goal set up for him. Many educators have challenged this assumption, stating that someone who possesses mastery performance already is in a better position than the student to point out the shortest route. The teacher's role, they argue, is like that of a friend telling you how to get to his house. Since he is there, and since he has also been where you are, he is the best one to tell you the quickest way to get to your goal.

On the other hand, although learner-controlled instruction does demand that a student learn to assess his own needs and to make his own decisions about the information necessary to him, it is a demand which the student will face quite often in the world outside the school. One example of Mager and McCann's approach are goal cards (Bauernfeind 1965). The

THE PRODUCTIVE THINKING PROGRAM

Although there are many individualized programs for teaching content in almost every subject in the school curriculum, there are few individualized instructional programs whose goal is to teach students the skills of solving problems for themselves. This is probably partly because behaviorists conceive of knowledge as building up from basic elements which begin with basic facts that have to be learned before higher skills such as problem solving can be mastered. Nonetheless, there have been some efforts to use programmed instruction to teach creative or productive skills to students.

One such effort is the Productive Thinking Program *(Covington et al. 1974), a series of self-instructional lessons designed to teach fifth and sixth grade students how to think productively. It is a sixteen booklet set of lessons in which the children are told semi-detective stories in cartoon form. Jim and Lila and their Uncle John go through a series of adventures, and the students are asked to try to solve the problems Jim and Lila encounter, such as figuring out how a large sum of money disappeared, what went wrong during a deep-sea dive of a rescue vessel, or what is really happening in an apparently "haunted house."*

The program is set up so that students learn increasingly complex skills, and using the key characteristics of programmed instruction—feedback, prompts, and sequenced progression—the student learns to organize information, ask questions, and generate and test hypotheses systematically. To help the students transfer the problem-solving skills they have learned to other areas besides those included in the cartoons, supplementary exercises are offered in which the student is asked to apply his newly acquired skills to problems in economics, politics, psychology, history, biology, or other subjects in the curriculum.

Research (Olton and Crutchfield 1969) so far indicates that the children enjoy the program immensely, and that students who finish the program show both increased enthusiasm for and ability to solve problems, not only in relation to haunted houses and deep-sea dives but in relation to the broad range of other school subjects as well.

students are given cards with behavioral goals on them. They are not given programs to guide their accomplishments but as each goal is accomplished by the student, he receives praise from the teacher and a personal incentive as he is able to mark off another card for the accomplishment list. Goal cards have been used successfully with children as young as those in the first grade.

Personalized System of Instruction (PSI)

The Personalized System of Instruction (Keller 1968), also known as the Keller Plan, the operant or behavioral approach, or the continuous progress concept, is currently the most widely used application of operant conditioning principles on the college level in this country today. It removes from the teacher, to a great extent, the primary responsibility for lecturing and replaces it with the responsibility for arranging the contingencies for learning.

The Keller Conditions of Learning. There are variations based on the exigencies of individual situations and teacher and student preference but what follows are the essentials of the Keller Plan. The professor sets up a detailed list of testable instructional objectives. These are given to the student along with the necessary text or other reading assignments through which he can achieve the objectives. The student proceeds to accomplish each of the objectives at his own place. When he is ready, he takes an exam in relation to the specified objective. If he achieves a sufficiently high grade in the test, which is scored immediately and returned to him at once, he moves on to the accomplishment of the next objective. If his grade is not high enough, he reviews the exam with his tutor, studies the assigned material further, and applies to take another exam on the same material when he again thinks he is ready. When a student has attained a certain number of objectives, or reached a level predetermined by the professor and announced at the beginning of the course, he automatically receives an *A, B,* or *C.* The student in this way determines what grade he wishes to receive and can continue to work within the boundaries of the college calender to achieve it.

Tutors. Tutors, usually advanced undergraduate or graduate students, are often assigned as assistants to the professor in providing individual guidance, testing, and feedback to the students. Lectures, if they are given at all, are simply to elucidate the essential reading, and attendance is not usually required. The same is true of movies, demonstrations, or other presentations that often supplement traditional teaching. In such a course, then, there is little emphasis on teaching but a great deal on learning. You might be interested to know that Fred Keller applied these same principles of learning to skiing and developed the graduated length method of ski instruction.

Resembles Skinner's Conditions. Leaf back to the characteristics of linear programmed instruction and you will see that PSI is based on almost exactly the same principles as Skinner's instructional method, but they have been applied differently. The learning goals are specified as *behavioral objectives:* each system demands an *actively response* student; each divides material into *small progressive units*; and in both, the student receives immediate feedback at the end of each unit. In both programs, the student proceeds at his *own pace*, and if he should fail, he has repeated opportunities to try again and achieve success without penalty.

BETTER BECAUSE IT'S BETTER?
OR BETTER BECAUSE IT'S DIFFERENT?

In a discussion evaluating the Keller Plan, Ryan (1974) asks whether personalized instruction would be as popular with students as it is now if all their classes that are now being taught by the lecture method were individualized instead. If most education was individualized, would the teacher who used the lecture method, giving only two tests a semester, and using reading to elaborate the basic points covered in the lecture sound as exciting, innovative, and rejuvenating to students as the personalized system of instruction sounds to many today?

What do you think? Is personalized instruction appealing to students more because it is unusual, or because students just find it a better way to learn than through traditional methods?

Computer-Assisted Instruction (CAI)

Although linear and branched programs can be presented by the computer, computer-assisted instruction includes a variety of other instructional activities of far greater complexity than either linear or branched programs. The marvelous thing about computers is that although almost everything they can do can also be done by someone or something else, the computer does most of these things faster and with less human effort and time. A computer is a little like a book, a calculator, a human tutor, a television, and a little like none of these.

Construction. To understand what the computer can do, it helps to understand how it is constructed. A computer has two main parts—a center and a varying number of terminals, usually one for each student. The terminals are plugged into the center and many terminals may be used at once, each operating in relation to the center. The student communicates with the computer through the terminal which is usually equipped with a typewriter keyboard and/or video screen which can be written on with a special pen. The computer communicates with the student through the video and/or audio system or printout in words or pictures. The student punches, writes, draws, or verbalizes his answers or questions to the computer through the keyboard, microphone or other device present at each terminal. A single computer may be connected through telephone lines to hundreds of terminals, sometimes thousands of miles away, and each terminal can interact individually with a different student.

The computer center provides a wide assortment of information to the terminal, and therefore requires a large fund of data kept in storage but retrievable at high speeds. The data kept in the center are of two types —content data and control data. *Content data* are the data that are communicated to the student. They include all the information about the subject which has been fed into it either in question or answer form. Thus the statement of the computer, "Denim, material out of which blue jeans are made, is one of the longest-wearing fabrics available on the common market," and the question, "Did denim originate in Germany or in France?" are both examples of content data.

Control data tell the computer the rules for communicating the content data. In other words, control data are the computer's instructions. "If student finishes Lesson Q with less than four mistakes in less than twenty-one minutes, go to section R; if student finishes Lesson Q with more than four mistakes or in more than twenty-one minutes, go to section P" is an example of control data. Since content and control data are separate, the teacher can improve or change a program by changing either or both, an advantage not offered by a book or by other instructional programs.

Computer As Teacher: Versatile and Inexhaustible.

The computer possesses an immense capacity for individualizing instruction for the student. It has at its disposal a vast amount of information that can be presented as pure information, directed dialogue, calculation, games, and drill and practice sessions, in form of questions, problems, tests, and simulations. It can communicate with the student through video-tapes, cassettes, films, records, and other media packets, through pictures, graphs, printouts, and visual and audio devices.

Like a *personalized tutor*, the computer can be programmed to keep a close and accurate record of the student's activities and progress, pointing out on request how long it has taken a student to finish a task, how many correct items he has completed, and the level of his accomplishment. It can be set up to suggest appropriate drills and practice areas for any individual student in any given subject, and can repeat problems endlessly without the slightest show of fatigue or impatience. It can take into account not only whether the student has given a correct answer to a question or problem, but can take into account the length of time it took the student to respond, and present additional problems accordingly.

The computer can *simulate problem situations* as well as carry on a *dialogue* with the student. This is an exciting capacity and sometimes seems more of a game than the hard work traditionally associated with learning. The computer has been used to run a dummy whose heart rate, blood pressure, and other bodily functions are varied for study and diagnosis by doctors in training. It has been used to simulate the operations of entire

A TALK WITH THE COMPUTER

Dialogues with computers can be versatile and fun. First the computer presents a problem or situation to the student, who decides what further information he needs or what course of action he wishes to follow. The computer responds by answering the student's question or telling him the consequences of his decision until the problem is finally solved.

In the following example of a simulation, the computer (C) has just made the student (S) the Ruler of Lagash, a city-state in the year 3500 B.C. The Royal Steward gives a regular report of the kingdom's economic condition to the Ruler who must decide how to use the available grain resources to feed his people.

C. *Initial Economic Report made to the New Ruler of Lagash by his Humble Steward:*

Total population now	*500*
Total farm land under cultivation, acres	*600*
Total grain in inventory, bushels	*900*
one season old	*900*
two seasons old	*0*
three seasons old	*0*
Total grain just harvested, bushels	*13000*
Total resources, harvest + inventory	*13900*

You must now decide how to use your resources.

How many bushels of grain do you wish to FEED your people?

S. *4000*

C. *How many bushels of grain do you want PLANTED for the next crop?*

S. *9000*

C. *This means that zero bushels must be removed from storage. Is this all right? Do you wish to (1) let your decisions stand or (2) revise them?*

S. *1*

C. *Resulting inventory*
The steward will execute the royal commands and return in six months.
Sir, I am sorry to report that 225 bushels of grain have rotted or been eaten by rats this past season.
Economic Report of the Ruler's Steward for the SPRING Season in the year 1 of Luduga 1.

Population at previous report	*500*
Change in population	*−55*
Total population now	*445*

The quantity of food the people received last season was far too little.

Harvest last season	*13000*
Harvest this season	*14396*
Previous inventory	*900*
Change in inventory	*−225*
Present inventory	*675*
Total resources, harvest + inventory	*15071*

You must now decide how to use your resources.

How many bushels of grain . . . .

This excerpt from "Two Computer-Based Economics Games for Sixth Graders," by Richard L. Wing is reprinted from *American Behavioral Scientist* Vol. 10, No. 3 (Nov. 1966) pp. 30–36 by permission of the Publisher, Sage Publications, Inc.

cities. One such educational "game" involves the entire school population and is set up in the school for a week or so, displacing all other activities, Each student is given or chooses a different role to play—the banker, the politician, the school board chairman, the policeman, the numbers man, the restaurant owner, the waitress, the lawyer, the priest, the rabbi or minister, the factory worker, the house wife. Interactions then take place for several hours during which the members of the community talk to each other. Compromises are reached, deals made, property exchanged, contracts signed, cases brought to court. At the end of the specified period, decisions are fed into the computer which processes the information and calculates what the outcomes would be had such decisions been made in a typical town in the U.S. New decisions are then made by the participants and new outcomes again announced by the computer—who was elected, who was defeated in the recent election, what property rose in value, what cases won and lost in court.

This kind of simulation can teach students aspects of a subject which are often difficult to communicate in books or lectures, and gives them opportunities to explore career roles before making a permanent commitment to them.

Computer As Teacher Aid. For the teacher, the computer can be used to increase his effectiveness and to reduce wearisome paper work. The computer can relieve the teacher almost totally of the tedious work of marking tests and giving grades, and we have already noted how many aspects of teaching itself can be taken over by the computer. Once the teacher has prepared a program for the computer, it can take over the task of teaching the student while the teacher can concentrate on improving and refining the program itself.

Besides doing what has traditionally been the teacher's work, however, the computer can provide the teacher with much information which can *guide improvements in teaching*, information that would take so long to gather without the aid of the computer that it would be virtually useless. The computer makes it possible for the teacher to find out in literally a matter of seconds whether students had trouble with any particular section of work, whether any questions were particularly difficult. Likewise, she can find out about the progress of any individual student, whether and where there are trouble spots, and smooth patches, how fast the student is going in relation to other students, and how much time is needed on an average to accomplish any particular task.

This information can guide the teacher either in changing all or part of the program for the entire class, and enable him to feed in particular instructions for a particular student. The paradox is that the more sophisticated the equipment with which the teacher and students work becomes, the greater become the possibilities for students to receive individual attention from the teacher.

Computer As Counselor.   Recently, computers have been set up to fulfill various counseling functions. The System of Interactive Guidance Information (SIGI for short) has recently been made operational in a series of colleges across the country to help students make career choices (ETS Developments, Fall 1974). The student answers questions for the computer, indicating what he wants to get out of a job most and what he considers less important—such things as stability, job-satisfaction, independence, free-time, good pay, etc.). The computer then lists various occupations that generally meet the student's specifications. Then as the student begins to narrow down his choice of possible careers, the computer helps him evaluate his chances for success in various fields in terms of grades, course programs, and job possibilities, indicates college training programs and financial aid available, and evaluates each occupation in terms of rewards and risks involved.

Gap Between Reality and Possibility.   Educators soon began to appreciate the possibilities of using the computer to teach, and in the 1960s, programs involving individual classes, whole schools, and even entire school districts were set up (Klausmier et al. 1968; Cooley and Glaser 1969; Atkinson 1971). Research into their effectiveness thus far indicates that although the possibilities inherent in CAI may be far-reaching, the problems in using it effectively are not easily or quickly solved.

There is research that indicates that when CAI is used to complement traditional instruction, students learn more quickly than they would using conventional means alone (Vinsonhaler and Bass 1972; Fletcher and Atkinson 1974). All the results are not as encouraging though. Oettinger and Marks (1969) studying computer use in schools, concluded that they are, on the whole, being used prematurely, that they are "much more primitive than is generally appreciated," that teachers generally simply do not possess the skills to use the computer as a teaching device well, and that institutional resistance to change is preventing the experimentation necessary to improve the situation. There is a shortage of tested programs available and much more time and effort are required for writing and checking them. In addition, at the moment, using computers to teach is simply too expensive for most cost-conscious school systems, although there is reason to hope that their cost per student can be reduced.

Progress Check 4.1:   Distinguishing Individualized Instructional Methods

Directions: In the spaces provided, fill in the name or characteristics of the individualized in-structional method which, according to the text, most accurately completes each sentence.

1.   Like learner-controlled instruction, _____ uses mastery performance as the principal reinforcer for learning behavior.

2.   A sentence with the correct word or words to be filled in by the learner is provided in each

frame of _____.

3.   _____ usually makes extensive use of student tutors.

4.   _____ is both the most expensive and versatile of the instructional de-vices discussed in this chapter.

5.–6.   The positive reinforcer used by both _____ and by _____ is feedback after each frame that the answer just given is correct.

7.   _____ is characterized by backward chaining.

8.   In _____, only the instructional goal is developed by the instructor while the means of attaining the goal is left primarily to the learner.

9.–12.   *All* behaviorist instructional methods are based on the same principles of learning and therefore they all:

_____;

_____;

_____;

and _____.

13.   Skip techniques are found in _____ programs.

14.   _____ can carry on a relatively versatile dialogue with the student.

15.   The *only* adjustment for individual learning differences provided by _____ is self-pacing.

16.   The _____ is an application of operant conditioning learning principles cur-rently in wide use on the college level in the United States.

17.   _____ use a multiple choice question in each frame.

SOME PROS, SOME PROBLEMS, AND SOME OBJECTIONS TO PROGRAMMED INSTRUCTION

We have seen that behaviorism promises us wonderful things if we follow its principles in education. Accordingly, students *ought* to learn better and faster when they are using good programmed instruction because it demands an active student who is continuously receiving feedback and positive reinforcement as his behavior is successively shaped to approach the final specific objective. How does the reality compare with these promises? In practice, what happens when students use programmed instruction? Do they learn as well or better than through other approaches? Research results are generally positive but there are curious exceptions which leads some educators to question exactly how or whether operant conditioning is the best possible explanation for the learning that occurs.

The Pros: Successes and Advantages

For almost twenty years there has been a heated controversy over programmed instruction and many attacks are still made on it, but it has become today one of the established methods of learning. Why?

Student Learning. Research with individualized instruction of all kinds clearly demonstrates that many students who use it learn at least as well, sometimes better (Johnston and Pennypacker 1971), and often, though not always, more quickly (Stolurow 1962; Roderick and Anderson 1968) than they learn through other kinds of instruction. Grades given out in courses using individualized instruction are often significantly higher than averages attained in traditional courses (Ryan 1974), and teachers are saved from repeating the same material over and over again for different sets of students.

The answer to the most important question—Can students learn through using programmed instruction?—then is yes. It is not the only method under which they learn, nor is it always necessarily the best or more efficient way for all students, all subjects, or all teachers, but research solidly supports the view that programmed instruction often achieves its learning goals, frequently better than do other methods. In addition, the behaviorist approach has other advantages to recommend it—students often like learning this way and it can be used with large numbers of learners.

Student Enthusiasm. Many students report that they positively enjoy learning through programmed instruction. At least eighty to ninety-five percent of the college students using the Keller Plan in a variety of subjects consistently report that this was one of the best learning experiences they have ever had (Ryan 1974). Students like being responsible for their own learning, and often develop a sense of achievement and self-confidence that they never felt before.

The self-pacing feature of programmed instruction frees the student from dependence on the lockstep pace of learning along with everyone else. Students who can and want to rush ahead can do so without distractions and without impeding students who want or need to move slower. Conversely, those who have difficulty grasping the material quickly are not penalized or encouraged to "fake" an understanding they do not possess just because everyone will resent being held back on their behalf. Also, because students work independently, absences are easily made up, and there is not the problem that there is with the lecture method of covering material that the teacher has already taught the rest of the class.

Many students find the constant feedback and frequent positive reinforcement of the program encouraging and motivating. The impersonal character of the feedback given by a program rather than by a teacher is also beneficial to many shy or anxious students who find the monitoring of a human teacher inhibiting, and to those students who fear—with justification, according to some research (Rosenthal and Jacobson 1968; Rubovits and Maehr 1973)—that teacher feedback is not always fairly and equally objective to all.

Modern Solution to a Modern Problem. Programmed instruction was not taken seriously on a large scale until the mid-1950s when the needs of mass education became acute. At a time when learning continued to extend beyond grade and high school, and even beyond college into graduate work and on-the-job training and retraining for larger and larger numbers of students, programmed instruction addressed itself to the specifically contemporary problem of teaching large numbers of students efficiently and quickly.

Programmed instruction is a means of giving a great deal of standardized basic information to students which they can learn on their own and at their own rates. It reduces dependence on the presence of a teacher and on the teacher's ability to actually teach well, while releasing teachers themselves to devote more energy to other aspects of education and learning. Programmed instructions also easily lend themselves to evaluation and need revision so often asked for by responsible and/or cost-conscious school boards.

In the midst of what appears to many as the confusing disaster and cross-purposes of our modern educational system, programmed instruction offers a clear goal and a specific way of getting there. Behaviorism is not content with grand schemes and high hopes with no guidelines to the teacher of how these lofty and admirable goals are to be reached in the raggle-taggle reality of a live classroom. It is based on a strong theoretical foundation, and offers specific instruction to teacher and students, sets up objective norms to evaluate whether goals have been reached, and makes concrete recommendations for change when goals are not achieved.

Some Problems: Practical Difficulties and Questions

Despite its advantages and record of success, individualized instruction is not without its severe problems and some profound questions about its usefulness. The existence of practical problems does not mean that the fundamental principles are necessarily wrong, but it does mean that behaviorism has not created a utopia in the classroom—at least not yet—and a teacher cannot expect a working prepackaged method to teach everything to everybody. There are still some students who hate school, who are unmotivated, and who have learning problems. And despite the plethora of individualized instructional programs, there are still unanswered questions about the best organization for a lesson, and how often to give students feedback.

Problem of Good Programs. Behaviorists believe that higher levels of learning such as those in the upper half of Bloom's taxonomy or Gagne's hierarchy are important. Unfortunately, programs on the market today concentrate almost exclusively on goals which demonstrate learning at the knowledge, comprehension, and sometimes application levels. There is a great scarcity of programs constructed to teach students how to engage in problem-solving, evaluative, analytical, or synthetic behaviors. The reason for the few programs to teach abstract thinking, conceptual thought, or creative behaviors is probably because these kinds of programs are more difficult to construct. However, programs have been used successfully to teach concepts and problem-solving techniques (Markle and Tiemann 1969; Covington et al. 1974) and demonstrate that the task is not an impossible one.

However, even of the programs available to teach factual information and behavioral skills, finding a sufficient number that both meet the needs of your particular students and that you can afford is difficult. Programs will all almost invariably promise unqualified success, but the truth is that simply arranging material in a programmed format does not make it an effective program. Program writers often have an inadequate knowledge of the subject for which they are writing, and even of the "good" programs, many have been tested and standardized on students who may be quite different from the students who are actually using it. Programs must, therefore, be evaluated by teachers who are in the best position to judge the effectiveness of a particular program for their own students, regardless of evaluations made by the program's publisher, writers, or psychologists.

Teachers can learn the principles of constructing their own programs, but the time, talent, and effort required of individuals to write and test sufficient numbers of these programs to meet their own needs is clearly prohibitive. Ideally, a teacher may need two or even three different programs to adapt to different levels of achievement in his class. The problem of obtaining good programs is compounded with CAI when the teacher needs to learn to program the computer to take full advantage of its capacities. Learning the language, the math, and the electromechanical devices that enable one to program a computer is almost impossible without training. Also (unlike books), using a computer program is jeopardized if the computer breaks down, and their use is limited to a single place when the room and school are open for use. Books, on the other hand, can be carried around for use at home, on the bus, or in the bath.

Problems with Self-Pacing. Self-pacing is one of the key advantages of individualized instruction. Unfortunately, it is not an undiluted blessing, and the same feature that is one of the prime advantages is also one of its problems. Students finish at different times, and teachers must decide what to do with students who finish first. On one hand, if quicker students are given mere "busy work" that does no more than keep them occupied and quiet in their seats so that students who are still working are not distracted, the time gained through self-pacing is wasted. On the other hand, whatever the students are doing after they are finished should not be so wonderful that the slower students are encouraged to rush through their own programs at inappropriately accelerated speeds in order to join them. Many teachers have not really come up with a viable solution to this problem.

Secondly, self-pacing, which was meant to reduce destructive competition, often has just the opposite result. Competition *is* a problem, particularly in grade and high school. Students know who is ahead of whom, and it is a matter of prestige to get finished first. To avoid the label of being "dumber," students sometimes resort to rushing, cheating, or haphazard guessing simply to get through the program as quickly as possible. This is a particular problem when students are using linear programs in which all they have to do is look at the right answer even before they have constructed their own, and then move onto the next frame.

The third problem with self-pacing is that is just doesn't seem to work with every student all the time. Some students do not find doing the program particularly reinforcing, and if the teacher does not find some other means of motivating them, students will dawdle, lackadaisically pushing any button until one works, or filling in any word that jumps into their heads. Kress (1966) documents the problem of using self-pacing programs with undisciplined students. Self-pacing for some students, then, can turn out to be not so much a means of learning at the pace that best suits the individual but an opportunity to learn as little as slowly as possible.

Most of us do not need to look at the particularly obstreperous student though to find that self-pacing can be a hindrance. Almost all of us have, at one time at least in our educational career, not finished an assignment—even one of particular interest to us—until some external pressure, such as the threat of failure or painful teacher dissatisfaction motivates us to finish the task. Self-pacing, then, is a good idea that sometimes improves the level of learning and enthusiasm for it, but it is not to be used indiscriminately as a magic cure for every ill because sometimes it creates problems of its own.

Students Who Do Not Like It. For some students, programmed instruction is not a successful or enjoyable learning experience. Most studies report that this is a minority while most students find programmed instruction exciting and liberating. Just how many students do not enjoy programmed instruction we are not sure. This is partly because researchers usually do not ask students how they have enjoyed or succeeded in a course until it is completed, and there is evidence that larger numbers of students drop out of programmed instruction courses than out of traditional ones (Keller 1967; Minke and Carlson 1972). This higher drop-out rate is apparently one reason why the average grades attained in this type of instruction are higher than in traditional courses as well since those who are dropping out are sometimes the ones who are earning the lowest grades (Born 1971).

Some students find the format of programmed instruction confusing and unstimulating. They find the prompts and constant feedback after each frame interferes with their understanding of the material they are trying to learn, and they dislike the frame-by-frame approach with its lack of initial overview of the material (Carpenter and Fillmer 1965). Other students feel pressured by the program and anxious because of the difficulty of retracing one's steps, particularly when they are using a programmed machine instead of a book. Still other students find the lack of personal contact with the teacher and other students during the learning process a distinct loss and complain that they cannot ask a machine questions or ask for clarification.

The problem of depersonalization is particularly acute if students are asked to use the programs for long periods. Naumann (1965) found that within a year at least 25 percent of his college freshmen felt ignored or expressed resentment against impersonal instruction. One instructor who was running a programmed course in a school where the same course was also offered in the lecture method had one student who groaned the first day of class, "Oh no, another rat class! I'm getting out of here. I was in one of these before and I felt like an animal in a laboratory box the whole semester!" Students who find programmed instruction too impersonal are apaprently responding to real and significant changes in their traditional learning enviroments that affects more than their learning behavior. A study by Feldman and Sears (1970) found that first graders who worked at a computer for only a half hour a day were significantly less socially oriented than their peers who did not spend part of the day working at the machine.

Also, the reduction of paper work and lecture time made possible by programmed instruction should make the teacher more accessible and responsive to the needs of individual students. But in practice, the paper work necessary to keep the program running smoothly and to submit required reports documenting individual progress sometimes is as time-consuming as the traditional demands of lectures and tests. This problem might be alleviated with better organization and teaching assistants, but it has not been as simply solved through the mere adaptation of programmed instruction as some had expected and promised.

What Are Small Units in Logical Sequence? Behaviorist instructional methods break material into small units, but research has not yet established the best size of a unit. Related to this question is the problem of how many errors students should be permitted to make as they go through a program in order to receive enough positive reinforcement for optimal learning. Skinner (1968) suggests that students should get about 95 percent of the answers right, but at the moment we have insufficient research testing this suggestion. To make matters even more complicated, there are probably great differences among students and the amount of feedback they need. Students who become easily discouraged in the pursuit of academia probably need a higher success rate (and so smaller steps) than students who are motivated by a harder challenge.

Behaviorists also have not been able to identify unambiguous characteristics of "logical sequence" that will maximize learning. Most teachers will agree intuitively that material should be well-organized but the order in which material is presented at the moment is based less on research results than on the hunches of the program writer. The problem is that the order of material presented in a programmed instruction often has not demonstrably been related to the level of the student's learning achievements. Schramm (1964) even made the disconcerting discovery that in eighty percent of the research studies he reviewed, order did not seem to affect learning significantly, and when items were mixed up in a linear program, students learned just as well as those students for whom items were in proper order.

Some cognitive psychologists suggest that the behaviorist difficulty with defining optimal organization is a result of a fundamentally erroneous view of the learning process which fails to take into account that it is the learner, not the teacher, who provides the distinctive organization of the material being learned. The behaviorists disagree and believe that continued study of the process of shaping learning behavior will unlock the problem.

Is Immediate Feedback Necessary? Since it is the key reinforcer used to increase learning behavior, immediate feedback is a theoretically crucial element in most behaviorist instructional methods. How important is it in practice? Some studies (Meyer 1960) have found that students learned better with immediate feedback, but others (Glaser and Taber 1961; Lubin 1965) found that immediate feedback made no difference and that students who did not receive feedback did as well as those who did. Some students find that immediate feedback actually confuses them and they want more time to "think" problems through themselves before the program gives them the answers (Sturges and Crawford 1964).

Do some students benefit more from immediate feedback than others? If so, when? Is feedback more important in teaching some subjects or some age groups? Frames in branching programs are longer than in linear programming. Is the relatively delayed feedback in the branching program, or even greater delay in the Keller system important? Can too much feedback actually inhibit learning? If it can, how much is too much feedback? Research does not yet provide us with sufficient answers to these questions.

Once again, nonbehaviorist psychologists suggest that these answers cannot be adequately found until researchers take into account that feedback can be either intrinsic or extrinsic. Intrinsic feedback is knowledge derived by the learner himself through his own examination of the problem that his answer must be either right or wrong. Extrinsic feedback comes from a source—such as the program, an answer book, or the teacher—outside the learner. Some students have said that they like programmed instruction because they can understand material that was almost always gibberish to them before. Do some students, then, respond so positively to programmed instruction because of the intrinsic feedback made possible for them by the frame-by-frame approach rather than because of the extrinsic feedback provided by the program? If the answer is yes, the presence of intrinsic feedback would explain why some studies have found that the absence of extrinsic program feedback does not retard learning.

Some educational psychologists believe that this is an important question theoretically because if it is intrinsic rather than extrinsic feedback that increases learning, it changes the emphasis of teaching from giving reinforcement to students for learning facts to presenting students with problems that are intrinsically reinforcing when they are solved.

Better than What? The most important, persistent, and difficult question facing researchers of any theoretical persuasion is that of comparisons. When we say that programmed instruction (or any other teaching method) is *better,* what is it better than? Most research has compared programmed instruction with "the lecture method," or "the traditional approach." But we need not have been students for many years to know that there is a great variation in "traditional approaches."

Is programmed instruction better than a poorly prepared or presented lecture? Probably almost always yes. But is a bad program better than a good lecture? Do students so often prefer the individualized instruction method only when lectures are typically poor? Which will students choose, and how will their learning be affected if they can opt for either a series of "excellent" lectures, or a "top-notch" individualized instructional program? To answer this question objectively researchers need to design studies in which the same content and same quality of teaching is presented in different methods, and money, study time by the student, kind of testing, and teacher preference, preparation time, and previous experience are all taken into account.

Even then, though, if we should carry out this ideal experiment, we still want to know if one method might not be better for some particular teachers, for some particular students, or some particular subjects.

Some Objections: A Matter of Values

There are some questions that probably will never be finally solved by research because they are, above all, questions of values. We will look at several of the most prevalent attacks on the values underlying programmed instruction. With whom you agree will be something you yourself will have to decide.

Is It Learning? In the previous chapter, we saw that some people disagree with the behaviorists that all learning can be stated in terms of behavior, and they, of course, objected to using behavioral goals for this reason. This same objection has also been raised against programmed instruction because it is based on the same concept of learning. Some educators believe that human education is not a process of learning a series of discrete behaviors, a more complex and sophisticated version of operant conditioning in the laboratory box. They radically disagree with the behaviorist position that the pigeon learning to press a bar when pressing is followed by a food pellet is a simple paradigm of human learning in which the student learns a verbal or written response when it is followed by a pellet of praise or positive feedback.

Fitzgerald (1969) accuses the programmed approach of leading to what he calls a "tendency toward infallibility," rigidity, oversimplification, and inappropriate reverence for fictional "right answers." It teaches students to think that somewhere out there is a world of correct answers, the more of which we know, the smarter we are. In real life, however, there are few "right answers" we can stock into a machine forever and then translate into the heads of succeeding generations of students.

Because programmed instruction is structured as if there were a set of permanent facts and truths, they encourage students to be passive, to let the system take over, to accept rather than question, to believe what they are told rather than verify and test. From this point of view, programmed instruction is constructed in such a way that it cannot challenge the student to bring to bear on the subject matter his own powers of constructive thought and critical evaluation. It can only teach him "right answers"; it can teach him to pass tests, but not to think for himself, to make his own decisions, to organize his own thoughts, to put information together in his own special way so that he might learn to make a unique contribution to society. It teaches him to memorize dead, predigested information, but it does not teach him to think new thoughts.

Is It Personalized?   Behaviorism has applied technology to the problems of learning in our technological society. As we have seen, many applaud this as a creative application of science to human needs, but not everyone. There are some educators who consider this part of an American mania with efficient production. They believe that because Americans have succeeded more than any other nation through standardizing and mechanizing the manufacturing process in the factory, that they have transferred the operations for making *things* to teaching *people*. We are a technological society obsessed with finding the most efficient way of putting students through school in the same way we assemble cars so efficiently on our factory lines. They believe that we are trying to produce students the way we produce products. Through programmed instruction we are setting up the mechanisms for students to roll off the assembly line, none perhaps brilliant, but all serviceable, all what was expected, all fitting neatly into the marketable package of the "average" American.

APPLYING BEHAVIORISM TO TEACHING

BASIC BEHAVIORIST PRINCIPLE	GENERAL EDUCATIONAL APPLICATION	WHEN YOU ARE DESIGNING INSTRUCTION	FOR YOU TO DECIDE
Scientific psychology defines concepts in terms of observable behavior.	*Learning is defined as the acquisition of reinforced behaviors.*	*Specify instructional goals in detail*	*Should all three components of an instructional goal be announced to students before instruction begins?*
Cues increase the probability of certain behaviors under specific conditions.	*Behavioral objectives should be made clear to students.*	*Begin instruction by informing students of behavioral goals and rewards for achieving them.*	*Should only the informational goal be announced?*
Operant conditioning begins with behavior already being performed.	*Effective instruction begins at each individual's own level.*	*Assess students' initial learning levels.*	*How might you assess entry behaviors besides through traditional tests?*
New behavior can be gradually acquired through shaping.	*Learning is acquired in gradual step-by-step progression.*	*Do task analysis organizing material and specifying each behavior to be learned.*	
Operant conditioning can occur only when the organism permits overt behavior.	*Students must respond actively during the learning process.*	*Provide for continuous overt student responses through verbal, written or other behaviors during entire learning process.*	*Besides taking tests and responding in class, what else might you ask your students to do as learning behaviors?*
Behavior followed by positive reinforcement tends to occur more often.	*Learning behavior should be followed by positive reinforcements; most common are feedback and mastery performance.*	*Provide liberal reinforcement, especially feedback through frequent questions, mini-quizzes, and other assignments.*	*What positive reinforcements besides feedback are available to a teacher to use?*
Organisms differ in the speed with which they are conditioned.	*Individuals learn at different speeds.*	*Provide opportunities for self-pacing through as much practice and reinforcement as necessary for each individual.*	*In what ways besides by using programmed instruction can you provide for individual learning speeds and needs for different amounts of practice?*

APPLYING BEHAVIORISM TO TEACHING (*cont.*)

BASIC BEHAVIORIST PRINCIPLE	GENERAL EDUCATIONAL APPLICATION	WHEN YOU ARE DESIGNING INSTRUCTION	FOR YOU TO DECIDE
Organisms can learn to discriminate and generalize.	*Prompts can reduce student errors.*	*Make directions clear; provide sufficient prompts to keep mistakes at a minimum.*	
Measurements and comparisons are essential to a scientific psychology.	*The achievement of behavioral goals can be measured and compared.*	*Provide for continuous assessment of learning goals.*	*When should tests be used only for feedback? How often should they count toward a student's grade?*

These educators accuse programmed instruction of depersonalizing and dehumanizing learning. Because each student has a different amount of time to finish a program, behaviorists call it individualized or personalized. The nonbehaviorists point out that there is no individual choice in terms of content, method, different answers, different ways of reaching a solution, no room for individual values, feeling, or judgements by either the student or the teacher. With the mechanization of learning comes the loss of the human dimension of human knowledge. Human enthusiasm, the richest, the most essential and fragile element of human thought, is lost. Learning from an impersonal program can never replace the value of interacting with a live teacher.

What Research Does and Does Not Tell Us

The different ideas about how human learning occurs and acceptance of varying values for education are some of the reasons why it is almost impossible to use research to prove in a final, conclusive way which teaching method is best. The behaviorists have produced a great deal of research which demonstrates that learning of students using programmed instruction is most often in the positive direction. On the whole, students like this approach and theoretically from a behaviorist view point, it should work. But suppose you are one of those educators who believe that the results found by the behaviorists just are not covering the things that you think are most important?

Some Pros, Some Problems, and Some Objections To Programmed Instruction

What if you do not believe that filling in objective answers has much at all to do with real education? What if you want to know how happy the student is in his job, or in his relationships with his family or friends? What if you want to know how much extra time he spent in the library, or how much enthusiasm for learning, or interest in a subject was stimulated by his learning experience? What if you want to know whether it increased independent problem-solving abilities? Or if he can write a better essay now, or has any better idea of what he wants to do in his life-career than he did before he took the course? Most of these questions are not answered by the research presented in relation to programmed instruction, partly because they are often difficult to evaluate, but often because they are not directly related to behaviorist definitions of objective, measurable learning behavior. In any case, the person asking these kinds of questions will not be able to go to available research for many of his answers.

But couldn't we do some research and find out which teaching method really works best in relation to just learning and not worry about other things that might be important but are too hard to measure? Probably not. Research can give us valuable information to guide our decisions, but it will not act as a final arbiter, because whatever our favorite theory, we can almost always explain research results to suit our own predispositions. For example, recently a teacher tried using behaviorist techniques in her class and reported despondently that "they didn't work." Subsequently a behaviorist psychologist examined what this teacher had done in class and argued that the teacher had not really applied behaviorist principles accurately. This is a single example, but it can be applied to any theory. One can almost always say that a theory did not work because it was not properly used.

The opposite process also occurs. One can use behaviorism (or any other theory) to explain the successes achieved by a method suggested by another theory. For instance application of some of Roger's humanist and nonbehaviorist ideas in the open classroom in ghetto schools has, on occasion, achieved astonishingly gratifying results in terms of students' academic and social behavior. These results do not disturb a behaviorist, however, who explains these changes in terms of behaviorist principles of reinforcement which they claim were inadvertently applied by the humanist teacher.

Research may guide, stimulate, astonish, delight, dismay, suggest, provoke, and even confuse. It should not be discarded or disregarded. But some decisions and some evaluations will always be left to you. Here is a short quiz which might help you at least make sure that your own evaluations are based on an accurate assessment of research results and an understanding of the positions taken by other educators.

Progress Check 4.2: Demonstrating Familiarity with Evaluations of Individualized Instruction

Directions: In the space provided, place a check beside those statements which accurately reflect statements made in the text.

_____1.   Research has shown that programmed instruction is unambiguously the best form of educational instruction developed thus far.

_____2.   One of the benefits of programmed instruction is that it gives many students an enthusiasm for learning.

_____3.   One of the most important contributions that programmed instruction has made to education is its major development of programs to teach problem-solving techniques.

_____4.   The fact that programmed instruction reduces the student's need for the continuous presence of the teacher when learning is taking place is offered as one of programmed instruction's advantages.

_____5.   The fact that programmed instruction reduces the student's interaction with the human teacher during a major part of the learning process is seen by some educators as one of programmed instruction's important disadvantages.

_____6.   Self-pacing is clearly a major benefit of programmed instruction and there are no research studies suggesting that self-pacing is not always beneficial to learning for everyone.

_____7.   Research indicates that we do not know for sure when the continuous feedback in programmed instruction is necessary for optimal learning to occur.

_____8.   A thorough review of current research indicates that students who take a programmed instruction course always like it.

_____9.   The market today offers so many programs that teachers should have no trouble getting programs to suit the individual needs of every student.

_____10.   We do not know how many errors a student should be permitted to make as he goes through a program if learning is to occur in the most rapid and efficient way possible.

_____11.   Because so much excellent research has been carried on in the last twenty years, we now know almost everything that is important about the human learning process.

_____12.   Some educators say that behavioral goals used in programmed instruction do not reflect the most important aspects of teaching and learning.

_____13.   An objection to individualized instruction is that it is not sufficiently individualized.

_____14.   Research will never be able to give us all the final answers about which teaching method is the best one under all circumstances for every student.

DESIGNING YOUR OWN INSTRUCTION

There are thousands of available programs written by professionals for almost every subject, every kind of student, every learning level, and every classroom situation. But there is often a scarcity of *good* available programs, and in addition, extensive use of professionally-produced programs is sometimes prohibitively expensive. Whether because there is a problem of getting good programs written by someone else, or because you wish to use the lecture method for teaching your students as well, you may wish to use behaviorist principles to construct your own lesson.

There are many different ways in which behaviorism can be applied to teaching. You have already seen some of the major forms of individualized instruction in which different behaviorists each have designed a method based on the general principles of learning through operant conditioning, and there is no reason why more methods cannot be developed in the future. The following five steps are offered, therefore, as guides for planning your lessons to insure that the essentials of behaviorist instruction—behavioral goals, feedback and positive reinforcement, active student response, and provisions for self-pacing—are included. However, exactly how you apply these principles will depend on your own preferences and ingenuity, the particular learning needs of your students, and lastly on the effectiveness of the method you may adopt.

Step 1: Specify Behavioral Goals. This is the first step of constructing a behaviorist lesson plan. If you did not skip the last chapter, you already know the three essential parts of a behavioral objective. If you did slide over it, you need to go back and learn it now.

Step 2: Analyze the Learning Task. This step is sometimes called *task analysis,* and it means sequencing the material you are teaching, arranging it in a step-by-step logical progression. It means analyzing the components of the learning goal, identifying each of the skills required to achieve the final learning goal so that you can shape your students' behavior toward that goal. Skinner (1961) promises that the discipline alone of planning a lesson in a sequenced pattern will improve the quality of teaching and learning.

Task analysis is really like setting up a detailed series of subgoals which are then learned and tested one by one just as they are learned and tested frame by frame in programmed instruction. The task analysis for teaching students to read, for instance, would begin by dividing introductory reading skills into at least the following major subskills: a. recognizing and distinguishing the individual letters of the alphabet; b. recognizing the phonetic sound represented by each of the letters of the alphabet; c. chaining the sounds of individual letters together; d. verablizing the words which are composed of sets of letters. This is, of course, a very broad breakdown of skills involved in reading, and each of these subgoals would themselves be divided into a series of additional subskills which would be taught over a period of some months.

How minutely the task is analyzed into its component parts is very much a matter of "try and test." Students vary in the size of the steps which they find optimal for learning, and you, as the teacher, must observe and make your own informed decision about this. Linear programmed instruction uses units that are no more than two or three sentences long, but the units in branching programs are much longer, and IPS uses whole chapters as units for learning. On the whole, though, it is a good rule of thumb to emphasize smaller rather than larger units when you are first preparing your lessons.

Step 3: Assess Entry Behavior. The next thing for you to do is find out what your students already know. Identifying your students learning behaviors before the lesson begins is called assessing entry or baseline behavior. To identify entry behavior, you should use the same norms that you used for behavioral goals: determine what your students are able to do and observe and measure their behavior in terms that can be understood in the same way by any objective observer or anyone reading your records.

One of the chief purposes of entrance examinations, age requirements, or other prerequisites is to help standardize entry behaviors but very often you will need to know more precisely exactly what your students know. An important aspect of assessing entry behavior, particularly with students with learning difficulties that are related to motivation, inappropriate anxiety or language problems, includes noticing whether some students may have learned inappropriate discrimination. Can they emit the behavior you want to teach in one situation but not in another? Can they add amounts of money, for instance, but not amounts of coffee beans or some other commodity which fill so many arithmetic word problems but not our real lives? Are they able to answer questions easily until they are told that it is a test? If the baseline behavior is different in important ways in different situations, then, of course, your lesson plan will be constructed differently than if these behaviors never show up at all under any circumstances. (Behavior techniques for reducing anxiety or discussed in further detail in chapter 6.)

Measurements of entry behaviors should include measurements of 1) skills you expect the students to possess as they begin the class, 2) all the intermediate subskills, and 3) the terminal behavioral objective you have listed in your task analysis. In evaluating prerequisite behaviors, test students' basic and essential skills, including—especially on the grade school level—whether and how well your students can see, hear, and read, and whether they speak and understand the language you are speaking. Each of the subskills you have listed in the task analysis should be tested as well. For instance, if your final goal is that "students should be able to complete correctly at least twelve of fifteen double-digit fraction problems," your entry behavior information should tell you exactly which students know what steps in the task of manipulating double-digit fractions.

Step 4: Plan Presentation: Provide Cues, Feedback, Reinforcement, and Self-Pacing. You are ready now to decide on your mode of presentation. You must already appreciate that the method of choice for presenting a lesson for the behaviorist is individualized instruction and not a lecture. However, if you decide to present a lecture instead of writing a program, there are several things that you can do to incorporate the principles of behaviorist instruction into your presentation.

Cues: Stating the Rewards of Achieving Learning Goals. Cues, as we saw in chapter 2, are "if certain behavior, then certain consequences" statements. The "if certain behavior" cues that you should give to your students at the beginning of a lesson are a statement of the behavioral goals of the lesson. The "then certain consequences" is an identification of the positive reinforcement that the student will receive when the learning goals have been achieved. "If you learn to read these five words, then you will receive a gold star beside your name," or "if you write a coherent and logical essay describing why the multiplication of water wells during the early 1960s among the desert tribes in Africa increased the starvation caused by the subsequent drought, then you will receive an *A* in this course," are two examples of such cues.

There is some controversy about the detail with which students should have learning goals presented before learning has begun since, as we saw in the last chapter, there is evidence that students who know a teacher's learning goals accomplish them better than students who don't know them, but at the same time their learning is also correspondingly narrowed to the limits of those goals. You will probably find that individual students respond differently to being told the exact details of what is expected of them. For students with a history of failure in school or whose lack of self-confidence inhibits learning, a more detailed specification of expectations will often be helpful. For almost all students, cues that the material is going to be "difficult" or "a challenge" which they will, with sufficient hard work be able to meet, are more effective in stimulating learning than cues that material is easy.

Feedback and Reinforcement: Stimulating Active Student Behaviors. Because learning is reinforced behavior, any effective learning environment must provide ample opportunity for students to respond with active and reinforced learning behavior throughout the whole lesson. Recent research (Abramson and Kagen 1975) provides support for the hypothesis that the more unfamiliar material is to students, the more active their responses need to be to bring about maximum learning. For instance, when students are just being introduced to new concepts, it is better for them to write out their responses than it is for them merely to choose the right answer from a number of possibilities offered to them. As a general rule, then, you will probably find that the more overt and active behavior you require from your students, the faster they will learn.

One of the most popular ways of assuring that your students are not turning into nothing more than well-behaved sponges but are actively engaged in learning during a lesson is to punctuate your lecture with frequent questions. These should be prepared ahead of time as an integral part of your lesson plan, and should be asked after each step of the task analysis. They should be sufficiently easy so that you have the opportunity to reinforce your students frequently for right answers but not so easy that they are too bored or uninterested to bother answering them. Both questions that are too difficult or too easy can retard learning.

Another important characteristic of behaviorist questions that sets them apart from the kind of questions frequently used in school is that behaviorist-type questions are related to material *already covered.* Programmed instruction asks students a question after each frame about material they have just learned. So should you. The whole point of the behaviorist approach is that students should be reinforced through positive feedback in relation to what they have already learned. Asking questions that the student can already answer about what you are going to teach next only demonstrates that you needn't bother teaching it. If the student can't answer the question, he will be punished or at best nonreinforced in relation to the material you are teaching, which, of course, is not in anyone's best interest either.

Beginning teachers often find it difficult to practice this kind of questioning. It might be because as students we have so often been exposed to the teacher who *began* the class with "Can anyone tell me. . . ?" And often, too, teachers feel that it is stupid to ask questions about what has just been said. *Of course* the student is going to know the answer! But a little practice in the art of this kind of questioning will demonstrate that students often do not know the answer as often as you would expect, and that their attention level can be raised if they expect to be asked at any moment to demonstrate that they have been learning what you have been teaching.

In some way or other, you should insure that all students have the opportunity to receive feedback to their answers. This means not calling on the same students all the time, and not concentrating on only the bright or verbal students. Feedback can be increased if you poll the class for many different answers to the same question and if you ask divergent questions which legitimately may have many different correct answers. Some teachers have each student write the answer to the questions interspersed throughout the lecture, and the correct answer is discussed immediately. The advantage of this approach is that each student must respond and cannot merely sit back and let another student do the work. Each student also receives immediate feedback to his individual answer and can ask immediately for additional clarification when his answer indicates that he has misunderstood the point. This approach also requires the teacher to eliminate fuzzy questions and to state them clearly enough that all students can understand them. A variation of this approach is to give frequent informal quizzes in class for which the student is not given a grade but through which he can receive feedback.

Feedback to questions should be delivered immediately. Wrong answers should not be punished or the answerer humiliated by even mild ridicule. Embarrassment at having given a wrong answer can be reduced by the teacher who emphasizes that the students are in the classroom to learn, not to demonstrate that they have already learned everything, and that mistakes are a necessary part of all learning. Right answers should be reinforced, perhaps with a smile, a "right," "that's good," or "correct." However, to reinforce is not to patronize and sensitivity to the exact response which will reinforce an individual is required from you.

Self-Pacing: Arranging for Individual Abilities. Whatever mode of presentation you choose, you will want to make some provisions for each student to proceed at his own pace with varying amounts of practice according to individual needs. Self-pacing may be facilitated by handouts which will give the students opportunities to practice material being covered, the opportunity to take a test or finish the required assignments within a period of time that gives the student some choice and self-determination in the matter, and providing a chance to take more than one test covering the material if the student does not receive a satisfactory grade the first time. Other learning supplements to class presentation which have been suggested (Bloom et al. 1956) are small group study sessions, individual tutoring, additional textbooks, academic games, and audiovisual aids.

Step 5: Evaluate, Record, and Adjust. Your last task is to evaluate the learning behavior of your students. How you evaluate should have already been determined in your behavioral objectives, and testing is discussed more fully in the next chapter. After the test or other measuring instrument has been administered, you should record the results in a way that makes comparisons and an evaluation of progress as simple as possible. This is usually done best either by graphing your results or writing them in table form. This is a critically important part of behaviorist teaching because it is only by looking at the results that you can tell if your lesson plan has been a good one or not. Then for those students who have reached acceptable performance, the lesson is finished. For those students who have not reached the goal, additional lessons and practice must be provided until *all* the students have reached the goal.

HOW INDIVIDUALIZING IS INDIVIDUALIZED INSTRUCTION?

PROVIDES THE FREEDOM TO LEARN IN ONE'S OWN WAY

The behaviorists say that programmed instruction reduces the excessive conformity imposed on students today by the use of mass lecture methods and textbooks uniformly assigned to everyone. At last there is a practical method in which students can learn at their own paces, with special attention from the teacher who has time for each student who needs him when he runs into difficulty.

CONSTRAINS EVERYONE TO LEARN THE SAME THING

Humanists say that programmed instruction doesn't allow people to be different; it just allows the student as much time as he needs to learn the same answers that everybody else is learning. Real individualization in education would mean that the student is allowed to learn different things in different ways, having different values about what he is learning, and drawing different conclusions about it. The behaviorists call it "individualized," say the humanists, but it is a way of covering up the fact that in programmed instruction everyone has to learn the same thing in the same way giving the same "right answers" to the same questions.

WHAT DO YOU THINK?

Is programmed instruction just another, more efficient way of making students conform? Or is it a very good way of covering essential material for everyone, leaving the teacher free to respond to individual needs? Does programmed instruction free students from the lock step imposed by textbook assignments and mass lectures? Or does it just put them into a different box? What do you think about trying to individualize learning for your own students by using programmed instruction in your classroom?

Here is another progress check for you to see if you have achieved the second goal of this chapter.

Progress Check 4.3: Recognizing the Five Steps of Behaviorist Instructional Design

Directions: List in their correct order the five steps suggested in this text for constructing a behaviorist lesson plan. Then, in the space following each of the characteristics listed below, indicate the number of the step to which it belongs.

Step 1: _____
Step 2: _____
Step 3: _____
Step 4: _____
Step 5: _____

Characteristics:

a. statement of conditions under which learning will be exhibited   Step _____
b. provisions for continuous feedback to student   Step _____
c. recording terminal test results   Step _____
d. positive reinforcement for learning behavior   Step _____
e. statement of what the student should be able to do at the termination of the learning   Step _____
f. organizing material into logical progression   Step _____
g. delineation of component skills involved in goal behavior   Step _____
h. process by which the level of each student's learning behavior is measured before teaching begins   Step _____
i. provisions for self-pacing   Step _____
j. statement of level of performance that will be considered successful for achievement of learning goal   Step _____
k. evaluating terminal behavior after instruction   Step _____
l. cues to students of expected learning goals   Step _____

SUMMARY

In this chapter we discuss the most popular forms of individualized instruction developed by the behaviorists. Although they differ in the degree of structure they provide for the student and are as varied as programmed tests, teaching machines, and computer-based instruction, they are all based on the principles of operant conditioning, include behavioral goals, positive reinforcement, consistent and immediate feedback to continuous student activity, and provisions for self-pacing.

Advantages of individualized instruction including research showing that students using it learn well and often better than in traditional methods. Student enthusiasm for this method of learning, and its provision for teaching large numbers of students are discussed. Some problems such as the difficulty of sometimes obtaining good programs, problems associated with self-pacing with some students, student dissatisfaction, and questions about good organization and feedback are examined along with possible objections to values underlying the concepts of personalized learning.

Five steps for designing instruction are suggested to incorporate the important principles of behaviorism in classroom teaching. They are 1) the design of behavioral goals; 2) analyzing and organizing the material being taught; 3) assessing students' initial learning levels; 4) making a presentation with provisions for cues, feedback, reinforcement, and feedback; and, 5) evaluating and recording learning behavior.

SUGGESTED READING

CROWDER, N. A. "On the Differences Between Linear and Intrinsic Programming." *Phi Delta Kappan* 44 (1963):250–254.

This is a short essential article comparing branching and linear programming.

GLASER, R. "Adapting the Elementary School Curriculum to Individual Performance." In *Proceedings of the 1967 Invitational Conference on Testing Problems.* Educational Testing Service, 1968.

Discusses the computer-based individual prescribed instruction (IPI) operating in Pittsburgh.

KELLER, F. S. "Goodbye teacher . . ." *Journal of Applied Behavior Analysis* 1 (1969): 78–79.

Presentation of the Keller Plan.

MAGER, R. F. AND J. McCANN. Learner-controlled Instruction. Palo Alto, Calif.: Varian and Assoc., 1961.

The original presentation of the principles of learner-controlled instruction.

OETTINGER, ANTHONY G. WITH SEMA MARKS. *Run, Computer, Run.* Cambridge, Mass.: Harvard University Press, 1969.

Oettinger believes that computers "might alter the course of science" but that despite their exciting and constructive potential they are being used prematurely in education with insufficient development of good programs and trained personnel.

SHERMAN, J., ED. *PSI: Personalized System of Instruction*. Menlo Park, Calif.: W. A. Benjamin, Inc., 1974.

A good collection of articles on the Keller Plan and individualized instruction in higher education.

SKINNER, B. F. *The Technology of Teaching*. New York: Appleton-Century-Crofts, 1968.

This is a must book for the background of linear programmed instruction and for the basic principles of operant conditioning applied to education.

For a look at some of the writings in relating behaviorist principles to creativity, look at the following articles:

COVINGTON, M. V. "Promoting Creative Thinking in the Classroom." *Journal of Experimental Education* 37 (1968): 22–30.

COVINGTON, M. V.; CRUTCHFIELD, R. S.; DAVIES, L. B.; AND OLTON, R. M. *The Productive Thinking Program*. Columbus, Ohio: Charles E. Merrill, 1974.

For evaluating, selecting or writing instruction:

GAGNE, ROBERT. Essentials of Learning for Instruction. Hinsdale, Ill.: Dryden Press, 1974.

JACOBS, P.; MAIER, M.; AND STOLUROW, L. *A Guide to Evaluating Self-Instructional Programs*. New York: Holt, Rinehart and Winston, 1966.

LYSAUGHT, JEROME P., AND WILLIAM, CLARENCE M. *A Guide to Programmed Instruction*. New York: John Wiley & Sons, Inc., 1968.

MARKLE, S. M. *Good Frames and Bad: A Grammar of Frame Writing*. New York: John Wiley & Sons, Inc., 1964.

For keeping in touch with what's happening, keep an eye on the following journals:

Journal of Educational Psychology
Journal of Educational Research
Phi Delta Kappan

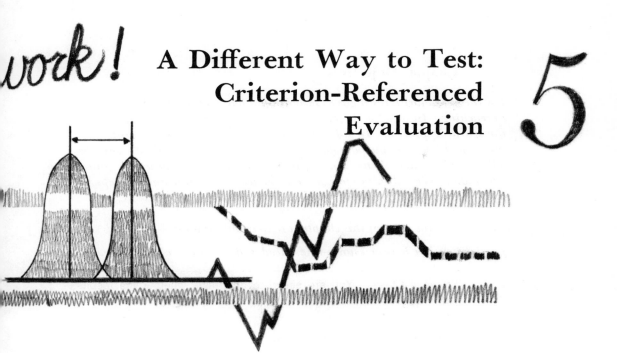

A Different Way to Test: Criterion-Referenced Evaluation

5

Chapter Objectives

For the behaviorist, testing is as important a part of the educational process as teaching. In fact, good teaching involves good testing at every point of the learning process. In this chapter we will see that behaviorism has broadened both the purpose and the way of evaluating students, and we will examine some of the kinds of tests you will be able to use in your classroom. We will also look at what makes testing fair and at steps for setting up a good testing program of your own.

The behavioral goals of this chapter are to enable you to:

1. differentiate between norm-referenced and criterion-referenced evaluations.

> *Progress Check:* You are asked to determine whether the results of six different testing situations are norm- or criterion-referenced.

2. evaluate five kinds of objective tests.

> *Progress Check:* You are asked to pick out among nine assorted test items eleven violations of the rules for good test construction.

3. apply the concepts of reliability and validity to testing procedures.

> *Progress Check:* You are asked to judge whether grades based on five different test results are reliable, and if they are valid.

4. use seven steps for carrying out a testing program in your own classroom.

> *Progress Check:* An 8-item multiple choice quiz in which you are asked to apply the principles involved in the steps.

WHY TEST?

Whether they want to or not, few teachers can avoid testing their students' learning. They are asked to give grades, make out report cards, suggest remediation, promote, pass, fail, encourage, admonish, provide feedback, and even occasionally improve their own instruction. All these activities are—or should be—guided by test results. The kind of test you give depends in part on your reason for giving it.

For the behaviorists, the most important reasons for testing have been redirected from the traditional one of ranking students' achievements in relation to each other to using testing as a teaching tool. With this expansion of the purposes of testing have come changes in kinds of testing as well. Feedback and evaluation have become an essential part of the learning process itself, and so, the skills of teaching well include to a great extent an ability to test well. Since entire college and graduate courses are dedicated to testing procedures and appropriate statistical analyses of them, reading this short chapter will not transform you into a testing expert. It should, however, help you understand the behaviorists' orientation to evaluation, and how their approach is particularly well-adapted to their theoretical approach to learning and instruction.

Evaluation for Selection: Norm-Referenced Grading

Norm-referenced grading is the kind traditionally used in our schools to compare the individual to the group, to determine how the individual stands in relation to the achievements of other students.

Reflects Different Learning Speeds. Norm-referenced evaluation is based on the assumption that there is a normal curve representing different learning aptitudes of individuals, and that grades should, on the whole, reflect these aptitudes. The normal curve assumes that in any large group of people, a small number will be very intelligent, an equally small number will be relatively unintelligent, and most of the people will hover in the vicinity of the "average."

Tests that are based on the normal curve reflect this distribution of smart, average, and not very smart people in the world, and they are constructed so that when they are given to at least 75 or 100 people, they identify which group a student belongs in. This is the chief purpose of some of the most important tests which you may have taken. SAT's, GRE's, and IQ tests are all based on the normal curve, and your grade tells you where you fit in relation to the achievements or the abilities of the rest of the group who took the exam with you. Norm-referenced grades are distributed so that roughly 15 percent of the students get *A*'s or high *B*'s, about 70 percent get low *B*'s and *C*'s, and another 15 percent get *D*'s and *F*'s. Unless you have gone to a nontraditional school, you have often been treated as a member of the "normal curve" and you probably have a good idea whether your grades place you in that group of relatively "smart," "average," or "below-average" students.

Behaviorists believe that there is a place for norm-referenced evaluation when information about student achievements relative to the group is necessary in order to select the most gifted or neediest students for a limited number of placements, scholarships, or training opportunities. They do *not* believe that it should be used as an instructional and evaluational device in regular classroom procedures. When norm-referenced grading is used in the classroom as part of the instructional process, the accent is on group-pacing rather than self-pacing. It is meant to spur competition among students and presumably to motivate them to do better than the other students in the class so that they will be reinforced with the praise attached to being in that group of "smarter" students—or at least avoid the punishment of being relegated to the group of "dumb" students. Norm-referenced grading is supposed to provide valuable self-knowledge and motivation. But many behaviorists (Miles and Robinson 1971) argue that it doesn't do either very well and that it creates additional problems of its own.

But What Has He Learned? Norm-referenced grading will tell anyone who looks at the grade approximately where an individual student stands in relation to other students in the group given the same test, but it does not communicate what a student has learned to do (Popham and Husek 1969). It tells how fast or how well, but not *what* the student has learned. The person who needs to know may make some sort of a guess behaviorists argue, but that is all.

The problem is made more difficult because different schools have different groups, so that to get an *A* in one school may be as difficult as it is to get a *C* in another. Does an honors mark from Harvard University mean the same thing as an honors mark from Kennewennybanga Community College? Educators, admissions officers, and perspective employers recognize this problem, and so they look at the results of tests such as the SAT's or GRE's which are given to students all over the country. These results make is possible to give less credence to the actual grades received by the student in school—which perhaps suggests, say the behaviorists, that school grades should be revised in some way to be more accurate reflectors to students of their real learning accomplishments.

Built-In Failure. Besides emphasizing how fast rather than what the student has learned, another problem with using norm-referenced grading in schools is that it dictates that in every group a certain number of students *must* come out at the bottom, and are therefore often labelled "failures" or "slow learners," or in the less elegant terms of less tactful students as "dummies."

Repeated research indicates that consistent failure interferes with learning. A student who is constantly told that he has failed or even consistently done poorly often gets into a rut that he cannot get out of. In behaviorist terms, he has had too few experiences of reinforced learning success and so this behavior disappears. Teachers who are using norm-referenced grading are apt to contribute to this unhappy outcome because they accept the assumption of the normal curve and the accompanying conclusion that the student probably got his low grades because he is just "naturally" less intelligent than the rest of the students.

Teachers who have the hunch that failing students all the time is not a very good teaching technique are often made to feel that they are "too easy" and are lowering the "standards." Faculties and administrators put pressures on teachers who do not grade sufficient numbers of students with low grades. A teacher who is trying to correct the supposed defect of giving out too many high grades will deliberately make tests harder and harder and will actually be delighted when the five or ten students who were formerly passing are now dropped to failed, and when the surplus of *A*'s have been turned into *B*'s and *C*'s. The behaviorists are not in favor of passing every student simply because it might damage their "egos" if they do not, but they have the nagging suspicion that something is terribly wrong when teachers who do not fail sufficient numbers of students may not be considered good teachers.

Grades Rather Than Learning. Because norm-referenced grading is based on the normal curve, there are only a certain number of high grades available to go around in any group. As a result, there exists—as you are no doubt aware—a very great competition for grades in most of our schools. Good grades are often connected with other goodies such as social prestige, scholarships, and often even good jobs, and so people try to get them. Low grades are connected with failure, sometimes personal and social, and lowered expectations, and everybody tries not to get them. Because in norm-referenced grading not everybody can get a good grade, it is like a giant game of academic musical chairs where everyone rushes and pushes everyone else out of the way so as not to be the last one without a chair. Students are not encouraged to help each other get good grades because they are all competing with each other to get one of those few available good grades.

This attitude, behaviorists argue, puts much more emphasis on getting a good grade through any means possible than on actually learning. If it is possible to get a good grade without learning very much, then students do not bother learning very much. The grade is enough. And if, as it sometimes happens, students must choose between looking as if they have learned (perhaps by being very quiet and never asking questions) and risking the possibility of looking as if they have learned little (perhaps by asking questions when they are confused or unsure), they will choose to look as if they have learned rather than actually learning. They choose the strategy that they expect will lead to good grades rather than to learning. One of the results of this attitude is an overdeveloped docility toward teachers.

For the Best Choice. The purpose of norm-referenced grading is to enable students, teachers, parents, and employers to identify individual capabilities and relative achievements. It is meant to help the student make realistic decisions about what he can do, and help educators and employers select those individuals who are most capable for further education and highly-skilled jobs.

With the broadening policy of open enrollment at increasingly higher levels of education, the behaviorists see the role of the school as something more than the means of identifying and selecting the fastest learners and most highly-gifted individuals. More and more students are finishing high school and going on to college and graduate schools. When students are attending school for as much as a third of their lives, behaviorist educators are arguing that schools can no longer be content with simply passing or failing a requisite percentage of students. The responsibility of the school must no longer be the learning of a few exceptional learners but rather the acceptable learning achievements of *all* its students (Bloom 1971). To meet this demand, the behaviorists offer criterion-referenced grading.

Evaluation for Mastery: Criterion-Referenced Grading

The purpose of criterion-referenced evaluation is to compare the individual not to the group but against some fixed standard or criterion of mastery.

Related to the Goal. Criterion-referenced grading reflects that extent to which the student has achieved the instructional goal that has been set up (Glaser and Nitko 1971). It does not rank students in relation to each other, but in relation to the fixed learning objective. It is based on the belief that the eventual achievement of the goals is possible for *everyone*. No one, given enough time, is so lacking in learning aptitude that he cannot reach the goal.

Unlike norm-referenced grading, grading for mastery does not require that somebody come out at the bottom either. Everyone can succeed;

everyone, in fact, can pass with flying colors. The fact that it may take some students longer than others to reach the goal is not counted against them or result in lower grades. Each student may take as long as he needs. The point is not that some students should be condemned to getting low norm-referenced grades but that every student should be encouraged to strive toward the final goal.

Criterion-referenced testing complements the learning definitions, goals, and instructional methods of behaviorism we have already studied. It is based on the assumption that learning goals can be specified and tested in terms of prespecified behavior, and that, given sufficient time, with practice and reinforcement, almost every student can achieve all the learning objectives the teacher has set up. As such, it is based on instruction which to some extent at least is individualized and self-paced, and it is based on a skewed learning curve. A skewed curve is one in which the majority of people are not in the middle, but are clustered at one end. In criterion-referenced grading, they are clustered at the high end of learning achievements.

Formative and Summative Evaluation. Besides emphasizing the relation of the individual learner to a fixed goal, criterion-referenced evaluation differentiates between the uses of evaluation. Evaluation used to *describe* learning is called *summative;* evaluation used to *increase or guide* learning is called *formative.*

Summative evaluation is used to test and summarize the student's overall learning achievements, and it replaces the traditional norm-referenced tests in this regard. It takes place *after* instruction is complete, and its

A COMPARISON OF NORM-REFERENCED AND CRITERION-REFERENCED TEST SCORES

A Skewed Curve

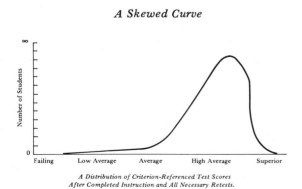

A Distribution of Criterion-Referenced Test Scores After Completed Instruction and All Necessary Retests.

A Normal Curve

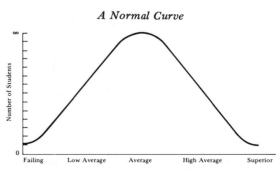

A Distribution of Norm-Referenced Test Scores After Completed Instruction.

purpose is to assess the total summary of the student's learning achievements in relation to a substantial unit of work in the curriculum.

Formative evaluation is not used as a test in the traditional sense but it provides feedback as an integral part of the learning process itself. Its primary purpose is to guide instruction by providing relevant information to identify special learning needs, abilities, or difficulties of the students, or instructional flaws in the teacher's lesson. Formative evaluation often takes the form of frequent practice quizzes or questions that check a student's progress but do not affect his grade. It should be tied closely to the task analysis and occur after each unit or subskill. The progress checks interspersed throughout this text are examples of formative rather than summative evaluations.

Formative evaluation is more specific, detailed, and frequent than summative evaluation, and should not in any way be the anxiety-ridden experience that traditional testing is for so many students. It is not given to motivate the student by pronouncing that he has or has not learned so much material by such and such a time, but to inform him of the progress he is making and how much further he has yet to go to reach the stated goal.

High Quality Success for Everyone. Behaviorists believe that criterion-referenced grading makes it possible to eliminate failure without eliminating or reducing quality of learning. Everyone is not passed or given a high grade because standards have been lowered by teachers fearful of the destructive effects of consistent student failure. Rather, every student gets a high grade because he is given the chance to keep trying until he succeeds.

The behaviorists believe this is a much more constructive approach than the built-in failure of norm-referenced grading. Most learning goals set up in our schools *can* be reached by everyone if they are given sufficient time and motivation. Sooner or later, most students do learn the rudiments of reading, writing, spelling, and arithmetic. There is little question that the great majority of students attending regular school are capable of acquiring these skills. But in the process of trying to acquire them, some students are given norm-referenced grades which indicate to them that they cannot learn, that they are stupid or slow, and this kind of feedback often actually interferes with learning, slowing it down or stopping it altogether.

The proponents of criterion-referenced grading believe that it encourages learning more effectively by giving positive feedback to *every* learner whatever his learning pace. It reduces the comparisons among students and shows the student instead how he compares with his *own* past performance, emphasizing how much he has improved, and indicating how much further he has to go to reach the final goal. Tests, instead of being used as a final gong that drops and sentences everyone to the grade he has earned at that particular moment, with little possibility of any further reprieve, encourage and monitor learning. Instead of sentencing the student to a certain grade no matter what he does in the future, discouraging him from continued work if he has not done well at first, criterion-referenced grading offers the learner another chance. He does not have to lug around with him the burden of an initially bad grade producing brilliant work just to balance out his first failure.

Encourages Cooperation. Instead of encouraging students to compete with each other for a limited number of grades, evaluation for mastery changes the emphasis so that students can help each other without fear of jeopardizing their own good grade. We saw in chapter 2 that Skinner believes that it is essential for the solution of humanity's most pressing problems that we learn cooperative behavior. Criterion-referenced grading is an attempt to reduce the rewards of competitive behavior, and insofar as studying together with other students increases learning, positively reinforce cooperative behavior.

Clarified Communication. Lastly, behaviorists believe that criterion-referenced grading will clarify the communication to the student himself and to others about what a student has learned, instead of simply communicating where the student stands relative to his group. A teacher who is trying to decide whether Johnny who is transferring from another school in another part of the country can look at descriptions of what Johnny has learned to do, and can decide more easily what grade he belongs to in the new school. Instead of learning that Johnny was at the top of his old second grade with-

---

Name: *John Smith*   Grade Level: **5**

The math achievements of this student this semester have been:

    A - Excellent
    B - Good
    C - Average
  (D)- Poor
    F - Failing

Comments: *Johnny is moving very slowly; in relation to the rest of the class he is in the bottom third.*

**A Student Report Card Based
on Norm-Referenced Grading.**

Name: *Jane Jones*   Grade Level: **3**

This student has successfully accomplished math goals:
    1-5   ;

She has yet to accomplish math goals:
    6-12   this term.

Comments: *Jane has learned to add double digit numbers since the last report. The next goal is to subtract double digit numbers.*

**A Student Report Card Based
on Criterion-Referenced Grading.**

out knowing what the second graders in Johnny's old school learned, the new teacher knows that Johnny has reached a specific level of math, reading and writing skills. Criterion-referenced grading, from this point of view, should make communication clearer, more precise, and ultimately more useful.

Which One Is Better When?

Using criterion-referenced grading is one attempt to solve the problems created by persistent and continuous failure imposed by norm-referenced grading, to reduce destructive competition among students, and to clarify communication about a student's learning. There are questions as well which have not been resolved and about which you as a teacher will have to make some decision. Some of these questions follow.

Will Everyone Benefit? There is research (Atkinson et al. 1960; Atkinson and O'Connor 1963; McClelland 1961) which indicates that individuals differ in how much or whether they are motivated by competition. Some students do their best only when there is competition, but others do their worst in competitive situations. Besides, we do not know to what extent trying to do better than other students, the motivation inherent in norm-referenctd grading, has the same effects as trying to do better than oneself has done before, the motivation inherent in criterion-referenced grading. In other words, is competing with oneself as rewarding for all students as competing with others? We need more research on the question but it may be possible that some students would operate better under norm-referenced grading, and others under criterion-referenced grading. Are there certain kinds of students whom you hypothesize would do better under one type of grading than under another? Or do you think everyone should be taught to compete only with himself? Should students of different ages be treated differently? Should younger students, perhaps those in grade school, be graded according to a criterion, while older students are graded according to a norm?

Is Competition Necessary? Is competition at the very heart of American progress, the source of American strength? Is it the motivating force challenging us to bring forth the very best of which we are capable? Do you think competition is an important ingredient of education? Or do you believe with Skinner that competition is too often destructive and that our schools would be better without it?

Some educators fear that by drastically reducing competition among students that there will be no standard of excellence, and that consequently, standards will be reduced. Because the goals will be within the reach of everyone, the most gifted individuals will remain underchallenged, content with achieving what is expected of the average student but not producing work of a quality of which only a few are capable. They fear that criterion-referenced grading could lower standards of the average student as well because teachers may simply lower their goals so that all students will reach them easily, rather than teaching better so that more students learn more.

Proponents of mastery evaluation say that the dangers of loss of excellence will actually be reduced because it will be clear when students have reached a specifiable goal. Teachers will no longer be able to hide shoddy teaching behind a facade that passes a certain percentage of students even when they have learned almost nothing from them at all. For those gifted students who reach initial goals more quickly, a teacher will be challenged to set higher and higher goals for him rather than simply getting by giving the student a high mark.

When Do We Need Information About the Norm? Whether or not one wants to use mastery evaluation in the course of ordinary teaching, there are times when it is important to have information about the norm. First of all, criterion levels for mastery evaluation are ultimately derived from information about what the average student can accomplish. Individuals and institutions often have valid needs to know about where the individual stands in relation to the group as well. Open enrollment on the college level is reducing the need for a strict selection process at this level, but students wishing to enter a course of training (such as medical school) where there are a limited number of spaces, are chosen on the basis of the norm. Such schools, and many employers, do not want to choose randomly among students who have reached graduation criteria, but want to choose those students who have been most outstanding within their group.

Students themselves often need norm-referenced evaluations as well, particularly when they are making career choices. If Albert has shown a sensitivity to music which is significantly superior to that of his peers, his ability to make an informed decision to be a musician or not will be increased by his knowing his standing in relation to other studens. So will Angelo's, who might enjoy music just as much as Albert but who appears to be almost tone-deaf compared to the rest of the class.

The question is when students should be compared to others and when they should be compared to an absolute criteria. Americans do not like to accept failure as inevitable to anyone willing to work hard enough to succeed. The American constitution is based on the assertion that all men are created equal, but the sometimes painful reality is that all men are not created the same. Each of us in the process of growing up realizes this to some extent, and one of the important places where children are introduced to these differences is in school. Some of these differences—sex, physical attractiveness, occupation of parents, skin color, artistic, musical, or gymnastic talents, social popularity, height or weight—cannot be hidden, and the school attempts to teach children that despite these differences, the basic dignity of every individual remains equal.

At what point, how clearly, and in what ways, should students find out that they are different from other students academically? When should a student be told that he is not very good at something at which he very much wants to succeed? Or conversely, when should a student be told that her achievements may be quite outstanding? In other words, when, how often, and under what conditions should norm-referenced grading be used, and when, by whom and for whom should criterion-referenced evaluation be used?

These are questions that you will have to address as a teacher. In the meantime, here is a short progress check to make sure that you have understood the basic differences between norm- and criterion-referenced evaluation.

BEHAVIORISTS BELIEVE THAT TESTS SHOULD MATCH THEIR PURPOSE

NORM-REFERENCED TESTS

Should be used to:
- *select students with the highest achievements.*
- *compare achievements of the individual to the average achievements of the group.*
- *describe students' learning relative to the group.*

Should not be used to:
- *motivate learning.*
- *evaluate effects of instruction.*
- *determine students' grades.*
- *describe what students have learned in absolute terms.*
- *test learning in ongoing classroom instruction.*

CRITERION-REFERENCED TESTS

Should be used to:
- *diagnose learning needs.*
- *guide instruction.*
- *motivate learning.*
- *describe students' learning achievements.*
- *evaluate mastery achievements.*
- *evaluate learning continuously during regular instruction.*
- *compare students to absolute goal.*

Should not be used to:
- *categorize students (as slow or fast learners).*
- *compare students with each other.*

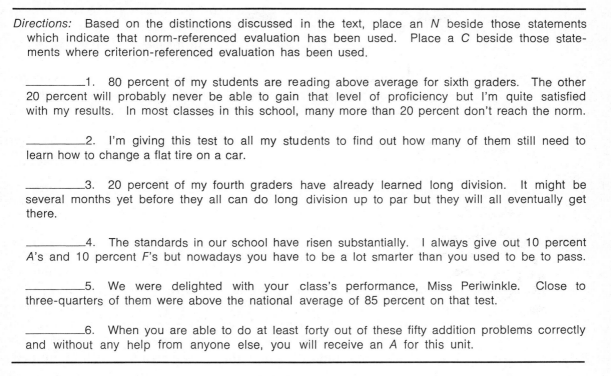

Progress Check 5.1:   Recognizing the Difference Between Criterion- and Norm-Referenced Evaluations

Directions: Based on the distinctions discussed in the text, place an *N* beside those statements which indicate that norm-referenced evaluation has been used.   Place a *C* beside those statements where criterion-referenced evaluation has been used.

_____1.   80 percent of my students are reading above average for sixth graders.   The other 20 percent will probably never be able to gain that level of proficiency but I'm quite satisfied with my results.   In most classes in this school, many more than 20 percent don't reach the norm.

_____2.   I'm giving this test to all my students to find out how many of them still need to learn how to change a flat tire on a car.

_____3.   20 percent of my fourth graders have already learned long division.   It might be several months yet before they all can do long division up to par but they will all eventually get there.

_____4.   The standards in our school have risen substantially.   I always give out 10 percent *A*'s and 10 percent *F*'s but nowadays you have to be a lot smarter than you used to be to pass.

_____5.   We were delighted with your class's performance, Miss Periwinkle.   Close to three-quarters of them were above the national average of 85 percent on that test.

_____6.   When you are able to do at least forty out of these fifty addition problems correctly and without any help from anyone else, you will receive an *A* for this unit.

EVALUATING WITH OBJECTIVE TESTS

The ways of testing learning include paper-and-pencil tests, take home assignments, simulations, demonstrations, speeches, painting, essays, and other original student constructions.   We are going to look particularly at kinds of objective exams you have the option of using for either norm-referenced or criterion-referenced evaluation because they are especially well-matched to the behaviorist concept of learning as a step-by-step process in which each step can and should be tested individually.   After looking at the kinds of tests you can give, we will examine the characteristics that make tests fair, and then at steps for planning your own tests.

Tests that are objective in the strict sense have only a single right answer for each test question, and each student is scored in exactly the same way as every other student.   These tests are often even scored by machine, and they are constructed so that it is not necessary for the scorer to understand how the student was "thinking" but only what the student has actually written. The right answer—in well-constructed tests, anyway—is so unambiguous that there is never any doubt about whether an answer is right. As we will see, a behaviorist evaluation program using objective tests is very much like a programmed instruction except that the immediate feedback after each frame—called a "test item" in an exam—is deleted in the exam situation.

We will examine specifically the essay test and the various means suggested to grade them more objectively than they are usually graded, and four other kinds of tests that are called objective. We will look at the advantages and disadvantages of using each of the tests, and will see that the advantages of using a loosely structured exam—such as the essay—are often offset by corresponding disadvantages, while the advantages and disadvantages of using more highly-structured objective tests are just reversed.

Essay Tests: Structured by the Student

In an essay test, the student is asked to discuss a topic, problem, question, or area of inquiry determined by the teacher. He is expected to use his own words, and develop his position logically, coherently, in a well-organized and comprehensive manner. The essay may be relatively long, or quite short. It may be written in class or taken home to be worked on for a day, a week, a semester, or even a year or more. The teacher may make general demands indicating only the general area in which the student should address himself ("Write about the economic situation in South Africa since Rhodesian Independence.") or may make quite specific and structured demands ("Delineate in about fifteen typewritten pages the changes in the eating habits of the Rhodesians as a result of the change of food importation policies of Tanzania since Rhodesian Independence.")

A Good Test of Complex Learning. Of all the standard exams commonly used today, the essay exam is the one that is least prestructured for the student, and therefore demands the greatest independent organization of material by the student himself. For this reason, essay exams have the advantage of enabling teachers to assess the development of relatively complex learning. Besides, essays are often highly motivating and intrinsically rewarding learning experiences for the students doing them. Students, for instance, often report that just having to write a paper or answer a series of well-formulated essay questions taught them far more than studying for an objective exam possibly could have. Also, it takes the teacher relatively little time to compose good essay questions. Essay tests are usually best used when the teacher wants to test the higher levels of learning such as synthesis or evaluation and when class size is small.

Often Unreliable. Essay tests are extraordinarily difficult to grade well, and they are also time-consuming. There are so many ways that a student can write a good answer that the norms for determining whether an essay is well-written or not are much more vague than the norms for scoring strictly objective tests. In fact, research has indicated that teachers who are asked to regrade essay tests which they themselves have graded just a few days before will often give the essay a very different grade on rereading. Extraneous factors such as the student's name, handwriting, grammer, and spelling often take on an influence all out of proportion to their importance. And while some students learn a great deal in the process of writing an essay, others learn the technique of writing an apparently coherent answer while carefully tip-toeing around any material they don't know.

Making It Better. There are a few techniques that you can use to improve the grading of essay exams. First, this is one kind of test where length does not usually lead to better grading but to worse, and so, especially in the beginning when you are just learning to grade essay questions, you should probably concentrate on assigning very *short* essays.

Secondly, concentrate on asking relatively *highly structured* questions that have clear and specific answers. As you become more proficient in grading essays, you will be able to move toward less structured assignments.

Third, delineate specific criteria for students' answers *before* you start grading. Make a list of points which must be included in a good answer and how much each point is worth. Decide whether you will deduct points for inaccurate information, and how much extra credit may be gained for inclusion of relevant material which you have not listed as absolutely essential. You should be able to specify exactly what percent of the total grade each aspect of the essay is worth, including spelling and grammar if you are taking it into account. The more thoroughly you structure your norms before you start grading, the more reliable will be your final results.

When you are grading the exams, refer to these specifications to make comments that relate to particular characteristics of the essay. It is unfair and not very enlightening to students to write something as general and vague as "fair development of idea but needs improvement" when it is possible to say that while two important concepts have been covered well that another is unclear, and the fourth omitted entirely.

Fourth, have your students put their *names on the back* of their answers where you can keep them firmly and permanently out of your sight until all the grading is complete. You will be surprised, if you are like most teachers, how much knowing who wrote a paper can influence the grade you give, even when you are trying not to be unduly influenced. This is a good practice even for grading objective exams, but it is especially critical for essays.

Fifth, if you give more than one question for each student to answer, *grade all of the answers to each question* at one time. That is, complete the grading of the first question for every student in the class before you begin to grade the second question each student has answered, and so on. This will keep you from getting "set" and being influenced by the grade you have just given the student on his previous questions. For this reason, it is a good idea to keep all grades out of sight along with the student's name when you are grading succeeding questions. This can usually be conveniently arranged by having each question answered on a separate page.

Sixth, if the grades to the essays are important, or if you are unsure of your grading procedures, check your grading by setting the papers aside for a sufficient length of time to forget the grades you have already assigned. This may not be for more than an hour or two. Then *regrade a random selection* of the questions without looking at your original grade and see how well your two different grades match. If there is a wide divergency in the grades, you need to develop more specific guidelines, and perhaps in the future, to concentrate on asking shorter and more structured questions. In any case, your grading is not objective, and your students would have a legitimate complaint if they were to feel they were not being tested fairly.

Fill-In Exams: A Move Toward the Objective

In a fill-in or completion exam, students are given a sentence or short paragraph and asked to fill in the missing word or words. Depending on the length of the answer required, fill-in exams resemble full-fledged essay exams or bona fide objective exams. When an entire paragraph must be written to answer the question, the completion test approaches the essay exam with its relative advantages and disadvantages. When the answer to be filled in is no more than a word or two, the completion exam closely resembles the other objective tests. Linear programs are composed of the kind of items that are used in short-answer fill-in exams.

More Reliable and Specific. The short-answer or fill-in exam is much easier to score reliably than the fully developed essay especially for inexperienced or hurried teachers. They also enable the teacher to ask a series of specific questions so that feedback is more precise and students cannot replace knowledge with writing facility as easily as in an essay. Also, as in the essay exam, the completion test requires that the student *produce* an answer, not just recognize it as required in the other kinds of objective tests we will be looking at.

Sometimes Irrelevant. The biggest problem with the fill-in test that requires short answers is that it is often difficult to construct them so that they test complex learning rather than memorization. They easily lend themselves to testing bitty pieces of useless and marginally irrelevant trivia picked up from the text by poor students but glossed over by better students who concentrate on key ideas rather than on amassing piles of unrelated facts. This disadvantage can be counteracted by asking for answers requiring a short paragraph, but then there are the problems accompanying essay tests of grading quickly and fairly.

Points for Improvement. Fill-in items can be improved by constructing items for which there is a single correct answer. If the item indicates specifically that the identification of a person, event, phenomenon, time, place, process, or thing is called for, the student is required to fill in an important concept rather than an irrelevant string of words which may nonetheless accurately complete the sentence. For example, the test item "Columbus discovered America in _____." can be completed accurately by filling in 1492, three ships, a hurry, confusion, or a state of starvation. The item can be improved by indicating that it is a specific *date* you are looking for such as "Columbus discovered America in the year _____."

Since completion items can also be confusing or invalid when the student is faced with too many blanks in one item or is alerted to the correct answer with grammatical tips, items should be constructed with a minimum of blanks and with as few unnecessary hints as possible. For example, an item such as "_____ began when _____ marched into _____ in the year _____." is better with fewer blanks: "World War II began when Germany marched into _____ in _____", and "The authors of *The Mikado* were _____." contains a grammatical hint not included in "_____ wrote *The Mikado.*"

True-False Tests: Tried but Not So True

In true-false tests, students are asked to evaluate the accuracy of statements. For instance, a student may be asked to indicate whether the following statement is true or false: "The sun is the main source of light on the planet Mars." True-false tests are very easy to construct and to score, but they have disadvantages of such magnitude that most testmakers are disinclined to use them.

Question of Clarity. The first problem is that it is amazingly difficult to write a series of true-false statements that are not legitimately subject to misinterpretation. Statements that seem perfectly clear to the person who wrote them have a way of looking for perfectly logical and coherent reasons like something entirely different to another reader. True-false tests, especially if they require an accompanying statement from the student explaining his evaluation, can sometimes be useful in formative evaluation. But if you use true-false tests for tests which count for a grade for the student, be prepared for a larger than usual number of requests for reconsideration of your grading procedures.

Good for Guessing. Besides the problem of composing unambiguous items, true-false tests give students a fifty percent chance of getting an answer correct using nothing more than pure uninformed guesswork. Again, the test can be doctored by asking students to state why they think the statement is right or wrong but then the test grader must deal with the same problems of grading objectively that beset essay or long fill-in tests.

Matching Tests: Usually Another Poor Solution

Matching tests ask the testee to pair items in two columns with each other. Each column may contain a statement, name, date, characteristic, description, or some other item. Each item in the column is related in some specifiable way to items in the second column, and the student is required to recognize which item in column one is best paired with an item in column two. Like true-false tests, matching tests are easy to compose and to score. It is particularly difficult to make up matching tests that measure more than the student's memorization of discrete facts but test more advanced kinds of analytical, synthetic, and evaluative learning.

Multiple-Choice Tests: Method of Choice

In the multiple choice test, a partial statement is made or a question asked in what is called the "stem." The student is asked to choose from several possibilities the one that best completes the stem or answers the question. The answers that are offered to the student as possible choices but that are incorrect are called "foils" or "distractors." Multiple choice tests are currently the best method of compromise most often used by examiners in need of a test that can be scored objectively and that also tests subtleties of learning.

A TEST TO GRADUATE?

For some ten years now, SAT and other nationally administered test scores have indicated that the achievement levels of the average high school student seems to be steadily dropping. Colleges across the country have subsequently found it necessary to offer remedial courses in basic skills such as math, reading, and writing to bring freshmen students up to a sufficiently proficient level to begin college work. The increasing dissatisfaction with results achieved by our schools has led to a serious consideration of criterion-referenced tests in which students must demonstrate a minimum competency in basic areas before a high school diploma is awarded. In some areas, including Arizona, Oregon, and Florida, legislation has already been passed to implement such a practice. Supporters of the plan say that these minimum competency tests will restore public confidence in the high school diploma, but to institute such a program, certain problems must be faced as well:

• What is minimum competency? Who should determine it? The school? Parents? Education boards? The state?

• How should competency be measured? How will it be determined that such measurements are culture-fair, not discriminating against already disenfranchised groups? What about students who do poorly on objective tests but do well in other demonstrations of learning?

• What should happen to students—perhaps as many as 25–30 percent—who do not meet minimum requirements when they are first tested? How many times should students be permitted to retake the test? For how many years should they be permitted to attend school? What will happen to those students who are never able to receive a diploma?

• If different standards are set by different educational districts and different states, is it fair to fail in one district a student who could pass the minimum requirements set up in a neighboring district with lower standards?

• When should the test first be given? Is it too late to wait until twelfth grade to test? Should students be tested as early as fourth grade in order to diagnose potential weaknesses? If some students pass the test as freshmen or younger, should they be permitted to leave school or go on to college?

WHAT DO YOU THINK?

Should basic minimum requirements be set up at various check points along the educational system? If so how would you deal with the practical problems a decision to take such a course of action would involve?

An Objective Test of Complex Learning. When they are well-constructed multiple choice tests can be used to test a student's ability to solve problems, perceive logical relationships, apply a principle, evaluate an argument, or analyze ideas better than any other kind of objective test we have already examined. It is a popular form of test because they can be scored quickly and fairly, and at the same time can be used to test all the levels of learning suggested by Gagne's hierarchy or Bloom's taxonomy.

Difficult to Construct. While multiple-choice tests may be easy to score, they are very very difficult to compose. In fact, some professional organizations require that their employees write only about one multiple-choice item an hour. If most teachers were to work at such a pace, they would never be able to produce the number of items they need. Often what is sacrificed is quality.

Helpful Hints. Just as there are some helpful hints to reduce the problems of essay testing, there are also some guidelines to the writer of multiple-choice tests. First, the stem may be in the form of an incomplete sentence or of a question, but in either case it should *state as much of a meaningful problem as possible*. The stems "According to the text," or "The United States," or "Animals usually" are poor because they do not initiate a meaningful problem to the reader. On the other hand, stems such as "According to the text, population in the Eastern countries of the world during the last ten years," or "The United States federal government is composed of," or "Animals are usually unable to digest" are better because they indicate the problem area with which the question is concerned.

Second, all the possible answers from which the student is to select the right answer should 1) be about *equal length* (many test writers are tempted to make the right answer longer), 2) agree grammatically with the stem, and 3) sound somewhat plausible to someone who does not know the right answer. This last requirement is sometimes a tough one. Most students who have had any experience with multiple-choice tests cultivate a garden variety of guessing known as "eliminating the obvious." Clearly, if the student can eliminate an obviously wrong answer just by recognizing that it sounds ridiculous, he has increased his chances of guessing the right answer considerably.

Third, now that the right answer and all the foils agree grammatically, are about the same length, and are at least plausible, be sure not to ruin the whole test by consistently putting the right answer in either the first or second place.

Fourth, check your foils and make sure that there is only *one right answer* for each stem.

Lastly, you may expect difficulties from at least some of your students if you state the problem in the stem negatively. If you want to test a student's knowledge of particular material and not his ability to reason with negatives and double negatives, you should probably steer *away from using no and not in the stem* at all. If you do use negatives and have some doubt about whether you should or not, take a special look at those items in which negatives were used and check to see if a disproportionate number of students answered them incorrectly.

To see if you understand what has been said about objective tests, here is a short one for you.

Progress Check 5.2: Evaluating Test Items

Directions: Among the following nine test items are at least twelve violations of rules suggested by the text for constructing good tests. In the space provided, indicate the errors and the items in which they occur. Do not assume there is an error in every item or that each item contains only one violation. For further feedback, try to improve poor items. Correct answers are marked with an asterisk (*).

Item a. Evaluation is *not*
  *a. criterion-referenced if it is norm-referenced evaluation.
   b. criterion-referenced if it is formative evaluation.
   c. criterion-referenced if it is summative.

Item b. Which of the following does not accurately describe a criterion-referenced test?
   a. tests which compare the individual's accomplishments to a fixed goal.
  *b. tests which compare the individual's achievements to the achievements of the group, showing whether the individual is above, below, or at about equal with the group average.
   c. tests administered during the instructional process to guide and motivate learning.
   d. tests in which the final results are not distributed in a normal curve.

Item c. Which of the following test results is norm-referenced?
  *a. Jane was scored in the ninety-eighth percentile of students across the country who took the SAT exams in April.
   b. John can spell ninety of the hundred words listed in the fourth grade speller.
   c. All thirty-two of Ms. Jones' statistics students know how to interpret a frequency graph correctly.
   d. None of the children in the first grade of PS 72 can recognize all twenty-six letters of the alphabet.

Item d. To find out whether Mary needs further practice to reach the spelling goal for her class this year, you should make use of the test results showing that Mary
   a. has an IQ of 110.
  *b. can spell correctly less than half of the words listed for this year's spelling goal for the class.
   c. are among the top third of the class in spelling
   d. did very poorly in spelling last year.

Item e. Given the following elements, which order does the text suggest for developing a behaviorist lesson plan?
  Elements: 1. present lesson
            2. evaluate students' learning
            3. provide positive reinforcement for students' learning behaviors
            4. specify informational goals
            5. set criterion of successful goal achievement

*a. 4, 5, 1, 3, 2.
*b. 4, 5, 2, 1, 3.
 c. 1, 2, 3, 4, 5.
 d. 5, 4, 1, 3, 2.

Item f.   In the light of the behaviorist principles of operant conditioning we have studied, indicate which of the following educational practices would meet with approval from a behaviorist educator.

   a. increasing promptness by hitting a child when he comes late to school.
   *b. increasing learning in the bright but unmotivated student by praising her every time she does one step better than before.
   c. solving discipline problems by being very careful not to notice or disturb a troublemaker on those rare occasions that he is studying quietly.
   d. wearing perfume to school.

Item g.   Write three essays of about fifty words each, evaluating the results of an extended use of programmed instruction to teach mathematics to fifth graders on:

   a. subsequent learning levels
   b. student self-concept
   c. students' problem-solving behaviors.

Write each of your essays on a separate page, writing the title of the topic you are discussing in the upper right hand corner of each page, and your name on the upper left hand corner.

Item h.   Criterion-referenced evaluation was first discussed systematically by _____.

Item i.   Indicate whether the following statement is true or false: "The important point in the instructional process according to the behaviorists where evaluation should be used is after the lesson."

Violation: In Item: Violates the rule that:

1) _____   _____

    (Can be improved by _____)

2) _____   _____

    (Can be improved by _____)

3) _____   _____

    (Can be improved by _____)

4) _____   _____

    (Can be improved by _____)

5) _____   _____

    (Can be improved by _____)

6) _____   _____

(Can be improved by _____)

7) _____   _____

(Can be improved by _____)

8) _____   _____

(Can be improved by _____)

9) _____   _____

(Can be improved by _____)

10) _____   _____

(Can be improved by _____)

11) _____   _____

(Can be improved by _____)

12) _____   _____

(Can be improved by _____)

CHARACTERISTICS OF FAIR TESTS

The behaviorists look to tests to provide information about learning to motivate and guide further learning, and to describe what has already been learned in an objective and verifiable way. Testing for the behaviorist is an integral part of the educational process, a procedure which must occur continuously throughout a students' career.

To get the valuable information tests have to offer, it is not enough simply to test students ad infinitum. Volumes of test results can be nothing more than volumes of neatly stacked waste paper if the tests given to the students were not good tests to begin with. To provide information that is worth anything, that is something more than an arbitrary justification for a grade handed out on the whims of all-powerful teachers, tests—all tests, whether they are norm- or criterion-referenced, whether for summative or formative evaluation—must be fair, and to be fair they must be both reliable and valid.

Reliability

Reliable tests can be *relied on* to give consistent results. You can count on information provided by reliable tests in the same way you can count on information from a reliable thermometer. Unreliable tests may work sometimes and other times may provide widely inaccurate information. Using them is like using an unreliable car that just might get you all the way across the United States, but also just might break down at the next corner.

IS IT A GOOD IDEA THAT WON'T WORK?

"I was once enthusiastic about [evaluation for mastery] . . . I thought it was moving us in a worthwhile direction. But as we tried to work with this idea in our research, we abandoned it. We abandoned the whole notion of time to mastery or time to reach criterion or rate of learning. Why? Because learning is multi-dimensional. It is multi-dimensional in a laboratory; it is far more multi-dimensional in the school. As we are teaching one thing, a lot of additional things are happening. . . .

Even in the subjects at the center of the curriculum, such as reading comprehension, achievement is multi-dimensional. There is the level of knowing what the author said, the level of knowing what the author meant, and the level of understanding things the author said that the author wasn't aware he had said. These aspects of reading comprehension are developed continuously and the child who has been 'brought up to mastery' on only one of the dimensions probably hasn't mastered the other dimensions. Nor does the teacher know what to do to cause him to 'master' reading in all these ways. The teacher can only hope that repeated interactions with material, discussed at whatever level the pupil can discuss these less obvious meanings, will successfully move the child along. This is what we speak of as growth or educational

development, and I, at least, have not been able to apply the mastery concept to it."

Lee J. Cronbach (1971)

What Do You Think?

Cronbach is saying that he thinks that behavioral goals and criterion-referenced evaluation initially sound like very good ideas until one begins to realize that learning is so much more complex than such goals and tests presume. He has concluded that they won't work for describing and measuring the richness of human learning as it actually occurs.

How validly and completely do you think all aspects of learning can be included in behavioral goals and tests? How confident do you feel that the results of such tests accurately describe how much a student has actually learned? Do you think subtle but important parts of the learning process will be omitted, narrowing learning into a barren one-dimensional field in which everyone must behave in the same way to demonstrate what he has learned? Or will specifying behavioral goals and using criterion-referenced tests insure that no important aspects of learning will be omitted?

Using reliable tests is important if the information they provide is going to have any meaning at all. Imagine if as a teacher you had the results of one IQ test that scored Maryann as a genius, and another IQ score that indicated that she was subnormal. One or both of the results are unreliable, and they would be of almost no use to you at all. You yourself have probably taken an exam whose results were unreliable by the fact that you were sick, or had just broken your glasses, or were worried about something happening at home. Sometimes, though, there is something wrong with the test, not the test-taker, that makes their results unstable.

Validity

Valid tests test what they say they are testing. To demonstrate the difference between valid and invalid tests, let's examine this example. Suppose a teacher lined up all her students in order of height, and then assigned reading scores, giving the lowest grades to the shortest pupils, the highest grades to the tallest. In other words, the test for reading skills was height. These results would be highly reliable; the test would yield the same results everytime it was given. But they would be very invalid, beaause the connection between height and reading is an *invalid* one. The *test* was for height, but the *grade* was for reading.

In valid tests, there is a legitimate connection between what the student is graded for, and what he was tested for. Since what a student is graded for is presumably what he has been taught, a valid test is also one in which there is a legitimate relationship between your learning goals which indicate what is to be learned, and the grade, which indicates what the student has learned. A test is valid when the student can pass the test if he has achieved the instructional goals, and cannot pass if he has not achieved them. If the student can pass the test without achieving your goals, it is invalid. Equally, if the student cannot pass the test when he *has* achieved your goals, it is invalid.

You have probably taken a test or two in your life which you thought lacked validity. In cooking class, for instance, your teacher may have said she was going to test your ability to cook an omelet but really tested your memorization of the recipe; her test lacked validity. You probably came away from such a test feeling that it was "unfair" because you really knew the material but hadn't had a chance to demonstrate it. Or it could have been that exam you "aced" even though you knew you didn't know the material, the exam that was easy for you to pass without "knowing a thing."

There are limitations to the reliability and validity of the best of tests, especially those that you construct yourself and that you probably do not have the opportunity to analyze sufficiently before they are given to your students. We will see in the section on designing your own tests that there are some reasonable steps you can take, however, to insure some measure of reliability and validity in your tests. First, here is a check point to make sure you have an accurate grasp of the basic concepts involved so far.

Progress Check 5.3: Evaluating Reliability and Validity of Testing Procedures

Directions: In the spaces provided, place a check next to each of the educational testing and grading procedures which are 1) reliable, and 2) valid. For further feedback give the reason for your decision that an item is either acceptable or not.

1. Ms. Jones passed out history grades to her sophomore class based on the number of history books they had signed out of the library during the fall semester.

_____ Reliable?   Because _____.

_____ Valid?   Because _____.

2. Students in the sixth grade physical education class received grades based on their weight increases between September and June.

_____ Reliable?   Because _____.

_____ Valid?   Because _____.

3. The report cards of the fourth grade reflected grades in arithmetic based on a single one hundred item exam in multiplication given one rainy winter Friday afternoon when many of the children were fighting severe colds.

_____ Reliable?   Because _____.

_____ Valid?   Because _____.

4. In educational psychology, Dr. Herman lectured and assigned readings on Piaget's four stages of cognitive development; the midterm and final exam contained one hundred objective items, ninety-five of which related to the influence of behaviorism in education, and five of which related to Piaget's theory of cognitive development.

_____ Reliable?   Because _____.

_____ Valid?   Because _____.

5. The grades Mr. Klein assigned to his seventh grade geography class were based on four long-term assignments in land use, industrial capacities, transportation facilities, and population distribution, and four objective tests on these same topics.

_____ Reliable? Because _____.

_____ Valid? Because _____.

Since evaluation for the behaviorist is an integral part of teaching, complete plans for evaluation should be included in your original lesson plans. If you recall, the last step in preparing your own lesson plan in the last chapter included evaluation. This chapter deals exclusively with that step of evaluation. In itself, it involves a series of additional steps.

Step 1: Plan Frequent Formative Tests. Look at your task analysis and mark off at which points formative evaluation (to guide and motivate further learning) will occur, and at which points or under what conditions evaluation will be summative (to see if learning goals have been achieved). Since the feedback provided by formative evaluation should function as a reinforcement delivered on a frequent ratio schedule to increase learning behaviors, formative tests should be relatively frequent. Unless they are doubling as summative evaluation when sufficient criteria are reached (as in the Keller Plan), they should not count toward the students' final grade.

How often you plan to give tests to your students will have to be determined as a result of some experience, taking into account students' learning abilities and histories as well as the nature of the subject you are teaching. You should decide at the outset at what points in the learning process tests will be given. They should be sufficiently frequent to motivate students with positive feedback rather than cause severe anxiety.

Step 2: Build a Table of Specifications. When evaluation is formal and not carried out informally in a casual question-and-answer verbal interchange among class members, you should construct a table of specifications. A specifications table is based on your behavioral goals and task analysis, and states 1) the content of learning to be evaluated, 2) the level at which it is being evaluated, and 3) the percent that each unit contributes to the final learning evaluation. You have already stated in your behavioral goal the kind of test you are going to give, but to complete your table, you may choose to include the information again here.

Step 3: Design Your Test. You have already specified the kind of tests and levels of success in your behavioral goals. Since the kinds of information provided by different kinds of tests—essay, take home, various objective exams, term papers—complement each other, it is a good idea to mix the kinds of tests you use as well as to use different kinds of items in a single test. Once you select the kinds of tests you are going to use and are actually designing the items themselves, the following rules will help you construct items that are valid, reliable, and provide you with the kind of feedback that is most helpful toward guiding the learning of your students.

Focus on Essentials. You want your students to learn key ideas rather than trivia. Since the kind of test you give will guide the future study habits of your students, you want to encourage them to look for central concepts, general principles, and essential processes. Your aim is not to trap your students or to fail a certain percentage of them but to help them *all* learn the important aspects of the subject.

Use Fresh Examples. If you use examples in your test that have already been discussed in class, you run the risk of testing memorization rather than comprehension, application, or other higher levels of learning. Remember this, too, in a re-test situation.

Construct at Least Two Items For Each Unit in Your Task Analysis. The purpose of writing at least two items for each unit of learning you are testing is to enable you to check the reliability and possible validity of your test items in Step 6. An even better way to check your test is to provide whenever possible a second *test situation* in which units of the task analysis can be examined. For example the units included in a task analysis dealing with learning to repair a car can be tested both in an objective paper-and-pencil exam and by asking the student to actually repair a car with specific defects.

Clarify Ambiguous Items. This is easier said than done because it is often difficult to recognize that items one has constructed oneself may be ambiguous to another reader. You can, however, read each item of your test over carefully several days after you have actually written it, and you can also ask another teacher to read the test over to screen for unclear wording. Lastly, you will have to be open to the possibility that some ambiguous items may slip by, and they may be pointed out to you by your students after the test has been administered. In that case, they must be deleted from the test, and of course omitted in future test administrations.

Step 4: Cue Your Students. As you recall, most behaviorist methods include informing students of the behavioral goals of a course, and as such, you will be providing them with guidelines about the nature of the tests they will be taking. The rationale for giving "surprise" exams to try to increase learning is weak. During the initial stages of learning, your goal is to increase learning by reinforcing it on a frequent schedule rather than by punishing its absence. Therefore, you should maximize the probability that students will do well on tests. Research supports this position, indicating that students learn less under a regime of surprise exams than in courses where tests and their contents are announced beforehand (Bigge 1964). So let your students know when tests will be given, what will be covered, and give them adequate time to prepare. Only after learning has become firmly established should you maintain it on an infrequent random reinforcement schedule—perhaps by an occasional unannounced quiz or in infrequent tests such as official midterm and final exams.

Step 5: Administer the Test. The conditions under which you administer the test will depend on the kind of test you have selected, on the number and ages of your students, on facilities and time you have available, on the subject matter being tested, and on the particular needs of your students. Room for your own discretion and ingenuity, then, is large. In deciding how and where tests should be given, however, the following points should be kept in mind:

- Testing conditions which cause high levels of anxiety will often interfere with the student's ability to demonstrate learning which he can demonstrate under less anxious conditions.
- Testing conditions which are too relaxed and casual may not be taken seriously, and thus may also interfere with the student's tendency to exhibit all the learning behaviors of which she is capable.
- Inappropriate suspiciousness on the part of educators can actually increase students' tendencies to cheat, but so can inappropriately high levels of trust. What may be too much or too little monitoring of test-taking can be judged only in relation to your particular students.

Step 6: Score and Analyze the Test. After the test has been administered, it must, of course, be scored. When scoring is done by you, keep all irrelevant information—especially the students' names—out of your sight. This is almost an essential procedure when you are grading essay exams, but since objective exams sometimes may be variously graded, it is a good procedure to follow for all test scoring.

After the test is scored, you are ready to proceed with an item analysis. You have constructed your test so that each learning unit was tested either by two different items in the same test or in two different test situations. It is this pairing that is going to enable you to identify at least the most reliable and/or invalid of your test items, and if your results are lined up correctly, can provide you at the same time with information about the effectiveness of your instructional procedures and of individual student needs and accomplishments.

Let us look at a short example of test results which have been tabulated to provide the maximum information most easily. A *c* indicates that the student's answer was correct on the item; *i* that his answer was incorrect.

TABLE 1. *Item Analysis: Test on Effects of 3 Environmental Contingencies*

LEARNING UNITS	1. POSITIVE REIN-FORCEMENT			2. PUNISHMENT			3. NONREIN-FORCEMENT			UNITS ACCOM-PLISHED (STUDENT ANALYSIS
Students:										
Item #'s:	1	2	(match)	5	9	(match)	3	4	(match)	
Ellen	c	c	+	c	i	—	c	c	+	1,3
Tom	c	c	+	c	i	—	c	c	+	1,3
Dick	c	c	+	i	i	+	c	c	+	1,3
Larry	c	i	—	c	i	—	c	c	+	3
Bernadette	c	c	+	c	i	—	i	i	+	1
Bob	c	c	+	c	i	—	c	c	+	1,3
Mary	c	c	+	c	c	+	c	c	+	1,2,3
Cathy	c	c	+	c	c	+	i	i	+	1,2
Dorothy	c	c	+	i	c	—	c	c	+	1,3
Totals Match: (test analysis)			8			3			9	
Totals Correct: (instruction analysis)	9	8		—	3		7	7		

Indentifying Unreliable or Invalid Test Items. There is no way to pretend that every test is perfect, and in practice, most teachers do not have the opportunity to pretest their tests before they are administered to their

A Different Way to Test: Criterion-Referenced Evaluation

students as a test of learning. This makes an examination of test items afterwards even more important, although it is a step that can be fruitfully performed even when you are using professionally-produced tests since invalid and even unreliable items still often slip through.

There are statistical analyses presented in tests and measurement courses and texts which can give you more precise information than the simple test suggested here, and you should be familiar with these techniques and how to use them. However, it is not always possible to perform the time-consuming task of a correlation test or analysis of variance, and using the technique suggested here will point out at least the most glaring errors in your test constructions.

Items or tests which you have constructed to test the same thing but which do not give the same information—that is, students get one answer right and the other wrong—may be a result of a poorly constructed item. It may be that one of the items is unclear, or that both items are not testing the same learning. To check the quality of test items, you can look at the "Total Match" row. Items which indicate that a high number of pairs were answered either both incorrectly or both correctly by the students are probably good items and are indicated by a + that they match. Items for learning units 1 and 3 have high matching scores—eight and nine out of possible totals of nine matchings. Unit 2 on punishment has a low number of matching pairs—only three of the nine gave similar results. On inspection of items 5 and 6 you may be able to identify item 5 as being unclear. At this point then, it should be dropped from further analysis, and of course omitted in any further administrations of the test.

What percentage of items should match? Unfortunately, because this is such a simple and quick analysis, it cannot do more than indicate to you either the best or worst of the items, and a definite criterion cannot be predetermined. For more precise analysis, you may carry out (and occasionally should) statistical analyses.

Identifying Areas of Poor Instruction. When the majority of the class does not reach criterion levels after instruction has been given, there is a strong possibility that the instruction provided for that unit was inadequate. The place in the item analysis to look for possible instructional weakness is in the row labeled "Totals correct." In the example given here, items 1 and 3 have relatively high totals, but the majority of the class did not do well on item 2. When there is a general weakness in the whole class like this, it is a good idea to ask whether your instructional planning is responsible. The checklist on pages 168 and 169 might help you identify some problems in instruction.

HOLDING YOURSELF ACCOUNTABLE

Besides evaluating your students, once in a while you should evaluate yourself as well. Sometimes too many students are learning too little too slowly, or sometimes an individual is learning at a pace that you know is below the level that he is capable. When one or more students are not learning as much or as quickly as they should, it is important to ask whether the problem is with your teaching. Is there something you can change to increase learning in your classroom? Here is a checklist that you can use to examine your own teaching methods from a behaviorist perspective either before or after a lesson has been presented.

Behavioral Goals

• Have you defined learning clearly, using action verbs and an observable product to define learning?
• Is the test for learning an accurate and adequate test of your learning goal, or have you taught one thing and tested another?
• Is your criterion of success too high or too low in relation to criterion employed by other teachers? Are you picking on trivial little mistakes or flaws that are unimportant, or are you glossing over important concepts?
• Would graduated criteria provide greater reinforcement and so more learning for some or all students?

Task Analysis

• Are the units of your task analysis too small? Are students becoming bored by too much repetition or unmotivated by having to learn bitty steps at a time when they are capable of comprehending more material in a single unit?
• Are the units too large so that students are getting lost and are not progressing on a firm

foundation of acquired learning? Have you left out any important steps?

Entry Behavior

• Did you assess entry behavior accurately and comprehensively? Are you sure students possess the intial learning behaviors they need?
• Does your lesson begin above or below the students' entry levels so that students may be either not ready to begin at the high level at which your lesson begins, or is your lesson repetitious because students already have learned what you are teaching again?

Presentation

• Do your cues tell your students both what learning is expected of them in terms of specific behavior, and the consequences, particularly in the form of positive reinforcement that will follow?
• After the lesson, do you check to make sure that your cues were reliable? Do you carry out your promises?
• Do you provide sufficient feedback to each student during the learning process, or did you just face them with a test at the end? Where some students left out because they find it too hard to speak out publicly in the classroom? Should you offer alternative sources of formative evaluation to them?
• Is the positive reinforcement you chose really working as a positive reinforcement for your students? Do any particular students find such reinforcers as praise, good grades, shows of affection, privileges either nonreinforcing or actually embarrassing or punishing?
• Have you provided for sufficient amounts of practice and self-pacing to meet the individual learning needs for both your fast and your slow learners?

EVALUATION

• *Have you tested the learning of all your students fairly and objectively? Are some students being evaluated more leniently than others because you expected them to do well and so overlook mistakes that are not over-* *looked in relation to other students?*
• *Have any students actually learned, but find it impossible to manifest that learning in a test situation? Are you making provisions to overcome this difficulty?*

Analyzing Student Learning. Your item analysis is set up so that you can also identify easily and quickly the learning strengths and weaknesses of individual students. In the example, except in the case of unit 2 on punishment where item 5 was deleted from the test because of poor construction, students were required to have answered both items testing a learning unit to reach criterion level. In the column "units accomplished" those units for which the student answered both items correctly are indicated. Obviously, units not listed for the student are units in which further instruction is required.

Information in this column is the basis of the feedback which you will give to the student, pointing out to each student exactly what they need to learn better and what they have already learned. For greatest effectiveness in guiding subsequent learning, feedback should be as specific and immediate as possible.

Step 7: Assigning Grades. Since many schools are still run on a norm-referenced basis and the grades you assign are expected to fit into the normal curve, a policy of criterion-referenced grading may be difficult to arrange. The kind of compromise you are able to make will depend on the policies in your school, and the leeway you are given. If you are permitted to assign grades on the basis of criterion-referenced evaluation, you have the following options:

1. Students are assigned grades which are either *A* indicating successful achievement of the mastery goal, or *I* indicating incomplete achievement of the mastery goal.
2. A more refined and more informative version of the approach described above is to indicate exactly how many of the total number of required steps have been achieved by the individual student. For example, the student who has achieved mastery performance will receive a grade indicating that he has achieved 10 out of 10 subgoals. Another student may receive a report indicating that he has accomplished 8 or 6 or 2 out of 10 subgoals. Since each student realizes that if he has not yet achieved

complete mastery he will be given sufficient practice in the future to reach the goal, the grade does not indicate that the student's work is of a particular quality. All work which has been accomplished is of criterion quality, and the grade indicates only the quantity of work achieved and yet to be achieved.

3. In some applications of criterion-referenced evaluation, students are given the opportunity to choose the grade with which they are satisfied. For instance, they may be told that if they achieve 6 of 10 subgoals of a course or test section, they will receive a *C;* students achieving 8 of 10 may receive a *B,* and students completing master of all 10 subgoals receive an *A.* Students may then accept the results of the first test they take, or may take subsequent tests on the same material in which they may receive higher grades. This last application is a popular one on the college level particularly.

Here is a short test that you can *take* to see how qualified you are to *give* one.

Progress Check 5.4:   Using the Steps

Directions: Circle the letter next to the phrase which best completes each statement or answers the question.

1. Which of the following statements reflects most accurately statements made in the text concerning text administration?
    a. When students become unduly anxious about a test it is usually because they have not learned the material well enough.
    b. The more relaxed the testing situation, the better students will do on the test.
    c. Cheating can be reduced only by vigilant monitoring.
    d. The conditions under which it is best to administer a test vary greatly from class to class and situation to situation.

2. In designing a test, you should
    a. use examples already used in class.
    b. construct at least two test items for each concept or learning unit being tested.
    c. be sure not to test the same learning unit in more than one test situation.
    d. be firm in rejecting any student arguments that a test item might be unclear.

3. The text recommends that cues to your students about tests
    a. not be given.
    b. be given with sufficient clarity and time to allow adequate preparation for the test.
    c. should be general rather than specific so that tests are usually something of an unexpected surprise to the students.
    d. should be clearly separated from behavioral objectives.

4. Which of the following includes the essential elements of a table of specifications?
   a. contents and levels of learning to be tested, and percent each will contribute to the total grade.
   b. contents, levels of learning to be tested, and kind of test to be given.
   c. kind of test to be given, and percent each test or test item will contribute to the total grade.
   d. contents, kind of test to be given, and percent each test will contribute to the total grade.

5. Which of the following educational practices *best* agrees with the behaviorist principles of evaluation discussed in the text?
   a. a planned program of frequent quizzes throughout the term; final course grades are the average of all grades received on the quizzes.
   b. a course with no evaluation of student learning except a midterm and final exam.
   c. a series of frequent unplanned quizzes given by the teacher every time the students seem to need it.
   d. a planned program of frequent quizzes for which students receive feedback but which often do not contribute to the students' formal evaluation and final grade.

Item Analysis: Test on Knowledge of Two Novels

Learning Unit:		1. Crime and Punishment			2. Brothers Karamazov			Units Accomplished:
Students:								
Item #'s:	1	3	(match)	2	4	(match)		
John	c	i	_____	i	c	_____	_____
Michael	c	i	_____	i	i	_____	_____
Kelly	c	i	_____	i	i	_____	_____
Jean	c	c	_____	i	i	_____	_____
Dan	c	i	_____	c	c	_____	_____
Mark	c	i	_____	i	i	_____	_____
Totals Match			_____			_____	
Totals Correct	___	___		___	___		

In order to answer the next three items, you should complete the item analysis above.

6. In the above item analysis, which item(s) should probably be dropped from the test as poorly constructed?
   a. items 1 or 3.
   b. item 2.
   c. items 2 or 4.
   d. item 4.

7. Using the above item analysis, what area(s) can you conclude have been poorly taught to the entire class?
   a. Unit 1: Crime and Punishment
   b. Units 1 and 2
   c. Unit 2: Brothers Karamazov
   d. Both Units 1 and 2 seem to have been taught well.

8. In the item analysis above, if the criterion for success in each learning unit was two correct items, which student(s) have accomplished Unit 27?
   a. John and Michael
   b. Kelly and John
   c. Dan
   d. John

SUMMARY

In this chapter we have seen that the behaviorists have added a new dimension to both the purpose and the kind of test used in education. The behaviorists believe that norm-referenced tests should be used only when it is necessary to compare the abilities or achievements of the individual to a larger group, but that in the course of ordinary instruction criterion-referenced evaluation which compares the learning achievements of the individual to a fixed standard should be used to guide, motivate, and describe learning behaviors. Criterion-referenced evaluation used primarily for feedback to guide and motivate learning is called formative and is generally more specific and frequent than summative evaluation used to describe and summarize larger units of learning.

Five different kinds of tests with which to evaluate learning were described and their relative advantages and disadvantages discussed. Because essay tests must be structured primarily by the student himself, they are a good way to test complex levels of learning but are difficult to grade reliably. Fill-in tests are usually more specific than essay tests but depending on the length, may either be difficult to score reliably, or to use to test higher learning levels. Both true-false and matching tests have problems which make them difficult to construct to test higher levels of learning reliably. The multiple-choice test is probably the best strictly objective test format for testing all levels of learning but they are often difficult to construct well. All tests, to be fair, must be both reliable—that is, must give comparable results on repeated testings—and valid—that is, there should be a legitimate connection between the description of learning in the behavioral goal and/or the final grade, and the test material.

In planning and administering tests in your own classroom, a detailed and specific plan, including a table of specifications based on the task analysis, should be made along with the rest of the instructional plan. After tests have been scored, an item analysis should be used to identify poor test items, areas of poor instruction, and to analyze student learning.

SUGGESTED READING

For a look at some of the differences between criterion- and norm-referenced testing, and the issues involved in them, see the following articles:

GLASER, R. "Instructional Technology and the Measurement of Learning Outcomes." *American Psychologist* 18 (1963): 519–521.

The first full-fledged discussion comparing the two kinds of referenced evaluations.

GLASER, R. "Evaluation of Instruction and Changing Education Models." In *The Evaluation of Instruction: Issues and Problems*. Edited by M. C. Wittrock and D. E. Wiley. New York: Holt, Rinehart and Winston, 1970.

STAKE, R. "Comments on Professor Glaser's Paper." In *The Evaluation of Instruction: Issues and Problems*. Edited by M. C. Wittrock and D. E. Wiley. New York: Holt, Rinehart and Winston, 1970.

For help in actually preparing and using criterion-referenced tests, the following suggestions are highly recommended:

BLOOM, B.; HASTINGS, J.; AND MADAUS, G. *Handbook on Formative and Summative Evaluation of Student Learning*. New York: McGraw-Hill, 1971.

A host of detailed suggestions for evaluating mastery learning on all levels and subject area.

GRONLUND, N. *Determining Accountability for Classroom Instruction*. New York: Macmillan, 1974.

———. *On Improving Marking and Reporting in Classroom Instruction*. New York: Macmillan, 1974.

———. *Preparing Criterion-Reference Tests for Classroom Instruction*. New York: Macmillan, 1973.

A how-to booklet giving you specific instruction for test making.

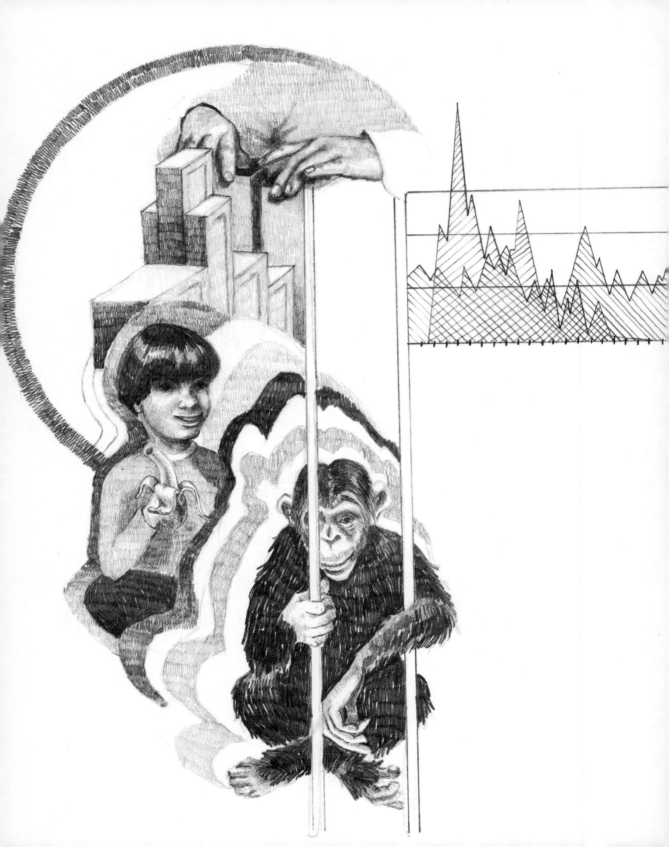

The Mod Approach to Behavior: Behavior Modification Techniques

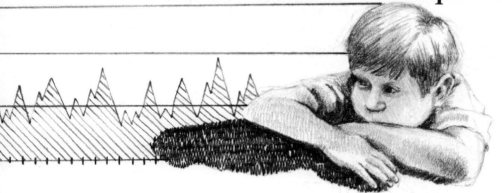

Chapter Objectives

In this chapter you are introduced to what is popularly known as "behavior mod," a set of techniques developed by behaviorists to control behavior through conditioning, which is being used with increasing frequency to control discipline, motivation, and behavior problems of students in our schools. This chapter examines a variety of techniques that have been successfully used to control or change both academic and nonacademic behavior, along with some ethical issues involved in the practical application of behavior modification programs, and seven steps for using behavior mod in your own classroom.

The behavioral goals of this chapter are to enable you to:

1. choose the appropriate behavior modification technique to achieve a variety of behavior changes.

> *Progress Check:* You are asked to read six vignettes of classroom behaviors and evaluate in a multiple-choice format the strategies used by the teacher to modify those behaviors.

2. recognize the ethical issues surrounding the use of behavior mod.

> *Progress Check:* You are asked to identify some of the controversial ethical issues involved in three applications of behavior mod.

3. to implement a seven step behavior mod program of your own.

> *Progress Check:* In a 7-item multiple-choice quiz, you are asked to evaluate an application of each of the seven steps in a classroom setting.

BEHAVIOR MOD TECHNIQUES

Behavior modification techniques have been developed during the last fifteen years to control, increase, change, or eliminate almost every kind of behavior. All of these techniques are based on the principles of classical and operant conditioning, and so they are concerned with changing behavior rather than changing what is on the "inside" of a person. Although we are discussing the techniques in this chapter primarily in terms of discipline and motivational behavior, they can be used equally well when applied to learning behavior, which is, actually, the behavior that teachers are most eminently and ultimately concerned about.

Increasing Behavior with Positive Reinforcements

The use of positive reinforcement to increase desired behavior is the behavior mod technique par excellence. It is the method, above all, found to be most effective in producing desirable and long-lasting results and it has resulted in a multiplicity of schemes designed to increase learning.

The underlying principle involving positive reinforcement is the experimental finding we looked at in chapter 2 that behavior when followed by a positive reinforcement tends to occur more often. Behavior mod makes sure, therefore, that a desired behavior is followed by a positive reinforcement. For a teacher using behavior mod, using positive reinforcement is the center jewel in the strategies available, and accompanies the use of almost every other technique discussed in this chapter.

A Positive Goal.   To use a positive reinforcer, you must first have a positive goal, a behavior that you want to increase. Positive reinforcement strategies, therefore, place an emphasis on the positive. The teacher must know what he *wants* ("I want Johnny to be able to recognize these ten prepositions") not just what he *doesn't* want ("I don't want Johnny to hit other pupils"). You might recognize this as the same principle underlying programmed instruction which uses feedback that an answer is correct as the positive reinforcement to increase the learning behavior emitted by the student in that frame.

Once the positive goal has been identified, reinforcers are administered after the behavior occurs to increase the probability that it will happen more often in the future. To the perceptive and ingenious teacher, there is a vast supply of cost-free reinforcers available in the typical educational setting. The following suggestions do not exhaust the possibilities within any particular class.

Social and Status Reinforcers.   Reinforcers that relate to the interaction between individuals or groups are some of the most powerful reinforcers you have available, and they are readily available. A social reinforcer may be a smile, a look, a touch, sometimes only a subtle nod of the head, a firm hand on the shoulder, a handshake, some appropriately chosen verbal comment such as "That's good work" or "I like the way you've been sitting in your seat this morning." In fact, any kind of attention can usually serve as a positive reinforcer.

Another powerful set of reinforcers the teacher has at his disposal are grades and other feedback about the student's work. Some teachers do not like to use grades to motivate student learning but there are few reinforcers within the school system with as much consistent power to do so when they are used well. Feedback in the form of comments about the students' work has also been shown to be a strong motivator of student morale and learning levels. In a well-known study (Page 1958) even brief comments such as "Good work!" or "Let's get that grade up!" made by the teacher on each pupil's paper significantly improved subsequent learning performance.

In addition, there are reinforcers available from other students. Chosen friends may be permitted to sit or study together, or may be given the opportunity to engage in status activities such as folding the flag, leading the class in song, carrying the teacher's books, or walking with her to her car.

Activity Reinforcers. Activities are another group of readily available reinforcers. The activities that are rewarding differ with the age of the student but they include such tasks as erasing the blackboard, carrying messages to the principal's office, passing out lunch milk, and taking down or putting up the bulletin boards. The ingenious teacher will find many more—feeding the fish in the bowl in the corner, watering the plants, returning books to the library, holding the door open when the class leaves for recess, or passing out papers.

Reinforcing activities can usually be discovered by using the principle of preferred activities as well. The principle of preferred activities is also known as the "spinach before dessert" or, more scientifically as the "Premack principle" after the man who first identified it (Premack 1965). According to the Premack principle, in order to engage in something one likes to do very much, people will often engage first in less-preferred activities. In other words, we will eat our spinach if that is the only way to be able to eat our dessert.

In the classroom, a teacher can identify preferred activities of students by watching what they do when they are given free time. Alec goes to play basketball; Alice combs her hair; Peter reads science fiction. The teacher can enlist the cooperation of students themselves directly as well and ask them to help construct a list of activities from which they later may choose when they have earned a reinforcer. As a teacher, you may also find it helpful to remember that the more proficient someone is in an activity, whether it be math or basketball, typing or painting, the more apt they are to find it enjoyable. Activities that a student is just learning or does not do well are not nearly as often reinforcing.

Atmosphere Reinforcers. Atmosphere reinforcers sometimes include elements of social and activity reinforcers, but their essential basis is a change in the classroom situation. Playing music, turning lights up or down, announcing free time or game time, reading a story out loud, having an interesting visitor in the class, or letting the students choose their own choice of activities for specified periods are examples of atmosphere reinforcers.

Token Economies. Token economies are a simulation of the real-life situation in which people are paid for working. Money is the positive reinforcement that keeps most of us—even those of us who generally like our jobs—getting up morning after morning to get to work. Money itself was not originally reinforcing. Who cares about having a grimey, dirty, well-used set of green pictures of presidents? But these pictures are powerful reinforcers in our society because they can be exchanged for so many other things that are reinforcing in themselves—food, clothes, a place to live, a stereo, a car, travel, or a night out.

In the classroom, a token economy gives the opportunity to students to earn tokens for specified behaviors. These tokens can then be redeemed for back-up reinforcers, either at the end of the day or at the end of the week. These back-up reinforcers may be such items as pens, pads, books, or a new ball, or cost-free reinforcers such as free time, extra hours in the gym, or many of the other reinforcers we have listed as available in the ordinary classroom. Behaviors that are reinforced are those behaviors that the teacher has listed—time spent in reading, completing assigned work units, keeping one's desk clean, and cooperating with others students. Token economies have been used successfully in many classrooms to improve motivation, productivity, and the quality of work of both student and teacher (Bushell and Brigham 1971).

THE IRREPLACEABLE REINFORCER

Behaviorists almost all agree that there is no substitute for a positive reinforcer and that a teacher can hardly function effectively in the classroom without using them generously. The text has suggested some positive reinforcers that research has proved to be effective in increasing behavior but there are many more available to the observant and creative teacher. List some reinforcers that you have experienced as a student or believe could be used by you as a teacher.

If you are having trouble filling up the list, ask other students what is reinforcing for them. Since we are different, we often find different things reinforcing.

Reaching an Agreement with Contingency Contracting

A contingency contract is an explicit agreement between the teacher and either individual students or the entire class. The contract assures that if the student engages in specific behaviors over a clearly-defined period of time, then specific rewards will be granted. Academic contracts may assure that if a student completes two work units, he may engage in one-half hour free reading. Or an agreement may be made that if no papers are left on the classroom floor by the time the bell ending the lunch period rings, the teacher will read the class the next chapter of *Gulliver's Travels*. Homme and others (Homme et al. 1970) who have worked with contingency contracting in the classroom have nine suggestions for making a contract effective:

- *Immediate*. The contract payoff or positive reinforcement should be given immediately after the agreed behavior is performed. This is of particular importance at the beginning of the program, and remains so for most contracts with young students. Some psychologists recommend that every hour or even more often the teacher fill in a card for each student indicating what he has done to fulfill his part of the contract.
- *Easy At First*. At the beginning of the program, it should be easy to earn the agreed upon reward. Homme (1966) found that carrying this principle to what seems an absurd extreme was an effective way of gaining control of a class of pupils who were almost always out of their seats, talking, screaming, and running. Homme finally gained control of the situation by beginning with a very small step. Using the principle of preferred activities, the students and teacher agreed that if the students were quiet for a short period of time, they could make as much noise as they wished. The teacher then began by asking the students to sit down and quietly look at the blackboard. Almost immediately after attention was given, the students were told that they could now get out of their seats, talking as loudly as they wished and running anywhere in the room.
- *Frequent*. If rewards are easy to earn, they will also be given frequently, and at the beginning of the contract especially, this is just as it should be for an effective change of behavior.
- *Accomplishment Not Obedience*. The agreed upon reward should be for the accomplishment of some behavior or the completion of some project. It should *not*, Homme suggests, be given for obedience to the teacher as such. What is important is the task, the school work, not blind submission to what the teacher tells the student to do. Therefore, the successful contingency contract will reward the student for finishing two arithmetic problems, or for reading the chapter of a book or for reciting a poem,

rather than for not talking, or for sitting in her seat, behaviors which the student will probably have to perform anyway to accomplish the assigned task.

- *Never Reward Before.* A reinforcer increases the behavior it follows, *not* the behavior it precedes. Therefore, the reward or contract payoff should be given *only* after the agreed behavior has occurred. Enticements such as "You can go to the ballgame tonight if you promise to do your homework tomorrow," or "You can go out to recess now if you will finish your arithmetic afterwards" defeats the effectiveness of the contract. It is important, therefore, to set up contracts that both teacher and students are willing and able to stand by. The strict rule to be enforced is "No behavior, no payoff."

- *Fair.* When Homme says a contract should be fair, he means that there should be a reasonable equation between the agreed behavior and the promised reward. Rewarding students with a picnic day in the park for completing five elementary exercises in gym class is not "fair" because the reward is out of proportion to the behavior. For the same reason it is also unfair to reward a student with a grade of *B* for work which is of exceptionally high caliber.

- *Clear.* Contracts should be specific and clear. The students should understand *exactly* what behaviors will be rewarded so that there is no confusion or misunderstanding between the teacher and the students about whether a reward has actually been earned or not.

- *Honest.* Honest means you keep your word. It means the teacher doesn't change the ground rules in the middle of the contract period or decide not to give the rewards that have been agreed on after the behavior is actually accomplished. Being honest means planning well so that agreements can be carried out.

- *Positive.* Positive means setting up positive goals so that behavior is rewarded rather than punished when it occurs.

Contingency contracting has been used successfully with children as young as preschoolers (Homme and Totsi 1971), and as old as college students (Dash 1970).

Changing Behavior Through Modeling

Bandura (1965) noticed that the behavior of one person is often influenced by the consequences of behavior observed in another person and consequently began to study how models can be used to control behavior. Research is available now that indicates imitation is a pervasive human behavior and gives us some suggestions of whose behavior and what behavior is most apt to be copied.

Imitate Reinforced Behavior. Models—those whose behavior is imitated —may be imagined or actually observed in real life, portrayed in films, books, or stories, but neither children nor adults imitate indiscriminately. Some models are more apt to be imitated than others. Models who are most often copied are people who are warm and nurturant, who are in positions of status and power in which they can give and withhold rewards (Bandura et al. 1963), and who are perceived to be similar to the imitator (Rosekrans 1967).

Children and adults both tend to imitate behavior of models that is rewarded and avoid behavior that is punished. If you have ever slowed down to within the legal speed limit after seeing the driver of the speeding car in front of you pulled over to the curb by the police, you recognize the principle involved here. People will also tend to imitate more when they are reinforced for imitating. For example, parents often reinforce imitative behavior of their children by responding with laughter, delight, praise, or other attention.

People also *learn* a great deal of behavior that they may not *imitate* for quite some time. People learn the behavior they see in others whether it is punished, rewarded, or nonreinforced. Later, if behavior that was initially punished is now rewarded, they will be able to perform it. It is not enough, then, just to make sure that children and students see that certain behaviors in the model result in punishment for the model. There are perhaps some behaviors that we do not want our children to learn at all under any circumstances.

Modeling in the Classroom. Because the ability to imitate is such a highly developed talent even in children, it is often an extraordinarily effective way of teaching. There seems to be no kind of behavior which under some conditions will not be imitated. Work has been done showing that agressive behavior, and the development of sex-role behaviors are greatly influenced by factors controlling imitation. Models affect the expression of fear, and of emotion, in general. They influence the selection of standards of achievement and self-evaluation, and the development of moral judgements. Complex behaviors both academic and otherwise, which should take many repeated reinforcements to teach through shaping procedures can often be taught in a single demonstration by using models, and reinforcing imitation of them.

As a model, teachers are in an extraordinarily influential position in the classroom. He or she is consistently in the presence of the students and as the person most fully in control of the dispensation of rewards, is most apt to be imitated. By exhibiting warm and caring behavior, a teacher can increase his influence as a behavioral model even more.

Reducing Fears Through Desensitization

Desensitization techniques were first pioneered by Joseph Wolpe (Wolpe and Rachman 1960). They are used when high levels of anxiety interfere with appropriate responses. The man afraid to get on an elevator, the woman afraid of crowds, and the child afraid of the dark are examples of people whose anxiety interferes with behaviors which most people accomplish with ease. The student whose fear of taking a test is so great that he is unable to demonstrate what he really knows in a more relaxed state is a person for whom desensitization techniques are particularly appropriate.

Relaxed Response. Theoretically, the aim of desensitization techniques is to uncouple the connection between some stimulus (such as the elevator, tests, or the dark) and the anxiety, and to create a new connection between that stimulus and the absence of anxiety. To do this, the anxious individual is taught a response which is apparently incompatible with the expression of anxiety. Typically, a nonanxious response is one in which the individual is relaxed, his hands are not perspiring, his muscles not tensed up, his forehead is not furrowed, nor his heart rate accelerated. A person who is physically relaxed, the behaviorists argue, cannot by definition be experiencing anxiety at the same time.

There are many ways in which the individual can be taught a non-anxious response. One is deep muscle relaxation. In a series of very simple exercises the person tightens up each part of his body as fully as possible for about five seconds and then relaxes it. Within a period of weeks he has learned to be able to put himself almost immediately into a state of physical relaxation. Another way to induce physical relaxation or non-anxiety is by emotive imagery. The individual is asked to imagine himself in a situation which does not cause him anixety—lying on the sand under the hot sun by a quiet shore, being in the presence of someone he trusts and enjoys, or carrying out the request of a friend which is both easy and fun. While the person is imagining himself in a nonanxious and enjoyable situation he cannot at the same time experience the anxiety he feels in an anxious one.

Once the individual has learned, in whatever way, to put himself into a relaxed position, the anxiety-producing stimulus is introduced very distantly. The stimulus may be presented in actuality, but often the person is asked simply to imagine it. Gradually the distance between the individual and the anxiety-producing stimulus is shortened and it becomes—either in actuality or in imagination—more and more vivid. Because the change is gradual, the person is able to remain physically relaxed, so that finally he can remain completely relaxed in the close-up presence of the stimulus or situation that formerly caused anxiety, and his problem is cured.

Anxiety in the Classroom. Almost every teacher at some time or other must deal with individuals whose anxiety seems to interfere with learning and learning activities. Students may be unable to take an exam without

---

LEARNING TO RELAX

Deep muscle relaxation is one way to escape immediate anxiety. The person who is completely relaxed cannot at the same time be anxious in behaviorist terms. The following are simple directions you can use to teach yourself to overcome anxiety while you are studying for an exam.

1. Lie down on your back in a comfortable room where you will not be interrupted. Close your eyes and imagine for a few minutes that you are in one of your favorite quiet places—lying on a beach, sitting in the woods, standing on a hilltop or mountain peak.

2. Very slowly tense the muscles of your right foot and leg as tightly as you can; keep your attention on your leg, feeling your muscles and hold them tense while you count slowly to five; now slowly relax, letting go of the muscle tension completely.

3. Now slowly tense the muscles of your left foot and leg, again holding them as tightly as possible while you count to five, and then slowly relaxing them completely.

4. For a count of five, tense up and then relax your right arm from your hand to shoulder.

5. For a count of five, tense up and then relax your left arm from your hand to your shoulder.

6. For a count of five, tense up and then completely relax the muscles of your abdomen and buttocks.

7. For a count of five, tense up and then completely relax your chest and shoulders.

8. For a count of five, tense and then relax the muscles in the back of your neck.

9. For a count of five, tense your facial muscles—jaw, cheeks, nose, and forehead—and then relax them.

10. Now lie absolutely still and reflect whether there is any part of your body which does not feel completely relaxed. Move your mind over each part of your body. If there is any tension anywhere at all, repeat the tensing and relaxing exercises until you are completely relaxed throughout your whole body. Remain in this relaxed state for up to five minutes.

11. Now you are ready to think about studying. Think about it for only a minute or so or until you feel any anxiety. Then stop.

12. Repeat this process every day beginning each study period with a relaxation exercise. As you learn to relax, it should take less and less time.

---

becoming so anxious that they inevitably do poorly. The anxiety and worry may even be so great as to interfere with even the preparation for the exam, and as soon as the student sits down to study he may begin to worry so that he is unable to concentrate on anything but his worry about his impending doom. Teachers may have pupils who are unable to speak out loud in class either to ask or answer questions, to perform publicly, or even sometimes to enter into play with other children because of destructively high levels of anxiety.

Desensitization techniques may be adapted to help such individuals. Students may be taught how to put themselves into a state of deep muscle relaxation and encouraged to do so at the beginning of each study period and to renew the relaxation frequently during the time study continues. Gradually the periods of time in which the student is able to remain relaxed as he continues to study will lengthen, and the number of relaxation periods reduced.

Teachers may help frightened children approach a situation which is threatening to them by emotive imagery, helping the student imagine himself in another situation in which he is confident and relaxed. Sometimes a method of successive approximations is all that is required. One student, for instance, was helped by his teacher to overcome a deeply-ingrained fear of public speaking by gradually bringing the child closer and closer to the initially fearful situation. Within the normal classroom situation a teacher dealing with such a problem can introduce the anxiety-producing stimulus in very small, almost imperceptibly increasing steps.

If a child is afraid to speak in class, the teacher can begin by giving the child opportunities to answer a question of which he is sure only in the teacher's presence. When the child is able to do this, then he may be asked to answer questions which he has already answered privately in front of one or two other children. If the child is less afraid of reading short passages out loud than he is in constructing his own responses, he can be given the opportunity to perform in this way at first. Gradually, through the series of such small steps the child is led to perform behaviors which are lengthened little by little in time, in front of larger groups of fellow students and requiring more individual creativity.

Stopping Behavior by Nonreinforcement

One of the most effective means of eliminating undesired behavior is by nonreinforcing it. We saw in chapter 2 that behavior followed by nonreinforcement was eliminated often more completely and permanently than behavior followed by punishment. It is sometimes a difficult technique to use partly because teachers and parents often feel intuitively that it won't work. However, once you learn to use it effectively you will probably find that it is often not only easier but more efficient to use than punishment.

Nonattention as Nonreinforcement. Much of what people do is an attempt to get the attention of someone else. Sometimes the attention itself is sufficient but often it is to get information, assistance of some kind, to carry on a conversation, or sometimes just to get the salt from the far end of the table. Whatever the reason, both positive and negative attention are powerful reinforcers. Nonattention, therefore, is almost always an effective nonreinforcer or punisher. The child who is trying to get attention by stamping and screaming and whose mother simply continues washing dishes, showing neither anger nor impatience, is often cured very quickly of stamping and screaming as a means of getting attention.

Always with a Positive Reinforcer. Nonreinforcement as a technique should *never* be used without making it clear that the child can obtain his desired reinforcement in some other way. Nonattention as a response can sometimes be a damaging practice if there is no other way for the child to get attention. The child, therefore, who is not given the attention he is seeking by shouting out in the classroom and interrupting others to express his own point of view should be told, "I am not listening to you when you talk without being called on first. If you raise your hand, I will call on you and listen to what you have to say." The learning can be increased by using the modeling process to implement the direct contingencies so that the child can learn by imitating other students who raise their hands and do have an opportunity to be heard. Cues from the teacher such as "I am calling on you because you raised your hand" can also speed up the learning process.

Time-Out. Time-out is a technique which is currently recommended particularly for children whose behavior is disruptive. Essentially, time-out is a period during which the child forfeits the opportunity to earn any positive reinforcers. There is often a time-out room where the child is taken if behavior—such as tantrums or extreme hyperactivity—interrupts other children. During time-out—two, five, or ten minutes—the child cannot earn points or other rewards which are available in the regular classroom. Surprisingly, *short* time-out periods are usually more effective than longer ones, and in addition do not disrupt the child's learning time in the classroom so severely. Like any effective nonreinforcement, time-out should be called *immediately* after the undesired behavior occurs and it should not be unduly prolonged after the disruptive behavior ceases.

Effective as nonreinforcement is in permanently eliminating behavior, there are times when it is not feasible and some form of punishment becomes necessary. As we saw in chapter 2, most behaviorists would argue that punishment is, on the whole, both overused and poorly administered in our society. The use of punishment is still surrounded by controversy and disagreement even among behaviorists themselves but lately there has been an increasing attempt to delineate when and how punishment, when it must be used, is effective.

When Should Punishment Be Used?   There is no doubt that punishment is often used today by those in positions of power or authority when positive reinforcement or nonreinforcement would be much more effective ways of modifying behavior. However, there do seem to be times when some form of punishment seems absolutely necessary. When someone is engaged in behavior that is *immediately dangerous* to himself or to others, there is rarely time to engage in nonreinforcement. A mother may be understandably hesitant about using nonreinforcement while her three-year-old gets tired of playing with matches. A teacher may not be able to wait for nonreinforcement to cure a student from throwing one-hour tantrums in the classroom, or nonreinforce a knife fight in the schoolyard by ignoring it.

　　Besides using punishment against behaviors that are dangerous, punishment is also often required to help eliminate behaviors which are *intrinsically reinforcing* in themselves. In these cases, the reinforcer following the behavior cannot be removed because the behavior itself is so rewarding. Eating too many desserts, biting one's fingernails, using immediately effective drugs, and tripping the kid going up the aisle are examples of behavior that may be very tenacious because they can be, in one way or another, so much fun in themselves.

How Should It Be Used?   The judicious use of punishment can sometimes be effective, and the following are some guidelines for using it constructively.

1. Use punishment *only when positive reinforcement* and/or nonreinforcement *are either ineffective* or inappropriate because the behavior is immediately dangerous or intrinsically reinforcing.
2. Along with punishment, *positively reinforce behavior that is incompatible* with the behavior being punished. Never use punishment without also reinforcing behavior which is a desirable alternative to the punished behavior. If Tommy is constantly out of his seat, and particularly enjoys

walking around the room stabbing other hard-working pupils with a pencil, he may be punished when he does not stay in his seat, and reinforced when he does, particularly when he actually stays in his seat and writes with the pencil.

There are advantages to this approach for both teacher and student. The teacher is forced to emphasize the positive, and the student, rather than concentrating on what he shouldn't do, has his attention shifted to what he should do instead. This alternative behavior should be *clearly available* to the student and it *should not be in conflict,* in so far as possible, with some other strongly reinforced behavior. Teachers sometimes make the mistake of inadvertently forcing students to choose between approval of peers and success in school, or even sometimes between approval of parents and approval of school authorities. Effective teachers will be aware of these potential conflicts and will try to reduce them as much as possible.

3. *Remove the reinforcer for the punishable behavior* if at all possible. Often classroom behavior is reinforced by attention—shows of annoyance or anger from the teacher, snickering from other students, or even crying from the injured.

4. *Punishment should be preceded by a verbal warning* that if the behavior does not cease immediately that punishment will be administered. Johnny with the pencil can be told, "Return to your seat immediately or you will loose your game privileges." Once the students have learned that these cues are reliable indicators of ensueing consequences, actual punishment often becomes unnecessary because the offending behavior stops.

5. The choice of punishment varies with the situation and the individual involved, but it should be *neither so lenient* as to make little impact *or so severe as to create other problems.* For some students a mere frown or verbal reprimand is all the punishment that is needed. For others, reprimands may be reinforcing, and loss of privileges or some other punishment is necessary. Punishments that are of no consequence to the student involved will obviously not effect behavior. Unjust or inappropriately strong punishment can cause resentment which will interfere with learning just as much as the behavior you are trying to eliminate. Punishment, in any case, *should not be prolonged* unduly but should be as swift as possible.

6. Punishment, when administered, should be *consistent, administered* when possible *after each instance of the undesired behavior,* and *immediate,* even interrupting the behavior when this can be done. Delays in punishment—"Wait until your father comes home," or "I'll deal with you later"—often drastically reduce the effectiveness of punishment but

increase fear and resentment. One does not want to be completely insensitive to extenuating circumstances or reasonable explanation, but on the whole once the puishment has been agreed on and announced to the student, it should be administered if the behavior occurs. The "Well, just this once but don't do it again" approach after you have warned that punishment is forthcoming will simply make the threat of punishment that much less effective in the future.

Self-Management Techniques

Self-management techniques are so called because they are the application of behaviorist principles to manage one's *own* behavior rather than the behavior of someone else. Self-management techniques have been pioneered only since the mid-1960s but they are rapidly growing in popularity to overcome personal behavior problems. Self-management techniques use the same principles as other behavior mod techniques but they have two special characteristics: they are used to control one's own behavior, not someone else's, and of all the behavior mod approaches, they uniquely can use internal contingencies—what the individual is thinking or feeling—to change behavior.

Self-Direction and Self-Control. The first distinctive characteristic of self-management techniques is that the individual whose behavior is being changed fully participates in the choice of the goal and in the administration of reinforcers (Thoresen and Mahoney 1974). Change cannot be imposed on the individual without his knowledge and cooperation, so that self-management techniques can be used *only* if the individual *wants* and agrees to change his behavior in some specific direction. To do so, he must learn how to control his own behavior.

Internal Events. The second major differentiating characteristic of self-management techniques is that the individual who is changing his own behavior can identify and use both external and internal events that are either preceding or following his behavior (Homme 1965). Since internal events such as thoughts and feelings can be observed only by the individual having them, they can be used to direct behavior change only in a self-managed program.

For example, if a teacher is trying to modify Jane's behavior in the direction of longer study periods, the teacher can observe and measure only what happens in the external environment around Jane. These observations may be helpful but they are limited. The teacher may observe that

Jane's studying lasts longer when she is concentrating on her math homework than when she is studying history. She may record that mornings are better study periods for Jane than afternoons. These are helpful observations and will guide the teacher in changing the environment in such a way as to increase Jane's studying, though Jane herself has a much greater fund of information available to her than the teacher observing her from the outside because she can observe her covert or hidden behaviors as well. Jane can observe directly and accurately what she is thinking or feeling while the teacher can only guess—not a very scientific procedure for the teacher but a very respectable one for Jane.

Jane can actually count the number of times she has a specific thought ("I would like to have another piece of pie"; "I want to stop studying"), or a feeling, whether it be positive "I felt wonderful when I finished changing the car tire myself") or negative ("I was very depressed after I checked the mail today"). Since thoughts and feelings of one's own can be counted and measured in a way that thoughts and feelings of another cannot, how and what a person is thinking and feeling becomes a manipulatable controlling variable in self-management programs.

Intrinsic Reinforcers. Because of the availability of internal events, self-managed programs can usually make much greater use of intrinsic reinforcers than other programs. This is because intrinsic reinforcers are usually internal events. For example, the intrinsic reinforcer accompanying a perfectly executed jackknife dive is the feeling of coordination in one's body and the sense of satisfaction that you sometimes feel when you know you have done something beautiful. The advantage of using intrinsic reinforcers is that the behavior will continue even in the absence of extrinsic reinforcers usually provided for by an external modifier. Because research indicates that intrinsic reinforcers do not tend to control behavior in the presence of extrinsic reinforcers (Notz 1975) there are advantages to beginning with intrinsic reinforcers.

Self-Verbalization. In a self-managed program, not only is the goal selected and internal controlling events identified by the individual herself but new controlling contingencies are self-selected and administered. Self-managed programs can and do make frequent use of changes in the external environment to change behavior, especially at the beginning of a program but a primary emphasis is placed on controlling internal variables. One of the most effective ways of directing internal variables is through a process of self-verbalization (Johnson 1971).

Self-verbalization is talking to oneself in a very particular way. It is a way of reminding oneself of the results of his behavior both before and

A SELF-MANAGED PROGRAM TO OVERCOME STUDY DISTRACTIONS

The following is an excerpt from the records of a behavior mod program self-managed by a graduate student to increase uninterrupted study time to two hours. The student recorded baseline behavior and found it extremely erratic ranging from ten minutes to sixty-five minutes, and averaging eighteen minutes. Initial observation produced the information that study periods lasting for at least thirty minutes were always followed by a sense of satisfaction and often by increased motivation of continued study, while shorter periods led to feelings of anxiety and disorganization. The circumstances under which study be-havior was prematurely shortened were iden-tified as anxious thoughts related particularly to her room not being clean or her bed not made, waiting for a phone call from her boyfriend, or an impending visit to relatives.

Since length of study time was so variable, she adapted a technique suggested by Fox (1972). Every time she became anxious and wanted to discontinue study, she resolved to finish one small task before leaving her desk. An examination of the record will indicate that study time after anxiety begins is in-creasing, while the frequency of anxiety attacks is decreasing.

RECORD

Date	Length of initial study before anxiety begins	Relevant circum-stances or thoughts	Time required to complete task after anxiety begins	Reinforcers (extrinsic and intrinsic)
11/24	8 minutes	room clean; bed made	4 minutes	coffee; feel disorganized
11/25	4 minutes	room in order	task not completed	none
11/26	19 minutes	waiting for phone	3 minutes	make phone call; feel efficient
11/27	15 minutes	anxious; too much to do	6 minutes	eat lunch; think maybe I'm improving
11/30	30 minutes	all straight	5 minutes	eat lunch; feel happy with progress
12/1	21 minutes	must write several letters	9 minutes	write letter; realize it is getting better
12/2	30 minutes	room a mess; mending to do	20 minutes	clean room (a mistake; felt good but now dis-oriented)
12/3	35 minutes	typewriter ribbon grey and annoying	15 minutes	play record; anxious to return to work

after it occurs. For instance, one individual completely cured herself of a two-pack-a-day cigarette habit by doing nothing more than concentrating for ten seconds just before lighting up a cigarette on the effect that it was going to have on her lungs, heart rate, and physical fitness. The procedure was repeated for another five seconds when the cigarette was finally stubbed out. No other resolutions about cutting down cigarette smoking were used at all but gradually the person began to dislike the taste and even the smell of cigarettes more and more until the dislike finally became stronger than the enjoyment she derived from smoking.

Self-verbalization can be used to provide both cues before and consequences after a behavior being either increased or decreased. The individual starts out first by listing the reasons he himself experiences as convincing for changing the specific behavior being modified. Then immediately before and immediately after the opportunity for these behaviors presents itself, these reasons are clearly and explicitly self-verbalized.

Self-managed programs have successfully been carried out to control eating (Goldiamond 1965), smoking (Upper and Meredith 1970), drinking (Sobell and Sobell 1973), study habits (Beneke and Harris 1972), academic productivity (Nurnberger and Zimmerman 1970), anxiety (Bugg 1972; Campbell 1973), and interpersonal relations (Rappaport and Harrell 1972).

Before you set up a program to modify the behavior of someone else, you are strongly urged to set up a self-management program to modify your own behavior. Also, you should engage in additional reading (some suggestions are included at the end of the chapter), and be aware of the ethical issues involved in applying behavior modification programs to the behaviors of others. Some of these ethical issues in relation to education are discussed next, but first here is a short progress check to allow you to see if you have understood the general principles of the different modification techniques we have just discussed.

Progress Check 6.1: Choosing the Right Strategy to Change Behavior

Directions: In each of the following hypothetical educational situations, the teacher has tried to control, change, or inhibit behavior in a way that violates at least one of the principles for applying behavior modification techniques just discussed. Read each vignette and circle the answer which describes best what the teacher did incorrectly or offers the most suitable alternative.

1. First grader Tommy had demonstrated an unfortunate talent for tattling on his peers to his teacher, Mr. Allen. Mr. Allen wanted to change this habit of Tommy's, which annoyed him and was making Tommy quite unpopular. Mr. Allen's modification program consisted of cues warning

Tommy of impending consequences as soon as a tattle conversation began if he did not stop immediately, and of punishment which deprived Tommy of five minutes of recess every time he tattled. Before using punishment to inhibit Tommy's behavior, Mr. Allen should have
  a. tried reinforcing Tommy for a behavior incompatible with tattling, such as reporting good things about other students.
  b. pointed out models to Tommy of children who did not tattle, and their consequent popularity.
  c. helped Tommy set up a self-management program.
  d. used nonattention as a reinforcement.
  e. done all of the above.

2. Close to one-half of Mr. Carolo's class regularly did not complete their homework assignments. He decided to use a program of positive reinforcement to increase homework behavior, and so, on the first day of the new program he let all the students who promised to do their homework that night to go to the gym as an activity reinforcer.
What did Mr. Carolo do wrong?
  a. He chose an activity reinforcer when a social reinforcer would have been more effective.
  b. He tried to use self-management techniques when he should have used a contingency contract.
  c. He tried to increase behavior by reinforcing it before it occurred.
  d. He tried to inhibit behavior by using punishment instead of nonreinforcement.

3. Johnny was very much afraid of reading out loud in front of the class and his reading grade was dropping as a result. First his teacher, Mrs. Carnaby, gave Johnny frequent opportunities to try to read in front of the class but he stuttered and delayed the rest of the class so much that she eventually began to call on him less and less, and since Johnny also volunteered very infrequently to read, his fear of reading never diminished. To help Johnny overcome his fear of reading out loud in class, Mrs. Carnaby should have
  a. continued to make Johnny read in front of the class as she had been doing at first.
  b. gradually acclimated Johnny to reading in front of the class by letting him read very short sentences out loud in less anxious situations first.
  c. administered nonreinforcement for stuttering more immediately and consistently than she did.
  d. set up a token economy so that Johnny could replace the negative reinforcements he was receiving for reading out loud.

4. Seventh-grader Jimmy made a good many clever remarks that made the class laugh but often they were out of turn and interfered with the class lesson. It made the teacher angry and he began by threatening that if Jimmy were not quiet he woud be punished. Jimmy did not desist and the teacher finally resorted to putting Jimmy out in the hall. According to the text, Jimmy's teacher should first try to change Jimmy's behavior by using
  a. desensitization techniques along with punishment.
  b. a positive reinforcement and self-management technique.
  c. nonverbal cues of impending punishment.
  d. prolonged punishment.

5. The whole class agreed to enter into an agreement with the teacher whereby for every fifteen problems that they finished in geography they would be given a free hour every fourth Friday to do whatever they wished. This contingency contract is a poor one because
  a. the reinforcer is out of proportion to the behavior it follows.
  b. the reinforcer is not being administered immediately.

c. the reinforcer is not being administered frequently.
d. all of the above reasons.

6. Mrs. Peter's class never continued to study when she left the room and she wanted to teach them self-control and self-discipline. She announced, therefore, that she was starting a new regime to teach them to be more responsible and that every time someone spoke when they were supposed to be silent she would subtract one point from their final grade. If Mrs. Peter's wants to teach the class self-control she should
a. punish dependent behavior.
b. reinforce independent behavior.
c. include class participation in the goal selection, and contingency identification and administration.
d. refuse to assume responsibility for the class' behaviors.

WHEN ISN'T BEHAVIOR MOD ETHICAL?

The number of successes reported by psychologists and other "behavioral engineers" as they are sometimes called, is immense. Many of the behavior changes have clearly been for the undeniable and great benefit of the individuals involved and for society in general. Children with learning problems are taught to read, autistic children have been taught to speak, many others have been cured of self-destructive habits such as biting themselves, banging their heads against the wall, or have learned toilet training when other means have failed and their school age made it imperative. The list could be lengthened almost interminably, and for accounts of specific behavior mod projects you may read some of the books or journals suggested at the end of this chapter.

In any event, as the success of behavior mod has increased and spread, so has concern about its use. The very extent of its success has brought it to the attention of both the unscrupulous and the untrained, and sometimes as a result of malevolent intent, and sometimes of misguided good will, abuses of behavior mod in which individuals are submitted to damaging controls, have been reported. Because they are often used to modify the behavior of individuals who are unaware of the procedures being practiced on them and are unable to direct their own behavior either in cooperation or against the will of the modifier, the use of behavior mod has instilled in many the fear of a clockwork orange, 1984 world. In such a world people have forgotten how to care for each other for their own sakes and are concerned only with learning how to maximize their own positive reinforcements by manipulating the behavior of others.

B. F. Skinner (1971) was unambiguous when he warned that behavior modification techniques were amoral, that they could be used both to create a better world or a worse one, to create more freedom or more tyranny, to create more happiness or more misery. As behavior modification programs move out of the laboratory into practice in medicine, government, industry, prisons, hospitals, and training programs of every kind, the possibility of the frightening abuse becomes increasingly evident, and the question of how and when, by whom, and on whom behavior mod may be practiced is being raised with increasing urgency.

The ethical questions underlying a teacher's use of behavior modification techniques are no less profound than it is in any other area. The teacher is and will probably inevitably remain in a position of vastly superior power to his or her students. A teacher's position by reason of superior education, age, and administrative support all contribute to the power to control and direct what happens in the classroom more completely than any other individual and usually more than the entire class as a united whole. The teacher, then, has a grave responsibility to use the power at his disposal for the good of his students, since in many ways, the students are highly vulnerable and have few ways to protect themselves from the teacher's manipulations or influences.

There is general agreement by everyone acquainted with behavior mod that it can be badly abused and a destructive force. The questions surrounding when and if behavior mod should be used at all are more controversial. To say that you must make your own decisions about behavior mod is not to say that one answer is necessarily as good as another just because you can probably find someone to agree with whatever position you may take. It is to say that the issues are complex and that as a society we have not yet taken a fully-defined legal or practical stand on the lines to be drawn. We will look briefly at several of the issues raging around behavior mod, but especially at the question of the kind of control a teacher ought to use in the classroom and examine some possible effects of using a predominance of extrinsic reinforcements to reach goals chosen primarily by the teacher.

What Kind of Control Should the Teacher Use?

While many opponents of behavior mod have no objection to the teacher being in charge in a class, they do object to the kind of control a teacher is encouraged to exercise in a unilateral application of behavior mod techniques to control students. The behaviorists on their part argue that it is much more ethical to change an environment than to set out to change a person's mind or inner being which, they say, is a far greater violation (Skinner 1971).

Opponents argue that the teacher is trying to *replace* the individual's control of his own behavior by manipulating the environment around him. The teacher is seen as a dictator—sometimes a benevolent one, but nonetheless as the absolute authority who decides what behaviors are best for the student and how they are to be acquired. Most applications of behavior mod in the classroom, they argue, do not emphasize the right of the student to be given the information he needs to make his *own* decisions about the behavior he wishes to perform. Instead, the teacher decides and imposes the decision on the student: he should study longer, she should read faster, he should be taught to fidget less, it would be good for her to play with other children more. In other words, teachers' values are imposed on the student. But besides choosing goals *for* instead of *with* the student, behavior mod practitioners, say opponents, attempt to impose their unilateral decision on students by some questionable means as well. The fact that they are so often effective makes them more rather than less dangerous.

Can Students Be Harmed with Positive Reinforcers?

Legislation in many states in this country forbids the use of physical punishment to control the behavior of students. Aversive techniques, or use of punishment, to control behavior is an important behavior mod approach. Many parents and legislators are asking today what protection the student should have against the possible abuse of aversive techniques. To what extent should teachers be permitted or encouraged to use punishment to control behavior? Should aversive techniques be outlawed for use in school?

However, the problem of how teachers should be allowed to control behavior is not limited to the use of punishment. Skinner (1971) points out the problem of using positive reinforcement to bring about apparently voluntary and even eager behavior changes in an individual which may not ultimately be in his best interest. Skinner's example refers to the case of prisoners who may be gently persuaded to participate as experimental guinea pigs in scientific endeavors with an offer to reduce their prison terms. This principle applies also to education. Can teachers gently convince students as well to behave in ways which are easier for the teacher but not necessarily better for the child?

Several writers have suggested that the very imposition of a conscious use of behavior mod techniques to control the behavior of others, even with positive reinforcement, is intrinsically dehumanizing because it robs the individual of his sense of control over himself and his own behavior. DeCharms (1968) argues that the thing man wants and needs more than anything else is to feel in control of himself, to feel that he is the cause, or director, of what he himself does. Extrinsic reinforcers, therefore, can rob man of this most central motivating need, and is therefore ultimately dehumanizing. We desire more than anything else to manage our own lives, not to feel like pawns manipulated by the fates around us. Thus, when a student believes that he has chosen to do something himself, he will value his behavior and his own education more than the student who feels compelled either under threat of punishment or weight of heavy external reinforcement to engage in a certain behavior.

Research supports DeCharms' hypothesis that when an individual is reinforced with extrinsic reinforcers such as money, praise, or special privileges, the effect of intrinsic reinforcers is reduced (Notz 1975). The individual seems to turn his attention away from or is not controlled by intrinsic reinforcers such as enjoyment, a sense of accomplishment, or a sense of rightness when external reinforcers are available.

At first, behavior mod sounds to some like a relatively simple formula for changing behavior. As a matter of fact, it isn't. Hundreds of attempts to change the behavior of students through behavior mod fail, partly because teachers are often unable to identify the positive reinforcers that are consistently effective. In the previous section of this chapter, we looked at some of the reinforcers available to the teacher in an average classroom. None of these reinforcers will infallibly control behavior. Why? DeCharms has suggested that the greatest reinforcer for the individual is to feel that he is in control of his own behavior, and that a plethora of extrinsic reinforcers will interfere with that belief. Students in search of self-direction and self-control, therefore, may reject every other apparent positive reinforcement simply to assert that they are determining the direction of their own lives.

The basic issue then, is first whether a teacher ought to set up a behavior modification program in which the student has not participated in choosing the goal or the means of achieving it, and secondly, to what extent the use of extrinsic reinforcers to modify behavior is ultimately a creative educational practice. How often, and how much extrinsic reinforcement is appropriate to the educational goals which we profess for long-range student behavior? At what point, and with what kind of student, under what conditions does it change the student's behavior in the desired direction, and at what point does it begin to deprive him of feelings of self-worth and self-direction? When might it have the opposite effect?

WHAT BEHAVIORS HAVE TEACHERS THE RIGHT TO MODIFY?

"Do the subjects know enough to realize what is going on? Parents might be told that their children will be encouraged to cooperate with teachers, and given small incentives to be attentive in class. They will get affection and other rewards for being good students rather than always being punished. Parents might agree to that. But then, if they were told that this shaping of on-task or attentive behavior really has no relation to academic performance, it only makes the student more docile for the teacher, how would parents react? And further, if they were told that modifiers do not know whether the youngster's newly learned docility will make a problem in other parts of his life or prevent him from being assertive when he should be later on, how would parents react to that?"

From *Behavior Mod,* by Philip J. Hilts

Your Evaluation

Several research studies (Cobb 1972, Lahaderne 1968, Samuels and Turnure 1974, McKinney et al. 1975) have demonstrated that task-oriented behaviors and attentiveness were positively correlated with academic achievements in grade school children. But Hilts is concerned about two things. First, he is concerned because there are no studies reassuring us that teaching students task-oriented behavior makes them better students. We know that better students on the whole tend to exhibit task-oriented behaviors at least some of the time but we do not know whether reinforcing students for such behaviors as looking at their papers instead of the ceiling, writing with a pencil instead of biting it, or reading instead of looking at the window with chin in hand creates better learners. Hilts is worried that it may even destroy a capacity for learning already possessed by some students.

Hilts second concern is whether the long-term effects of behavior changes wrought through behavior mod programs may be detrimental as well, another question about which there is insufficient research.

Are either of Hilts' concerns valid?

What Behaviors Should Be Modified?

By whatever method, what behaviors should teachers be allowed to try to change in their students? Are there some behaviors that teachers should be forbidden by law to try to change? The question becomes particularly acute in relation to behaviors that are not strictly academic. The educational system has a clear social mandate to teach academic learning, but the right of the educational system to change and shape nonacademic behaviors is a question of much greater dispute among various groups in society. One of the gravest doubts about behavior mod is the extent to which it seems to lend itself to making students conform simply because conformity is more convenient for the teacher, not because it is better for the student. Schrag and Divoky (1975) believe that schools today are labeling more and more children as misfits, hyperactive, or behavior problems only because teachers do not like or do not know how to deal with absolutely normal exploratory, though sometimes restless, behavior of children who perversely do not like the teacher's narrow notions of adults.

What Are Students' Rights to Privacy and Protection?

Recent federal legislation has made it illegal to maintain files on any individual which is not open to inspection and challenge from the individual. There are citizens who believe that the private recordkeeping of teachers engaged in behavior mod programs violates the legal rights of students.

Related to rights of access to records which concern them are the students' rights to be protected from coerced participation in experimental programs. Many researchers argue that behavior mod is still in the experimental stage and that we have no right to treat captive students like experimental subjects. Teachers are equipped with a few principles which even trained psychologists may use only tentatively and are free to do whatever they like in the classroom. Are students deprived in such situations of a basic right to refuse to participate in the experiment without jeopordizing their grade or academic record? The question is how fully parents and students have the right to be informed of the procedures being used to modify behavior. Does the academic freedom of the teacher give her absolute control over the means adapted to increase academic learning? Or are some means to be prohibited, and if so, which means are acceptable, which not?

In gaining permission from parents to modify their children's behavior in school through behavior mod programs what information should be given to the parents? Hilts (1974) reminds us of the research (Milgram 1963) demonstrating the shocking extent to which many people trust scientific authority and willingly cooperate with advice given by apparent experts such as psychologists and professional educators. How fully do parents appreciate what may be really happening in a behavior mod situation? Do they appreciate how sparse much of the research in support of the beneficial effects of some of the behavior changes being brought about in their children may be?

The need to be adequately informed in a world of experts and technological knowledge, much of it beyond the scope of many to understand fully, is a crucial one for a democratic society but one that can be docilely handed over to the "scientists" to solve only at the risk of endangering the real roots of self-determination and freedom.

Being Managed Versus Learning To Manage

When the student participates in choosing a goal for himself and helps design the contingencies to achieve it, many of the most severe ethical problems surrounding behavior change engineered solely by the teacher dissolve. The teacher's role becomes that of a guide to the student rather than that of a dictator or absolute outside force. Instead of controlling the behavior of his students, the teacher shows students how to learn to control their own behaviors instead.

A cooperative approach such as this has several positive advantages. First are the benefits attached to using any self-management technique, notably the ability of the individual to identify and use internal events that control his behavior. Also, since students are actually participating in the program, they will be less prone to feeling manipulated, less helpless in the hands of external powers, and more self-directed, more responsible for their own actions. Indeed they will be because they will be learning not only how to submit to environmental forces but how to identify and control these forces for their own behavioral benefit.

As a teacher you will find that your students will need help at first in learning how to set up realistic behavioral goals and how to identify the positive reinforcers which effect their particular behavior, since research suggests that many of us do not know what reinforcers will control our behavior most effectively (Atkins and Williams 1972). However, because the students themselves are directing their own program under your guidance, the identification of contingencies will be able to proceed more quickly and accurately. Besides this, you will be able to teach the students to rely on intrinsic and covert reinforcers as well, so that many of the possible dangers of an overdependence on external contingencies will be reduced. You will be teaching students how to keep records of their own behavior changes, too, so there will be no question of your private recordkeeping which could interfere with students legal rights. Also, you will probably be saved a great deal of paper work.

The following is a short quiz to see if you can identify some of the practices some people object to for being unethical in the apparently well-meaning attempts of those in a position of authority to modify the behavior of those in their charge. You may try to restructure each program as a self-management project and see how many of the ethical problems you can eliminate in this manner.

Progress Check 6.2:   Analyzing the Ethics of Behavior Mod Projects

Directions: In each of the following behavior mod situations, the modifier is engaged in a program that, in the light of the issues we have just discussed, would be questioned by some as unethical. Read each situation and in the space provided, list as many of the objections as you can which might be offered to the program.   Since the use of behavior mod will often be left to your own discretion, space is also left for you to write in your own evaluation of each approach as well, indicating which of the practices you agree or disagree with and why.

1.   The teacher's goal was to teach sixteen-year-old Cindy, who almost always preferred to play or read by herself, to play with her peers for at least an hour a day.   The teacher decided to remove the apparent positive reinforcement Cindy derived from being alone by limiting the number of books she could sign out of the library to two per week, and to increase the positive reinforcements of playing with others by putting up a public chart in which every student in the class received a point redeemable for free time in the gym for every ten minutes of "brotherly or sisterly" behavior—ie: playing or working together with other students.   What objections may be raised against this program?

1. _____

2. _____

Your evaluation: _____

Reasons: _____

2.   In the summer of 1975, the British press carried an article reporting the alleged admission of a Pentagon employee who said that he had helped run desensitization procedures for foreign agents for the U.S., training them through a series of forced exposure to violence to be able to kill without feelings of nausea, guilt, or hesitation.   He allegedly reported that the desensitization was successful with only a percentage of men, and that a certain number always inevitably "failed" to become sufficiently desensitized.   The new report was subsequently denied by a Pentagon spokesman and there is no evidence available to the public that such a program was actually carried out.   Let us suppose, however, that the government was consulting you and others about the ethics of such a program.   Are there objections that might be made to it?

1. _____

_____

Your evaluation: _____

Reason: _____

3.   It was the teacher's opinion that Jerry was a fidgety child whose attention span was too short to enable him to engage in effective study.   The teacher, therefore, set up a program for him.

Since Jerry's hyperactivity was probably intrinsically rewarding, the teacher decided to punish Jerry every time he got out of his seat without permission by making him stand in what was called the "dunce corner" for one minute. When he remained in his seat for five uninterrupted minutes, he was reinforced by a touch on the shoulder from the teacher and a short comment of verbal praise. Can you identify any objections that might be raised against such a behavior mod program?

1. _____

2. _____

Your evaluation: _____

Reason: _____

BEHAVIOR MOD IN YOUR CLASSROOM

You are now familiar with both the basic principles and many of the common applications of behavior mod techniques. Which strategy or combination of strategies you use will depend on the particular behaviors you are modifying, on your own individual students, and your ethical position in relaiton to applying behavior mod. The following steps can be adapted as a general guide whether you are applying behavior mod to modify your own behavior or the behavior of your students. However, since there are both ethical and practical reasons for using behavior mod techniques only when the student actively consents and participates in the process, the steps here are designed to include both teacher and student. They can be used to modify academic learning behaviors as well as nonacademic behaviors. You will notice that the steps suggested here are similar in many ways to the steps suggested in chapter 4 for teaching new learning behaviors.

Step 1: Select the Target. If your students are participating in setting up the target your first step is to talk the goal selection over with them. If the goal you as the teacher want to achieve is of little or no interest to your students, discard it at least temporarily and start out with a goal that the students themselves are interested in. After you have worked together in achieving goals that are important to them, their confidence will increase and you will probably find that previously impossible goals begin to be suggested by the students. Your most important contribution as a teacher at this point is in guiding the individual student or class in setting up realistic and workable goals. If you have understood the three components of behavioral goals you should not find target selection a new process, since they both include three components—specification of behaviors, the circumstances under which they should appear (called test conditions when you are designing an instructional goal) and statement of criterion or success level.

Behavioral. The target should be stated in terms of observable, measurable behaviors. Increasing study time, reducing class noise, increasing reading speeds, improving math skills, increasing student cooperation, reducing playground fights are examples of behaviors that can be observed and measured.

Many initial suggestions coming from your students may be potentially behavioral, and part of your task will be to help them specify their targets clearly in terms of specific behavior. "Getting along better" may be restated as "helping someone with their arithmetic problems when you have finished your own," or "not taking things out of another person's desk." "Liking school better" may be changed to search for those things that would make school better—"earning a good grade in reading," "writing a class newspaper," or "having a clear classroom."

Attainable. The goal you and your students select should be attainable, and when students are new at setting up their own goals, should be attainable in a relatively short time so that they do not become discouraged or loose confidence in their ability to set up and achieve their own goals.

Beginning with behaviors which are already occurring with some frequency can help increase the probability that the goal can be attained. You will probably find that students at first will want to set inappropriately high goals that are simply unrealistic. Do not be too swayed by their optimistic assessments of what they can do because if the goal is not achieved you will pay for their optimism with consequent discouragement. Instead, try to select a more attainable goal on the way to the higher goal, and promise that the higher goal can be achieved after the lower one.

Positive. The behavioral target that is chosen should always include the acquisition of some behavior. Even when part of the primary target is to eliminate certain kinds of behavior, the acquisition target of an opposite and positive behavior should be included. This way you can use positive reinforcement rather than concentrating exclusively on manipulating punishments and nonreinforcements.

For example, if the agreed upon target is to be "less noisy in the classroom" the target can be restated either as a two-fold goal "to reduce noise and to increase quiet," or simply "to increase quiet." "To stop hitting other students" may be accompanied by the positive goal of "playing well with others;" "reducing irrelevant or out-of-turn comments in class" can be accompanied by the positive goal of "increasing relevant remarks made in turn in class." In any case no program should ever be set up just to *eliminate* some behavior.

Circumstances. Besides agreeing on the behavior of your target, the target specification should include a statement of the circumstances of when the behavior should or should not appear. It is all right, for instance, to run and shout during recess but not during reading. Limiting the circumstances under which the target behavior will be relevant is one way of making sure that the goal is practical and attainable. Instead of reducing class noise all day, for instance, your first goal may be to increase quiet only during reading period. Instead of agreeing that "better grades" is a goal across the board, you may agree to concentrate on learning behaviors at first in that class that is most interesting to the students.

Criterion. As with behavioral goals, targets must include a statement of the *level* of behaviors that are to be attained as well. How *much* quiet is enough quiet? How *long* should a student be able to study with a good attention span? What *level* of reading abilities are you trying to reach? If you can assign a number to the target you have selected, you can be sure that it is measurable and observable. If you can do that, you will also be able to carry out the next step which is to count the occurrence of *present* behaviors.

Step 2: Count Baseline Behavior. Counting baseline behavior is comparable to assessing entry behavior. If you are not able to count baseline behavior, that is if you and your students are not able to measure current behavior, your behavioral target is probably not stated clearly enough. If your target is clear, baselines can be measured in one of three ways.

How Often It Occurs. Some baselines can be measured best by counting the number of times a behavior occurs. "How many times did Tommy hit someone else this morning?", "How many times did Sylvia bite her fingernails while she was doing her arithmetic problems," or "How many times did someone in the class offer to help someone else with their math this morning" are examples of behaviors that are suitable for counting in this way. The period of time in which the behaviors are counted will vary with circumstances. Sometimes observation for two fifteen minute or half-hour periods a day for a week are sufficient. Sometime less is required. In any case, observation of baselines should be done for as long as is required to get a reasonable estimate of correct behaviors.

Length of Time. Sometimes baselines can be measured by observing the length of time the behavior continues. Study time, crying, playing with others, or reading are examples of behaviors that can often be measured best in terms of the length or duration of time they last.

Products of Behavior. The third way to count baselines is to look at the product of behavior instead of at the behavior itself. Number of arithmetic problems finished correctly, reading test scores, or completed homework assignments are examples of behavior products.

Who Should Count? The baselines behavior may be counted by you as the teacher, by the students themselves, or students of each other. Again, you will have to use their own judgement of the situation, the behavior being modified, and the capacities of your students in deciding who and how baselines should be counted.

Step 3: Identify Current Contingencies. While baselines are being counted, it is usually possible at the same time to observe and record current contingencies as well. You want to help your students identify the forces in the

---

A BEHAVIOR MOD CHECKLIST

Behavior mod programs do not always work. If you have set up a program to change your own behavior or behavior of your students which is not changing it, here is a short check list that might help you spot the problem.

• *Are your targets and mini-targets realistically attainable? Are you trying to change behavior too fast?*

• *Are the contingencies operating the way they should? Are positive reinforcers really reinforcing or do you only think they should be? Are the punishers really punishing? Are contingencies in conflict with one another, so that in order to avoid punishment, a very important positive reinforcer must be given up as well?*

• *How effectively are your cues operating before the relevant behavior actually occurs Should you verbalize them out loud?*

• *Are inadvertent cues and contingencies operating that you failed to identify? Have you studied your baseline record sufficiently well?*

• *Are you keeping a clear record so that you really know if and how much behavior change is actually occuring as a result of exactly which contingencies?*

• *Have you begun to use internal contingencies alone when they still need the additional support of overt and possibly external contingencies?*

---

environment that are both cueing and maintaining their behaviors. This means observing and recording both *when* the behavior occurs and what happens *afterwards*. This step is important whether the target is to increase or eventually eliminate a certain behavior because in either case, these are the contingencies that you want to alter. Students are usually capable of making these observations themselves and doing so will increase their awareness of forces controlling their own behaviors.

Exactly how you record baseline behaviors and current contingencies will depend on the details of the practical situation. However, the more specific and complete your initial observations, the more successful your subsequent behavior modification is apt to be. Every recording should include, however, 1) a description of the relevant behavior, 2) the date and time it occurred, 3) the circumstances under which it occurred, and 4) its consequences, or what happened after the behavior occurred.

Step 4: Design a Series of Mini-targets. This is a shaping plan comparable to the task analysis in your lesson plan. It is occasionally unnecessary in a behavior mod program but usually the final target is too far away to be achieved all at once and gradual approximations to the final target is more effective. For instance, to change a student's uninterrupted study time from ten minutes to two hours will be accomplished more quickly and more effectively if the change takes place gradually than if you and the student try to make the total change in one step.

If you have identified the criterion level of your target correctly, it has been stated in terms of a number or in numerical terms. (Criterion levels such as "never" or "whenever. . ." or "always" are numerical for our purposes here and are placed either in the zero position or at the other end of the number series.) Your baseline measurements are also expressed in terms of a similar number. The mini-targets fill in the numbers between the baselines and criterion levels. Let us suppose, for instance, that the target behavior is one hour of uninterrupted study behavior, while the baseline at the moment is fifteen minutes. Your series of mini-targets should stretch from the baseline of fifteen minutes to the criterion level of one hour. How big the steps between current and goal behavior are depends on the individual circumstances and adjustments can be made if steps are either too big or too small.

Each mini-target will be reinforced until it is a stably occurring behavior. A path of realistically designed mini goals that are achieved one by one will increase the probability that the final target eventually be achieved. It may make you and the class feel better at first to go after the final goal all in one piece, but the result may be disastrous.

Step 5: Arrange New Contingencies. Now that you and the class or individual student have identified your target, recorded baselines and current contingencies, and designed a series of minigoals, you are ready to plan positive changes in the environment affecting behavior. You do this by studying the results of Step 3 and by changing the contingencies that are currently controlling the behavior. You will want to study both the circumstances under which the behavior has occurred so that you can introduce new cues to either increase or decrease the relevant behavior, and what happened after the behavior occurred in order to introduce, increase, or change controlling reinforcers, punishers, and nonreinforcers.

New Cues. To introduce new cues and make them as effective as possible is your first change. Old cues, whenever possible, should be eliminated. If you have recorded in Step 3, for instance, that Tommy reads comic books instead of his geography book when he is seated next to Edward, you can begin to increase geography reading by keeping Tommy's proximity to Edward at a minimum during geography period. Often, however, old cues cannot be eliminated completely. If Marjorie "gets sick" every time math class begins, you may eliminate the cues presented by the math class by letting Marjorie drop math. This will keep Marjorie from getting sick over math but it won't solve the problem. What usually happens, therefore, is that you and your students must use new cues that are more salient than the old ones.

Cues will be effective if they clearly indicate a relationship between specific behavior and its conseqences, and if they are repeatedly brought to the attention of the person whose behavior is being changed. Giving students frequent opportunities to hear and verbalize for themselves the consequences that have been agreed on is a powerful way of increasing the effectiveness of cues. In particular, cues should be repeated *just before* the relevant behavior might occur.

Cues may also be nonverbal. One class that was trying to reduce its noise level (and eventually did so) agreed that whenever a student noticed that the noise had increased beyond agreed levels that he or she would flash the overhead light as a cue to keep voices lower.

New Reinforcers. As with cues, reinforcers must be adjusted as well. When you are trying to reduce or eliminate behavior, *reinforcers should be removed* if possible. Attention response, for instance, to the student seeking attention by speaking out of turn, making irrelevant comments, or disrupting other students should be withheld. Similarly, new reinforcers should be *added* following behavior to be increased and inadvertent punishers removed. This may take a great deal of ingenuity and study on the part of both you and the class.

Your plans for new reinforcements should be based on a careful study of the recordings made in Step 3. If you are trying to increase behaviors which are currently occurring only infrequently, study those circumstances under which the behavior *did* appear. What happened? Was the student laughed at? Was he ignored? Did he or she have to forego some other desirable reinforcer? Was the behavior more apt to appear in reading class than in history? In the presence of one particular pupil or certain pupils? In other words, is the behavior not being reinforced at all, being reinforced only weakly, or are the reinforcers competing with punishers? A similar set of questions should be asked about behaviors that you want to eliminate. How is it being reinforced now? Is it punishing or nonreinforcing for the student when he does *not* engage in the behavior? Once you and your students have answered these questions, you are in a position to change the contingencies to direct behavior toward your goal.

We have already seen that within the classroom there is a plethora of positive reinforcers at the disposal of the inventive and perceptive teacher. In a student participation program you will want to use reinforcers chosen by the students themselves. There are several ways of finding out what positive reinforcers your particular students want to use. Often no more than a class discussion is required. Or you yourself may construct a list of possible rewards from which individuals may choose when the specified behavior is accomplished. Best of all, the list may be generated by the students themselves. Remember also that simply becoming aware of behavior changes is often reinforcing so that a chart of progress kept by the students themselves is often a way of reinforcing progress.

Increasing Effectiveness of Reinforcers. Once the reinforcers and other contingencies have been selected, you should make sure that they are being used as effectively as possible. If students are applying the new contingencies themselves, help them make arrangements to administer the new reinforcers *immediately* after the target behavior appears. A delay of as much as ten minutes can be totally defeating. Also, the schedules of reinforcements should be such that reinforcements are administered *frequently* and *consistently* as behavior is being built-up. This is particularly important at the beginning of any behavior mod program.

Step 6: Record Your Progress. After you and your students have introduced new cues and contingencies, you should continue to record the dates and times the behavior occurs, its circumstances and consequences. This is an extremely important step because it is the way you are going to be able to tell if behavior changes are actually taking place, or to diagnose the difficulty if changes are not taking place. The most sensible way to record your progress in this step is as a continuation of the recordings you made while you were observing baseline behavior and its contingencies. It is also often helpful to graph the behavior changes as well in order to highlight more clearly the changes that are taking place.

If in a week or so after the new contingencies have been introduced behavior levels have not changed, you should study carefully the record you have kept. Have the new contingencies actually been used, or was the plan not really carried out consistently? Are the reinforcers really reinforcing? The punisher really punishing? The checklist above will point to some of the other questions you should ask as you are planning what changes you should make in your program to bring about more effective changes.

If regular changes are occurring in the target behavior, continue to carry out the program as you have designed it until the final target behavior is reached.

Step 7: Reduce External Contingencies. Once the target has been reached and is occurring at a fairly stable rate, you are ready to reduce the overt contingencies controlling the behavior and substitute less obvious but equally effective controllers.

Thin Out Reinforcements. The process of reducing external controls begins by using a less regular and less frequent rate of reinforcement. Instead of rewarding study behavior after every fifteen minutes, rewards should gradually be given only every two or three fifteen minute periods, and then perhaps not every night. Rather than giving positive feedback to a study after every problem completed correctly, feedback can be given more randomly and less frequently.

Introduce Covert Reinforcements. While overt reinforcers are being reduced and randomized, covert and often intrinsic reinforcers can be steadily introduced to take the place of the overt reinforcers. It is at this point that self-management techniques have their greatest value because students are able to continue to maintain behavior changes by reinforcing themselves with covert cues and reinforcers when the teacher or other external source of reinforcement is no longer present.

If the target behaviors should begin to diminish or unwanted behavior begin to reappear—as it most often does—a return to Step 6 should be repeated for as long and as often as necessary.

The best way to see if you know how to apply the steps to implement an effective behavior mod program is to try to put them into practice to modify some aspect of your own behavior. In addition, here is a short progress check in quiz form for you.

Progress Check 6.3: Implementing a Behavior Mod Program

Directions: Circle the letter next to the answer which best answers each question.

1. Which of the following student-selected goals *in their present form* meet the requirements for target selection included in Step 1 in the text? (For further feedback, indicate how you would go about making poorly stated or incomplete targets more acceptable.)
   a. "I want to learn to read better so I can get my homework finished faster."

(Improvements: _____)
   b. "Let's have the whole class work at being quieter during arithmetic class."

(Improvements: _____)
   c. "We could get it so the classroom is clean after lunch every day. It's clean when there aren't any papers at all on the floor."

(Improvements: _____)
   d. "I simply can't do math; I'm no good at it and I never will be."

(Improvements: _____)
   e. "I want the other kids to like me better."

(Improvements: _____)

Below is an example of a record of baselines and contingencies kept by a fifth grade class whose goal is to have a classroom with all the papers picked up after lunch. The teacher helped the students decide what circumstances and consequences to look for and record.

Record

Date:	# papers on floor:	Where?	Did anybody do or say anything after the paper count?
Monday	10	around basket: 5 aisle 1: 2 aisle 2: 0 aisle 3: 3	Alice picked all the papers up; Tom asked her why she was doing that.
Tuesday	12	around basket: 6 aisle 1. 1 aisle 2: 0 aisle 3: 5	Alice yelled at the boys in aisle 3, and said they were sloppy. They laughed.

Wednesday	9	around basket: 3	A student in aisle 3 threw
		aisle 1: 2	another paper on the floor
		aisle 2: 1	and pointed it out to Alice
		aisle 3: 3	and Mary who picked it up.
Thursday	14	around basket: 8	Alice and Mary began
		aisle 1: 1	to throw papers at
		aisle 2: 3	aisle 3 and a squabble
		aisle 3: 2	began.
Friday	25	around basket: 10	The boys in aisle 3
		aisle 1: 3	said it was nice to
		aisle 2: 3	have the girls looking
		aisle 3: 9	after them.

2. According to the above record what is the class' daily baseline behavior?
   a. 25
   b. 8
   c. 14
   d. 10

3. Which of the following conclusions may be validly drawn from the recorded contingencies above?
   a. Alice's anger at Tom serves as an effective punisher for dropping paper.
   b. The teacher's neatness during the past week serves as a model for aisle 3.
   c. The wastepaper basket serves as an effective cue for keeping papers off the floor.
   d. Aisle 3's untidiness may be being reinforced by Alice's subsequent clearning up and verbal attacks.

4. Based on an examination of the recorded contingencies above, which of the following would be the most reasonable arrangement to increase neatness?
   a. Begin by putting Alice in charge of picking up dropped papers.
   b. Begin by promising a special story period after lunch on those days that no paper is left around the basket.
   c. Begin by cueing aisle 3 that if they do not pick up their papers there will be trouble.
   d. Begin by taking away five tokens redeemable for free time from each aisle that has paper in it after lunch.

5. If you and the class agreed that every time the after lunch target for the day was met they would have a ten-minute period of music, when would be the most effective time to play the music?
   a. the first thing in the morning.
   b. the last thing in the school day.
   c. immediately after the paper count.
   d. just before lunch.

6. While the behavior modification program was being carried out, which of the following recording procedures would be most recommended?
   a. Alice should keep the paper count and report it to the teacher.
   b. The teacher should keep the record privately.
   c. No additional record would be necessary.

d. A public record including date, paper count, circumstances, and consequences should be kept.

7. After the target behavior had been accomplished and the paper strewing of the class completely terminated, what should the teacher do?
   a. Keep the program going unchanged so the behavior does not reappear.
   b. Drop the program because it is finished.
   c. Begin to replace music with verbal praise and encourage self-reinforcement.
   d. Arrange the music to be played on a frequent fixed interval schedule.

SUMMARY

In this chapter we examined several common behavior mod strategies, both to increase or decrease behavior. All behavior mod techniques are based on conditioning principles, and therefore modify behavior by changing factors in the environment to which the behavior is a response. Techniques to increase behavior all use a form of positive reinforcement following desired behavior. Two particular classroom applications of this approach are contingency contracting and token economies. Behavior can be decreased by using nonreinforcement when this is possible. Some form of punishment is sometimes necessary, however, to terminate behaviors that are intrinsically reinforcing or too dangerous or disruptive to be allowed to continue until extinction occurs through nonreinforcement. Punishment should never be used without an accompanying positive reinforcement available for the execution of a behavior incompatible for the behavior being punished and should be administered as immediately and consistently as possible. Self-management techniques apply the principles of behavior mod to the management of one's own behavior and frequently make use of internal contingencies such as thoughts and feelings to change behavior.

Behavior mod techniques have often proven successful when other means of behavior change have failed, and are therefore becoming increasingly popular. Concern about their ethical use is being expressed as a result and issues to which answers must be found include decisions about who has a right to determine a behavior target for an individual, whether teachers have the right to modify all academic and unacademic behavior which may occur in the school, students' rights to privacy, the conditions under which a behavior mod program should be used at all, and whether some methods of positive or aversive conditioning may be harmful to the individual whose behavior is being changed. Self-management techniques avoid many of the ethical problems involved in programs set up for others.

Several steps are delineated for setting up your own behavior mod program. They are target selection, measurement of baseline behavior, identification of current contingencies, specification of minitargets, selection of new contingencies, recording progress, and reducing external contingencies after behavior has been successfully modified.

SUGGESTED READING

For research and case studies:

BECKER, WESLEY C., ED. *An Empirical Basis for Change in Education: Selections on Behavioral Psychology for Teachers.* Chicago: Science Research Associates, Inc., 1971.

A collection of papers on basic concepts, and control of both academic and nonacademic behavior.

GRAZIANO, ANTHONY M., ED. *Behavior Therapy with Children,* vol. 2. Chicago: Aldine Publishing Co., 1975.

A book of collected papers dealing with the social and political issues of behavior mod and its application to a diversity of children's behavioral problems in the school and family.

ULLMAN, LEONARD P., AND KRASNER, LEONARD, EDS. *Case Studies in Behavior Modification.* New York: Holt, Rinehart and Winston, 1965.

A classic collection of research studies modifying severely-disturbed, neurotic, and deviant behaviors in children and adults along with studies with behavior of retarded or mentally deficient.

For additional research in behavior modification, the following journals are particularly relevant:

Behavior Therapy
Journal of Applied Behavior Analysis
Journal of Behavior Therapy and Experimental Psychiatry
Journal of Educational Research
Journal of Experimental Education

Some easy to read guides:

ACKERMAN, J. MARK. *Operant Conditioning Techniques for the Classroom Teacher.* Glenview, Ill.: Scott, Foresman and Co., 1972.

Nontechnical, simple guide for work with individual behavior problems.

GIVNER, ABRAHAM, AND GRAUBARD, PAUL S. *A Handbook of Behavior Modification for the Classroom.* New York: Holt, Rinehart and Winston, 1974.

Like Ackerman's book, this is a short simple guide with concrete instructions.

HOMME, L. E.; CASANYI, A. P.; GONZALRE, N. A.; AND RECHS, J. R. *How to Use Contingency Contracting in the Classroom.* Champaign, Ill.: Research Press, 1970.

An indispensable guide for contingency contracts.

PATTERSON, GERALD R., AND GULLION, M. ELIZABETH. *Living with Children: New Methods for Parents and Teachers.* Champaign, Ill.: Research Press Co., 1968.

Written as a programmed text, a simple guide for using behavior mod.

ROSE, SHELDON D. *Establishing a Token Economy in the Classroom.* Washington, D.C.: Jossey-Bass Publishing Co., 1974.

Not written specifically for educators but many relevant practices for school use are suggested.

STAINBACK, WILLIAM C. ET AL. *Establishing a Token Economy in the Classroom.* Columbus, Ohio: Charles E. Merrill Publishing Co., 1973.

For establishing a token economy in your classroom.

WILLIAMS, ROBERT L., AND ANANDAM, KAMALA. *Cooperative Classroom Management.* Columbus, Ohio: Charles E. Merrill, 1973.

A cooperative approach between teacher and students to classroom management.

WILLIAMS, ROBERT L., AND LONG, JAMES D. *Toward a Self-Managed Life Style.* Boston: Houghton Mifflin Co., 1975.

The best guide for self-management available on this level.

For some reservations about behavior mod:

BURGESS, ANTHONY. *Clockwork Orange.* New York: W. W. Norton & Co., Inc., 1963.

A novel later made into a movie about the fears that one man has about the possible applications of behavior mod at its worst

HILTS, PHILIP J. *Behavior Mod.* New York: Harper and Row, 1974.

For an eminently readable exploration of some of the best and some of the worst results of a behavior mod approach. I would say don't miss reading it.

The Student as a Special Person: Individual Differences

7

Chapter Objectives

Students are alike in many important ways, but in equally important ways they are different. In most of this book, we have talked about the learner as if every student were similar, but each student also brings to the classroom a unique constellation of characteristics that make her different from any other student you will ever know. They are different in terms of sex, age, rural or urban residence, socioeconomic status, cultural heritage, race, personality characteristics, intelligence, and family background. Students have been variously labeled as deprived, disadvantaged, hyperactive, retarded, intellectually deficient, exceptional, gifted, learning disabled, emotionally disturbed, underachieving, overachieving, introverted, extroverted, and intrinsically or extrinsically motivated.

In this chapter we do not examine every possible category into which your students may be divided, but we do look at two particularly important groups—the culturally different, and the exceptional learner—and present some steps to guide you in your own perceptions of the varied learning assets and liabilities of each of your own students.

The behavioral goals of this chapter are to enable you to:

1. *recognize cultural differences among students and their subsequent educational implications.*

   Progress Check: In a 6-item true-false quiz you are asked to pick out statements which accurately reflect facts about the culturally different student.

2. *recognize characteristics of exceptional students and relevant teaching strategies.*

   Progress Check: You are asked to pick out the correct categories of exceptional students described in ten fill-in items.

3. *differentiate between fact and fallacy in teaching approaches to the exceptional student.*

   Progress Check: You are asked to pick out the correct statements made by teachers of exceptional students in a 4-item quiz.

The Student as a Special Person: Individual Differences

THE CULTURALLY DIFFERENT STUDENT

Who Is Culturally Different?

When we are talking about the culturally different student, we are talking about the student whose family or outside-the-school culture differs in important ways from the predominant culture of the school, with its accompanying values, practices, and expectations.

Many Different Groups. Culturally different students are not all alike. In fact, they may be as different from each other in their learning styles, reinforcement preferences, and school achievement as they are from the dominant group. The major groups of subcultures in our country alone include blacks, American Indians who themselves have diverse cultural traditions, Latin American groups such as the Mexicans, Puerto Ricans, Haitians, Cubans, along with members from every other Latin American country, Asian Americans including Chinese, Japanese, Vietnamese, and Filipinos, and European Americans from every country in Western and Eastern Europe.

Differences Are Not Always a Disadvantage. The average academic performance of many culturally different groups is below the average performance of the students in general. This is not surprising since many culturally different students have to learn much more than other students, often struggling with even such obvious differences such as language. However, cultural differences do not always put the student at a disadvantage and some culturally different groups often do better than average.

In addition, *no* group is disadvantaged as a whole. In every cultural group, there exists outstanding individuals who achieve well above the norm among students in general, and there is a considerable overlap among all the cultural groups in our educational settings. In other words, there are average differences among some cultural groups, but since there are also such immense differences among individuals *within* cultural groups, cultural background will be an inadequate guide in determining the learning achievements of any individual student.

What Differences Are a Disadvantage?

The average middle class student does better academically than the average lower class one; so does the average white student compared to the average black student; and, so does the average urban child compared to the student from a rural area. But not all lower class, black, or rural students are disadvantaged. Socioeconomic background, race, or place of residence are not totally determining factors, and something else must mediate the difference among these groups.

Culture, Environment, and Race. It is a fashionable hypothesis today to ask whether differences in intelligence test scores among races are genetically based. While there exists a genetic contribution to intelligence, the environmental differences among blacks, whites, and other racial groups are immense, and many behaviorists (Skinner 1971) believe that an extended discussion of the genetic issue draws our attention away from the social, economic, psychological, and other environmental differences which are so important in educational achievements, and provides an unjustified excuse for refusing to identify the causes of much school failure as environmental. We will examine, therefore, some of these environmental factors.

Language. Most culturally different children speak two languages—one in the home and one in school. Sometimes the language is clearly accepted as a foreign one—Spanish, Chinese, Italian, German. While bilingual students possess a better grasp of two languages than the average American who has completed a second language on the college level, this kind of bilingualism often involves problems as well. Many children do not appreciate the value of their parents' languages, and second generation children almost inevitably feel ashamed of their parents' "foreign ways," and experience consequent feelings of inferiority.

Language spoken in dialect English is different from the language used in school as well, but it is often more difficult to recognize as possessing the characteristics of a foreign language. Yet language spoken by black children, for instance, is demonstrably different from standard usage. Until recently, studies focused on what seemed inherent deficiencies of this home language—short repetitive sentences with ungrammatical usages and limited abstract concepts. Recent studies today, however, tend to argue that black language is not inferior but different (Dillard 1972), and that teachers, not understanding the language in anymore than the most superficial way, have mistakenly labeled it as underdeveloped.

Socioeconomic Status. Many culturally different people are poor, and there exists a culture of poverty as well. To be poor is to be different in ways that go far beyond the difference between having two televisions or none, three outfits or one, six pairs of expensive shoes or sneakers. Some of the most obvious influences of poverty on educational achievement include the effects of substandard nutrition and health care, poor housing (and subsequent poor home-study conditions), and what Levine (1971) calls the pervasive insecurity of the poor. To be poor is often to be insecure financially, to be close to unemployment, crime, sickness, and other dangers which create attitudes of suspicion, frustration, lowered self-concept, and hostility.

In addition, the effects of poverty with its consequent crime, hopelessness, and reduced expectations, reinforce the effects of the negative stereotypes held by both the disadvantaged themselves and by employers and teachers, and make it even more difficult to break out of a vicious cycle that begins and ends with poverty. Davidson and Lang (1960) found that when teachers expected students to do poorly, for instance, they continued to think of those students as low achievers *even when* school work demonstrated the opposite. This means that poor children, exposed to poverty at home, will often in some way or other be exposed to more than their fair share of discrimination against their achievements even when they are not inferior. Yet, everybody who is poor does not do poorly in school. In fact, the Coleman report (Coleman et al. 1966) concluded that the quality of teachers was not nearly as important in school achievement as motivation, and Miller (1970) even concluded that poverty was a vastly overrated cause of school underachievement. What else, then, is important?

Family Influences. Family interactions apparently vary in subtle but crucially important ways in determining the educational achievements of children. First of all, if the family expresses a highly favorable attitude toward education the children will do better than if the attitude toward school is indifferent or negative (Miller 1970). If children are expected to do well and to go on to college, they will achieve higher academic success than if they are expected to drop out of school and go to work or walk the streets. If a family has a history of personal accomplishments, as opposed to a history of repeated failure in the academic realm, the child will tend to reflect these histories in his own.

However, attitudes toward education are not the only important family interactions. One study found that orderliness in the home was positively related to school achievement. Davidson and Greenberg (1967) found that among Harlem boys, those whose homes were most orderly were also the highest academic achievers, and Miller (1970) found that in families where discipline was stricter more educational achievements were found. Another important variable seems to be the amount of verbal interchange between parents and children. Parents who talk to their children more—apparently from birth onwards and even before the child could possibly understand what the mother is saying—tend to have higher achieving children.

Locus of Control. Another differentiating characteristic between high and low achievers is their locus of control. Locus of control describes what the individual believes to be the most important source of power controlling what happens to him. Individuals vary significantly in the degree to which they believe and experience the ability to direct what happens to them. Lower achievers tend to believe in "luck," and in forces outside them or beyond their control. They tend to feel that no matter what they do, it won't matter, that their fate is controlled by someone or something else anyway.

It has not been demonstrated whether high achievers have a firmer conviction that they control their own destinies because as high achievers they in fact do have more control, or whether they are high achievers because they possess an internal locus of control, feeling that they themselves determine a great deal of what happens to them. Whatever the causal direction (and it may very well operate in both directions, each increasing with the strength of the other), Rotter et al. (1962) has shown that, although lower income students and blacks tended to have an external locus of control, those students from lower income and/or black families with an internal locus of control do better in school than white and/or middle class children with an external source of control.

Teaching Strategies for the Culturally Disadvantaged

As we have already said, to be culturally different is not in itself to be disadvantaged. However, when significant groups of students consistently underachieve in school, they may be considered disadvantaged relative to the school environment. How can you, as a teacher, minimize that disadvantage?

Insure Success. Most learning-disadvantaged children will be laboring under a history of school failure, not only for them personally but often for many members of their group. A history of failure becomes self-perpetuating as both teacher and student come to expect it as inevitable and inescapable simply because it seems to have been so in the past. Your job as a teacher is to break this cycle of failure by beginning at realistic baselines, designing effective task analysis, and choosing meaningful reinforcers.

Begin at Real Baselines and Adjust Learning Speeds. Children with histories of failure probably come into your class with lower baseline behaviors in relation to most subjects you will be teaching. Starting points, therefore, must be lowered. This is not the same thing as lowering standards which is the lowering of the *end* point of criterion level. In fact, beginning at the true baselines is one realistic way of increasing the possibility that the final standards will not be lowered.

Task analysis should be quite differentiated. Students with many experiences of failure get much more satisfaction (and subsequent motivation) from a series of slow but steady successes than from taking a major step filled with a great risk of further failure.

Choose Meaningful Reinforcers. If one of the major contributors to academic success is motivation then the selection of effective reinforcers is critically important to the learning achievements of the culturally disadvantaged. Evidence seems to indicate that these students are disadvantaged in part because they are motivated by different reinforcers than children of the majority culture, and probably by reinforcers that the teacher has not been taught to use or respond to herself.

The research on the effectiveness of various reinforcers is quite large and the results are complex. You will find many exceptions to the following generalities but as initial working guidelines you may find them helpful.

1. External reinforcers will be more effective than symbolic or intangible reinforcers. External reinforcers may be material objects such as a gold star or new pencil, or may be some other concrete expression such as a verbal statement of praise, or permission to sit in a preferred seat (Zigler and deLabry 1962).
2. Feedback emphasizing praise ("That's a terrific job" or "This is very good work") is more effective with low socioeconomic classes than feedback emphasizing the correctness of a response ("That is correct" or "These three answers are right") which is more effective with middle class children (Zigler and Kanzer 1962).
3. Reinforcers delivered *immediately* will be more effective than delayed reinforcers. Delayed reinforcers for the disadvantaged are demotivating, perhaps because he has good reason to believe that delayed reinforcers never arrive.

Use Intrinsically Interesting Material. Some time ago, a conscientious second grade teacher called the parents of one of her students to report that the child was not learning to read with the rest of the class. "That's absurd," replied the little girl's father. "She's been reading here at home for over a year." "Well, there is no evidence here in school that she knows how," replied the teacher. So the conscientious parent sat the wayward child down many evenings beside him on the couch and helped her "learn to read." It was soon discovered that she indeed did know how to read but had decided that the books given to her in school were much too boring, and so she was making up her own stories to go with the pictures instead.

Many children do not appear to learn because the material in their texts and in teacher's lectures is of no concrete interest to them. Many concepts can be taught about Dick and Jane in a suburban home, or about Frank and Johnny out on the city street. Adapting the material to the real interests and life experiences of your students requires that you get to know them, and this will probably lead to increased learning on their part.

A Consistent and Highly Structured Classroom. If children are learning disadvantaged when they do not believe that they have control over what happens to them as Rotter's research suggests, they will continue to feel out of control in an erratic or disorganized classroom. Disadvantaged students often do better in highly structured, fair, and strict classes where the rewards and punishments for specific behaviors are clearly delineated and put into practice. This structure enables the student to see that his behavior is indeed related to what happens to him, and he can predict and control the rewards and punishments that come to him. Guided self-managed behavior mod programs can increase the student's internal locus of control as well.

We will look next at exceptional learners but first here is a progress check for you.

Progress Check 7.1: Distinguishing Facts About the Culturally Different Student

Directions: Place a check beside those statements which accurately reflect material in the text concerning the culturally different student. For further feedback, correct unchecked statements on the line provided.

_____1. Communication and language problems may still exist even if children speak some form of English in the home.

_____

_____2. To be culturally different is to be culturally disadvantaged in our school system in the United States.

_____

_____3. Children from different cultural backgrounds will often respond to different kinds of reinforcements.

_____

_____4. Skinner believes that our energy should be spent primarily on studying the genetic rather than environmental contributions to educational success.

_____5. Some researchers have found that such factors as order in the home, family expectations, and locus of control are more important in determining educational achievements than socio-economic status as such.

_____6. Behaviorists believe that standards should be lowered for the culturally disadvantaged.

EXCEPTIONAL LEARNERS

Exceptional learners are those students who in one or more ways learn either at a significantly faster or slower rate than the average rate. Children who proceed more slowly in some ways are sometimes called learning disabled, sometimes handicapped, or retarded, or emotionally disturbed depending on the nature and scope of the learning difficulty. Children who proceed at an unusually accelerated level are called gifted. Boys outnumber the girls in all these categories.

The Emotionally Disturbed Student

The emotionally disturbed student is not a child whose behavior is merely highly active, undisciplined, or disturbing to you. Neither is the child emotionally disturbed when a mild behavior disturbance erupts occasionally, particularly when it can be connected to some source of anxiety for the student in the home or among his peers. It is easier to say who the emotionally disturbed student is not than who he is because the definitions of emotional disturbance vary so widely. A wide discrepancy in definitions makes the estimate of the number of emotionally disturbed students vary from ten to twenty-five percent. Generally, although he may be more disruptive to you as a teacher, the child who "acts out" and boisterously demonstrates his disturbance is usually in less danger of becoming severely disturbed in later life than the withdrawn, excessively shy student.

The severely disturbed student should and probably will be removed from the regular classroom. Moderately disturbed children will often be in your regular classes. Such students have been helped by individual behavior modification programs, often under the guidance of a psychological consultant.

The Retarded Student

The intellectually deficient or retarded student is a student whose intellectual development has been impaired, and who is either slow or unable to learn such essential activities as walking, talking, and dressing. Intellectually deficient students often have accompanying emotional problems, often a side-effect of poor treatment or disregard.

The Educable Retarded. Students with IQs below 50 will probably not be in a regular school although the student with an IQ above 25 can learn the simple tasks of caring for himself, and sometimes even to read and write on an elementary level.

Students with IQs between 50–75 can usually learn up to about the sixth grade level, and so are capable of becoming self-supporting adults holding regular jobs and often supporting families.

Students with IQs between 75–85 are considered slow learners but are capable of continuing their education several years beyond students whose IQ ranges only around 50.

Teaching Strategies. Retarded students learn by the same principles as intellectually normal students but they learn more slowly. They need much *more repetition,* often in short but repeated drill periods carried on for much longer periods than is necessary for other students. Also, an emphasis on the *practical and concrete,* rather than on the abstract and theoretical will lead to greater success. It is important, as well, that the intellectually deficient child is not prevented from learning all that he can because of labels which interfere, leading teachers to expect too little, or other students to treat him with ridicule or disdain.

The Learning Disabled

The learning disabled student is one whose learning performance, usually in only one or two areas, is not equal to learning that is expected on the basis of his tested IQ. Learning disabled children often have minor speech, sensory-motor, or reading deficiencies, and they often possess unusually short attention spans with an excess of physical energy expressed in hyperactivity. Learning disabilities are often the result of minimal brain damage

(MBD) during pregnancy, childbirth, or infancy, and often (though not always) disappear as the child reaches puberty.

Teaching Strategies. The learning disabled child often does not need special remediation in his entire educational repertoire, unless his problem is a long-standing, untreated inability to read or some other deficiency which interfered with progress in every subject. The behaviorist approach to the learning disabled child is to attack the problem as a specifically behavioral one. If the child has trouble learning to read, the special drill must be

---

SHOULD SPECIAL STUDENTS BE IN SPECIAL CLASSES?

Grouping students according to ability so that slow learners are working with other slow learners is a common practice which must be evaluated in terms of both its possible advantages and disadvantages.

SUGGESTED ADVANTAGES

• *Retarded students are given a chance to focus upon the successes which they can accomplish rather than experiencing consistent failure when they are compared to non-retarded students.*

• *Motivation and morale will remain at a high level because it will not be constantly assailed by frustration and feelings of inferiority.*

• *Special training in relation to personal and social habits often required by retarded students can be given for as long as necessary without disrupting the normal class or bringing attention to apparently unusual needs.*

SUGGESTED DISADVANTAGES

• *Instead of categorizing individuals, special classes categorize whole groups, and slow or retarded learners come to believe that they cannot learn anything.*

• *Teachers have found that groups that think of themselves as "slow" are difficult to motivate and students rarely do better academically in special classes than they do in regular classes.*

• *Research indicates that slow learners are often stimulated by being in the presence of brighter students. This incentive is denied when students are grouped according to ability.*

• *Ability often leads to racial grouping with the consequent social disadvantages of such an arrangment.*

A COMPROMISE

Because of the disadvantages of ability grouping on a large scale, it is being abandoned by many educators today and a resource room *is taking its place. A resource room is a place for special instruction where the student spends a short period with a special instructor every day. For the rest of the time, the student works in the regular classroom with other students.*

---

given to him in reading. If his problem is sensory-motoric, then he must be taught, step-by-step, the motor skills—either gross or fine movements—which he does not possess. This special drill often takes place in what is called a resource room where the student goes for a short period for special practice every day.

The Gifted Learner

The gifted learner is one whose IQ is about 140 or over, and is surprisingly hard for teachers to identify. One study (Pegnato and Birch 1959) found that when teachers were asked to select the intellectually gifted students in their classes, over 50 percent of the gifted students were passed over by the teachers, and 30 percent of those identified as gifted were not. Group IQ tests are not much more accurate, although individual testing is. About one out of every two hundred students will have an IQ over 140, but in some schools the incidence will be higher.

Teaching Strategies. Teaching the gifted learner is in many ways as difficult as teaching the retarded student. The gifted student will more likely than not be poor in writing and art but far better than average in verbal comprehension, original thought, and abstract reasoning ability. You might find that she is more than usually critical both of herself and others, and becomes bored and frustrated with subjects—especially those requiring rote memorization—that do not challenge her intellectually. The intellectually gifted, of course, learn faster than the average student, and this is often a challenge to a teacher who sometimes finds himself faced with a student who knows more than he knows. Teachers of gifted students are expected to provide more work and challenge than the teacher of average students and this is additional work as well.

For this reason, gifted students, when they are recognized, are sometimes put into accelerated classes or given advanced standing. This helps to relieve the teacher of the burden of preparing what amounts to special classes for the gifted student, but it is often accompanied by the disadvantage of socially disorienting the student himself. Other students often feel as if the gifted student were too different to be a friend, and gifted students sometimes themselves, while excelling academically, may be retarded socially.

We will look at a short checklist for you when you are dealing with the exceptional child, but first, here is a progress check.

Directions: Fill in the spaces, choosing your answer from the following list:
emotionally disturbed
retarded
learning disabled
gifted
exceptional

1. The _____ student will usually have a learning problem only in a restricted area.

2. The principle problem of the _____ student is that he learns more slowly than average.

3. While excelling in abstract thinking and logical reasoning, the _____ student is often poor in sensory-motor subjects such as art and penmanship.

4. The _____ student usually should be taught by using concrete and practical, rather than abstract or theoretical, examples.

5. The _____ learner has an IQ of about 140 or over.

6. The behaviorist approach to teaching the _____ student is to provide extra drills and practice for the particular area of learning difficulty.

7. The _____ student is characterized by a relatively long-standing and recurrent behavior disturbance.

8. The definition of the _____ student is that she learns in one or more areas at a speed significantly different from the average.

9. Placing the _____ student in accelerated classes may provide necessary academic stimulation for him but may retard social development.

10. Teaching the _____ student should be characterized by unusually large amount of repetition.

A CHECKLIST FOR THE TEACHER OF SPECIAL STUDENTS

A teacher faced with an exceptional student needs to learn more about his special problems and abilities than this chapter includes. This chapter does not make you an expert on individual students, and additional reading and consultation with the educational psychologist are strongly recommended when you are actually teaching them. The following suggestions are offered as guidelines.

Setting the Goal

The goal that you would set for the average student is probably not appropriate for the exceptional student. The slow student will take longer, the gifted student less time than most. It will be a matter of experimenting yourself and learning to be sensitive to the needs of individual students, but be sure that you have not set the learning goal either too high or too low for your students. You may find it possible to keep all your students covering somewhat the same material if you concentrate on developing goals at the higher levels of Bloom's taxonomy for your gifted students, and at lower levels for your slower students.

Diagnosis

Your baselines or entry behaviors among exceptional and disadvantaged students will be further from the norm than you may expect. Students with histories of failure may have surprisingly low entry learning behavior for their grade levels, gifted students exceptionally high levels. Disadvantaged students may have language and writing problems which interfere with further learning. Since they are usually handicapped by a single learning disability, learning disabled and physically handicapped students may have low entry behaviors in a single area—hearing, writing, seeing, sensory-motor capacities, arithmetic, or speaking. You will have to search more carefully for an accurate assessment of entry behaviors among disadvantaged and exceptional students than among your average students.

Behavior Not Labels

In this chapter we have looked at various labels which have been attached to students. The behaviorists would emphasize that as a teacher you should concentrate on looking at the student's behaviors, not at his label. A label is not permanent, but we have seen how teachers too often tend to see students in terms of the category into which they have been placed, and are unable to interpret behavior change as taking the student out of the category into which he has been placed.

One of the advantages of a behavior mod approach is that teachers learn to concentrate on behavior instead of labels, and to expect behavior change rather than to ignore or disbelieve it. This principle is important particularly when you are relating to disadvantaged or exceptional learners who have had an extra large burden of labels already placed on them.

Choose Reinforcers Carefully

Do not expect the same reinforcers you use with the average students to work automatically as well with disadvantaged or exceptional students. Gifted students may find tangible reinforcers ridiculous, while disadvantaged or slow learners may find abstract or delayed reinforcers too unreal to be effective. We have already looked at some differences in reinforcement preferences but there are many more. Do not expect all reinforcers to be effective. Expect differences among students and look for them. Here is a short progress check.

Progress Check 7.3:   Recognizing Teachers' Fallacies About the Exceptional Student

Directions: Below are four opinions expressed by different teachers of exceptional children.   Place a check beside those which reflect statements made in the text.   For further feedback, correct unchecked items in the spaces provided.

_____1.   "Research supports the practice of setting the same goals for both exceptional and average students in the same schools."

_____2.   "A teacher with exceptional or disadvantaged children in his class will probably have to deal with widely divergent entry behaviors."

_____3.   "An emotionally disturbed child will probably remain so permanently."

_____4.   "The exceptional child often has reinforcement preferences which differ from those of the average student."

SUMMARY

Although the disadvantaged and exceptional student learn according to the same principles that all other students learn, adjustments in teaching strategies to meet their special needs are usually necessary.

The culturally different child is disadvantaged to the extent that behavioral expectations of his home culture differ from that of the school culture. He is often characterized by a history of failure, and one of the teacher's most urgent tasks is to overcome a syndrome of failure by beginning at realistic baselines, and using sufficiently small units in a task analysis to allow for frequent administration of effective reinforcers.

The exceptional student includes: retarded students who learn more slowly than average and may not be able to achieve beyond a maximum grade level; the gifted student who academically excels the average student; the learning disabled child who has a normal IQ but is unable to perform adequately in some areas; and the emotionally disturbed student whose learning and behavioral difficulties are not primarily caused by an exceptional IQ but by physical or environmental factors. Teaching exceptional students requires that particular attention be given to goal setting, entry behavior assessment, learning styles, and reinforcement preferences.

SUGGESTED READING

GARDNER, WILLIAM I. *Behavior Modification in Mental Retardation: The Education and Rehabilitation of the Mentally Retarded Adolescent and Adult.* Chicago: Aldine Pub., 1975.

Behavior mod applied to an older age group than the book above, including a research review and examples of actual clinical studies.

GARDNER, WILLIAM I. *Children with Learning and Behavior Problems: A Behavior Management Approach.* Boston: Allyn and Bacon, 1974.

A guide for the teacher applying behaviorism as we have studied it here.

HAMMILL, DONALD D., AND BARTEL, NETTIE R. *Teaching Children with Learning and Behavior Problems.* Boston: Allyn and Bacon, 1975.

This book is special in that it presents approaches for teaching specific subjects such as reading, arithmetic, spelling, and writing.

HASLAM, ROBERT H. A., AND VALLETUTTI, PETER J. *Medical Problems in the Classroom: The Teacher's Role in Diagnosis and Management.* Baltimore: University Park Press, 1975.

The emphasis in this book is not primarily the treatment but the recognition of various physical, neurological, glandular, and drug-related problems which can impair learning.

HEWETT, FRANK M., WITH FORNESS, STEVEN R. *Education of Exceptional Learners.* Boston: Allyn and Bacon, 1974.

A detailed book discussing the origin, diagnosis, incidence, treatment, and special capacities and needs of exceptional learners including the emotionally disturbed, mentally retarded, socially and economically disadvantaged, physically handicapped, and gifted student.

SAFER, DANIEL J., AND ALLEN, RICHARD P. *Hyperactive Children: Diagnosis and Management.* Baltimore: University Park Press, 1975.

Includes diagnosis and modes of treating the hyperactive child including use of drugs and behavior mod and their relative success in school and family setting.

SCHRAG, PETER, AND DIVOKY, DIANE. *The Myth of the Hyperactive Child, and Other Means of Child Control.* New York: Random House, 1975.

The authors present real-life cases in support of their position that "hyperactive" and "learning disabled" are being attached wholesale to normal children, and argue against the quality of research supporting some practices to "cure" them, particularly in the form of medication and behavior mod programs. A painful reminder that behavior mod can be used destructively, more for the convenience of the system than for the good of the student.

Current research can be found in the following journals:

Exceptional Children
Journal of Special Education

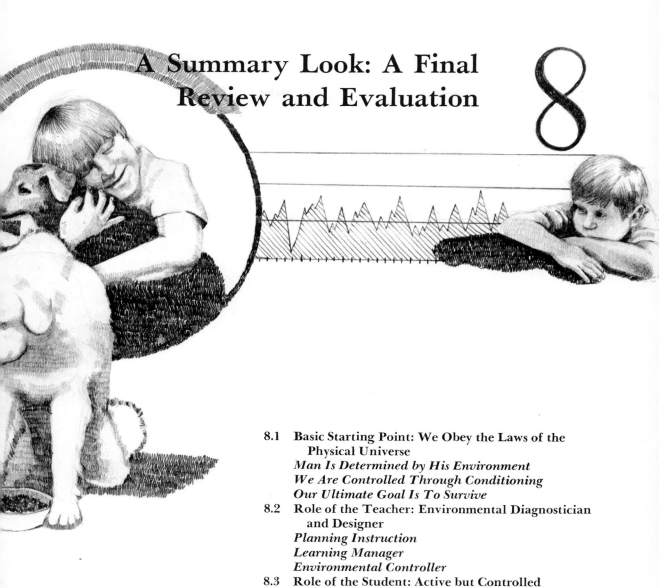

A Summary Look: A Final Review and Evaluation

8

Chapter Objectives

The purpose of this chapter is to take a final overall look at behaviorism in the field of education. Then you have the opportunity to take a final summary quiz covering material from all the previous chapters. A final item analysis has been set up as well so that you will be able to identify both your strong and weak points, and possibly reread those sections in which you have not achieved complete mastery. Before you take the summative quiz, there is a brief review of the major concepts we've dealt with throughout the book, looked at from the point of view of the roles of the teacher and the student.

BASIC STARTING POINT: WE OBEY THE LAWS OF THE PHYSICAL UNIVERSE

We have seen for the behaviorist that since man is part of the physical universe, his operations are similar to the operations of the rest of the material world, and he can be understood by applying many of the same principles that are applied to an understanding of that world. To study man, then, behaviorist psychology follows the same procedures physics uses to study, control, and predict the workings of the physical universe.

Man Is Determined by His Environment

We are controlled by the forces in the environment around us just as surely as the sailboat is moved by the wind in its sails, or as the clay is formed by the potter's hands. What behaviorism tries to do is to identify what forces in the world around us control our behavior, how they work, and how in turn, we can control our environments in order to control our own behavior.

We Are Controlled Through Conditioning

The forces in the environment that control us do so through the process of conditioning, which is either classical or operant. Classical conditioning controls respondent behavior which is behavior that is elicited at first automatically by a particular environmental stimulus, and through a process of repeated pairings, is finally elicited by a different and previously neutral environmental stimulus.

Operant conditioning is probably much more prevalent and controls much more of our behavior than classical conditioning. The forces in the environment that control operant behaviors are called "environmental contingencies," and they occur *after* the behavior that is controlled has already occurred. Obviously, contingencies do not control the behavior that has already occurred but they do determine whether the behavior will tend to occur again in the future. Behaviors that have been followed by a reinforcement tend to occur again. Behaviors followed by nonreinforcement do not tend to occur often again, and behavior followed by punishment is highly variable, sometimes disappearing permanently, sometimes temporarily, and sometimes simply changing so that the punishment is either avoided, terminated, or diminished.

Our Ultimate Goal Is To Survive

The kind of behavior that has the highest value of all for the behaviorist is behavior that increases the likelihood of our survival as a human species. That is why the ultimate goal of the school is to condition those behaviors that will make it possible for us to solve the problems that face us on this planet. Particularly, schools can do this by teaching people practical job skills, cooperative rather than competing behaviors, and by developing individuals capable of solving original problems who will use these skills for us all.

ROLE OF THE TEACHER: ENVIRONMENTAL DIAGNOSTICIAN AND DESIGNER

Education achieves its goals by designing environments that condition behaviors that are desired, and extinguish behaviors that are not desired. The design of an efficient, effective learning environment is the primary responsibility of the teacher, and it can be carried out only by extensive planning by teachers who understand how the environment controls the students in the classroom. The teacher is the learning manager, the environmental controller, the behavioral engineer who plans in detail the contingencies necessary to bring about learning behaviors.

Planning Instruction

Every aspect of behaviorism's implementation in education demands extensive, careful, and detailed planning. Behavioral goals and target selection require the teacher to specify clear, predetermined behavior objectives. Lesson plans must be organized so that material is taught in small, logically progressing units, and complemented by a continuous series of tests giving feedback and reinforcement that establishes learning. When goals have not been fully achieved, more observation and planning are required because, for the behaviorist, the mastery goals set up by the teacher are to be reached by everyone, not just by the brightest, or quickest, or apparently most motivated students. Because planning is so important, much of the teacher's most vital work is not carried out in the classroom, but in preparation.

Learning Manager

Programmed and individualized instructions may be available to assist teachers and we have seen that behaviorists support their use. Behaviorists also repeatedly emphasize that their system is not one in which the teacher is programmed for obsolescence. It is the teacher who must select programs to meet the particular needs of his students, and then must constantly monitor the effectiveness of the programs selected. The teacher is expected to direct students into areas of special interest, and to see that reinforcers provided by the program and used elsewhere in the classroom are working effectively.

Behaviorists have provided the basic research to guide the teacher, but it is still the teacher who must use her ingenuity and creativity to construct those specific conditions that will bring about learning in the individual student in her charge. Only the teacher can identify and dispense positive reinforcers that are uniquely effective with an individual student, who can pinpoint areas of individual difficulty, and so arrange specific conditions tailor-made for the individual's problems. Only the teacher can lead class discussions, counsel students, answer questions not directly related to the text, and above all, best serve as a behavioral model.

Environmental Controller

Because environmental conditions rather than individual abilities are seen as the primary cause for learning, the teacher is not excused from teaching the student whose record shows a low IQ, who has a motivation problem, or who has consistently failed to learn in the past. These problems can be overcome by and are even usually caused by the environment. The teacher's role is to diagnose and change the environment, not to diagnose or change the individual directly.

When a teacher using behaviorism wants to motivate a student, he applies behavior modification, a process of redirecting environmental contingencies that are controlling the behavior. It is not a question of giving, or *finding* the proper motivation as if it were some elusive and precious thing inside someone. The cause of the problem and its solution lie in the environment and so that is what must be changed. The environment is rearranged by manipulating reinforcement, punishment, and nonreinforcement, and by setting up the right schedules of reinforcement.

ROLE OF THE STUDENT: ACTIVE BUT CONTROLLED

Above all, the learning student in the behaviorist school is an *active* student. He is *doing* something.

Reinforced Doing

Since an individual can be reinforced only for behavior he actually performs, the student who is forced to sit silently doing nothing that anyone can observe cannot be reinforced for learning behaviors. If behavior is not reinforced, it will not increase. Therefore, the student who is not an active participant in the learning process, according to the behaviorists, does not learn anything.

The role of the student is one of activity. The educational system that wants to increase learning but lines students up in rigid silent rows of desks for hours at a time is in Behaviorist terms a contradiction. Students must be given every possible opportunity to emit learning behavior. He must be encouraged to act, to do, to attempt to solve problems, to give the right answer, and to test himself. Correct behaviors can then be strengthened through reinforcement, and incorrect learning extinguished through nonreinforcement.

Molded and Shaped

Although almost all educational theories call for high levels of student activity, the *kind* of activity recommended differs with different theories. In the behaviorist school, the activity of the student is deliberately and carefully controlled and guided.

Through prompts, the students are encouraged to emit one kind of behavior rather than another. Through the carefully sequenced material, his activity is logically directed by the program to previously determined objectives. In this sense, the active student is also a molded student, and it is the responsibility of the educator to mold that behavior in a manner required by and for the human community.

Students do not become the kind of people they are as a result of sterling characters, or base selfishness, or intrinsic wretchedness. People do not obey the law or even perform apparently generous or heroic behavior because they are in some way intrinsically superior, nor do they disobey it because they are intrinsically bad. People do what they do because of conditioning. Diagnoses such as "Martha is an intellectual coward," or "Joey is a spoiled brat," which try to explain a problem as a result of intrinsic qualities retard the discovery of those factors in the environment that are really molding that behavior. Students are individual, they are different from each other, but they are different far more because of their environments than because of original genetic differences.

A SUMMARY SUMMARY

This book has been written mostly for those of you who have wanted to understand how behaviorism can be used to guide and improve your teaching. By now, you should be able to begin to put into practice the use of behavioral goals, and individualized approaches to instruction. You should have an appreciation of the purpose and nature of criterion-referenced testing, and how to use it for both formative and summative evaluation. You should be able to see by now how behavior modification techniques are an application of the same principles of behaviorism applied to programmed instruction, and have some idea of how to use them creatively.

Lastly, you should understand that, although the role of the teacher within behaviorism is a controlling one, it is not a rigid one, one in which all the answers are already provided for you, because effective teaching on your part will demand much ingenuity, much energy, creativity, and a continuous and alert perception of exactly how your students are responding to the environments around them and how you can best change that environment to increase their learning. The task is clear but it is not easy or simple, and it can be accomplished only by the teacher who continues to experiment, observe, adjust, and respond to the everchanging individuals in the classroom.

Now, as a final evaluation of your learning behaviors in relation to all the areas of concern to you as a teacher covered in this book, here is a final, though short, summative quiz, and an item analysis that you can use to identify your own potential teaching strengths within the behaviorist perspective.

A Summative Evaluation

Directions: Circle the letter next to the answer which best completes each phrase or answers the question asked in each item.

1. Which of the following general educational goals reflects a non-behaviorist orientation?
   a. The development of individuals with secure, self-directed identities and strong egos.
   b. The development of behaviors which will contribute to a culture in which the human species can survive.
   c. To provide each student with requisite skills necessary to take advantage of job opportunities available in modern society.
   d. To encourage students to cooperate in finding solutions to their common problems.

2. A behaviorist would object to the teacher's hypothesis that a student's problem is "a need to be understood" because
   a. the student may really have a need to be loved rather than understood.
   b. evidence shows that athletic achievements are usually more important that being understood for most students today.
   c. "a need to be understood" is not a scientifically valid concept for the behaviorist.
   d. the teacher should not develop an hypothesis for which he has not yet provided evidence.

3. When you are designing your own instruction based on behaviorist principles, the text suggests that
   a. the first thing you should do is to assess entry behavior.
   b. you should not specify your behavioral goals until you have analyzed the learning task you want to teach.
   c. you should plan to provide cues, feedback, reinforcement, and self-pacing.
   d. you should eliminate testing as a means of motivating learning.
   e. all of the above are recommended by the text.

4. Which of the following ethical issues is shared by behavior modification programs whose goal is to modify the behavior of others *and* in a self-managed program carried out by a student with the cooperation and guidance of the teacher?

    a. Whether the student should participate in the target selection.

    b. Who should administer the internal contingencies.

    c. The question of the subject's right to privacy.

    d. Possible harmful side effects of some environmental manipulations.

5. Compared to nonreinforcement, punishment

    a. may have bad side effects.

    b. may be used to increase desired behavior.

    c. is sometimes necessary to terminate dangerous behavior immediately.

    d. has longer lasting effects.

6. A discrepancy between IQ and performance in a restricted area of the student's learning abilities usually characterizes the student who is

    a. retarded.

    b. learning disabled.

    c. gifted.

    d. emotionally disturbed.

7. After a test has been scored, it should be analyzed in order to

    a. find out what the student has learned.

    b. eliminate any test items that might be unclear, invalid, or unreliable.

    c. discover whether the teacher has provided poor instruction in any area.

    d. all of the above should be analyzed.

8. The essential components of a complete instructional objective are

    a. learning behavior, testing conditions, and success level.

    b. teaching, learning, and evaluating.

    c. knowledge, application, and evaluation.

    d. active student response, formative feedback, and summative evaluation.

9. All forms of behaviorist individualized instructions

    a. use positive reinforcement, self-pacing, and backward chaining.

    b. use a frame-by-frame approach.

    c. are based on principles of conditioning.

    d. eliminate the need for a teacher.

10. The behavior mod technique that uses internal events as manipulatable contingencies to change behavior is
   a. contingency contracting.
   b. self-management.
   c. modeling.
   d. aversive conditioning.

11. In Bloom's taxonomy, knowledge is the ability to
   a. receive what is being communicated and make effective use of it.
   b. use abstraction, rules, principles, ideas or methods in many different situations.
   c. remember, recall, or recognize ideas and facts.
   d. break down concepts into their component parts.

12. When Linda starts crying on her first day in kindergarten in order to get the attention of the teacher she is probably
   a. discriminating between home and school.
   b. discriminating between the teacher and her mother.
   c. generalizing between her home and school.
   d. generalizing between the teacher and other pupils.

13. Research has shown that students from lower income families often do better academically if
   a. they possess an internal locus of control.
   b. the discipline in their homes is not strict.
   c. they are expected to get a job at an early age.
   d. they can speak two languages.

14. In order to be fair, tests must be both reliable and valid, that is they should give results which are
   a. consistent, and which are legitimately related to the the behavioral goals.
   b. based on a large number of items.
   c. a result of both formative and summative evaluation.
   d. criterion-referenced.

15. A behaviorist educational psychology is based on the assumption that
   a. animal and human learning have nothing in common.
   b. animal and human learning are controlled by the inner decision mechanism of the learning oragnism.
   c. learning cannot be controlled by the teacher.
   d. learning is controlled by the environment of the learning organism.

16. The teacher of the exceptional student should

a. not expect anything unusual.

b. disregard different entry behaviors.

c. use predominantly covert reinforcers.

d. concentrate on student behavior rather than student labels.

17. To build up learning quickly and then maintain it at steady and high levels with few reinforcements the following reinforcement schedules should be used:

a. frequent fixed, then infrequent random.

b. frequent fixed, then frequent random.

c. infrequent random, then frequent fixed.

d. frequent random, then frequent fixed.

18. For the behaviorist, psychology is scientific if it

a. studies what can be observed.

b. assumes that man directs his own behavior.

c. is clearly differentiated from clinical psychology.

d. does not confine itself by the belief that man is determined.

19. Compared to negative reinforcers, positive reinforcers

a. increase instead of decrease behavior.

b. usually do not have the undesired side effects often accompanying negative reinforcers.

c. are almost always more difficult and time-consuming to administer than negative reinforcers.

d. cannot be administered repeatedly without danger of damaging the student.

20. One of the problems of using punishment as a means of controlling classroom behavior is that

a. punishment does not directly strengthen desired behavior.

b. it rarely works.

c. punishment works temporarily but never lasts.

d. punishment always interferes with learning.

21. The kind of test which can be used to test all levels of learning and can be most easily scored objectively is the

a. fill-in exam.

b. essay test.

c. multiple-choice format.

d. a true-false quiz.

22. The purpose of norm-referenced grading as opposed to criterion-referenced grading is to

a. encourage cooperation.

b. compare the individual to a fixed standard of learning.

c. provide both summative and formative evaluation.

d. compare the accomplishment of the individual to the average accomplishments of the group.

23. According to the text, which of the following statements provides the most effective guide for implementing your own behavior mod program?
    a. A baseline behavior should be measured before new contingencies are introduced to change it.
    b. The target selection for a behavior mod program is made most effectively after baselines and current contingencies are recorded.
    c. It is usually not necessary to measure baseline behavior for behavior to be decreased instead of increased.
    d. A behavior mod program should begin by using internal reinforcement contingencies on an infrequent schedule and gradually change to external reinforcement administered on a frequent schedule.

24. Frame-by-frame feedback is used as the principal reinforcer in
    a. learner-controlled instruction.
    b. PSI.
    c. mathetics.
    d. linear programmed instruction.

25. The purpose of using prompts in individualized instruction is to
    a. reinforce learning.
    b. assess the student's individual criterion level.
    c. insure that few mistakes are made during the learning process.
    d. decrease the possibility of negative reinforcement.

26. The last three types of learning in Gagne's hierarchy are
    a. signal, concept, and rule learning.
    b. concept learning, rule learning, and problem solving.
    c. discrimination, problem solving, and concept learning.
    d. rule learning, chaining, and problem solving.

27. For the most effective use of punishment in the classroom, it should be
    a. preceded by a verbal warning during which time the punishment may be avoided if the undesired behavior stops.
    b. delayed for as long as possible after the undesired behavior has begun.
    c. as severe as possible.
    d. as lenient as possible.

28. A test in a course on English grammer in which students are required to complete four mathematical proofs is probably
    a. unreliable.
    b. invalid.
    c. not objective.
    d. norm-referenced.

29. A teacher who is following the steps suggested by the text for designing his own lesson plan, and who has specified subtraction of single digits as his behavioral objective would then
    a. teach the first logical step in subtraction.
    b. begin by teaching to be sure all students know how to add.
    c. develop a norm-referenced test of subtraction behaviors.
    d. determine what steps each student has already learned in the subtraction process.

30. One of the difficulties of using programmed instruction is that
    a. the results rarely justify the expense.
    b. programs are helpful only to very bright students.
    c. it is difficult to obtain an adequate number of good programs.
    d.most students do not like them.

31. To increase a desired behavior, a teacher should at first make frequent use of
    a. external reinforcements.
    b. punishments.
    c. gifts of candy.
    d. time out.

32. If a student has reached the highest level of Bloom's taxonomy in relation to specific material he can
    a. evaluate it according to some specific criteria.
    b. restate it in his own words.
    c. apply it to a new situation.
    d. organize it into a coherent whole.

33. According to the behaviorists, learning may be defined as a process whereby an organism
    a. changes its behavior as a result of thinking.
    b. undergoes maturation.
    c. changes its behavior to receive few external reinforcements and increased internal reinforcements.
    d. responds reliably to contingencies in the environment.

34. The best way to get your student to do his homework each night would be to praise him for doing it
    a. every Friday afternoon before he leaves for the weekend.
    b. randomly.
    c. sparsely.
    d. very frequently.

35. According to the behaviorists, research indicates that punishment
    a. can be used to increase learning if applied effectively.
    b. inhibits hostility.

c. cannot change thinking.

d. often has undesired side effects.

36. The first step suggested by the text in a behavior modification program is to

    a. record date, time, and contingency of relevant behavior.

    b. select and specify the target behavior.

    c. select new cues and contingencies.

    d. record baseline behavior.

37. Which of the following goals is appropriately stated for a teacher's behavior mod program for changing a student's behavior?

    a. The student will feel more enthusiastic about reading.

    b. The other children will like this student better.

    c. This student will spend at least fifteen minutes each day playing with his peers.

    d. The student will do better in arithmetic.

38. The reason Gilbert designed mathetics as a teaching strategy was because

    a. mastery performance is a powerful reinforcer.

    b. he wanted to prove that Skinner's theory was wrong.

    c. Skinner's daughter was doing poorly in school.

    d. his dog was often hungry.

39. According to the behaviorists, programmed instruction is a good approach to teaching because it

    a. identifies the smarter students quickly.

    b. is very inexpensive.

    c. provides feedback so that wrong answers are not reinforced and right ones are.

    d. is norm-referenced.

40. One can use covert behavior in a behavior modification program in relation to

    a. the mentally retarded.

    b. children two or three years of age.

    c. close friends whom one knows well.

    d. oneself.

41. Everytime Johnny eats his spinach, his mother gives him dessert. This is an example of reinforcement on a

    a. fixed interval schedule.

    b. fixed random schedule.

    c. fixed ratio schedule.

    d. random ratio schedule.

42. The most perferred way for a teacher to increase learning, according to behaviorists, is by using
   a. negative reinforcement.
   b. positive reinforcement.
   c. either of the above.
   d. delayed threat of punishment.

43. According to behaviorists, learning is primarily a result of
   a. genetic predetermination.
   b. science.
   c. early childhood mothering.
   d. conditioning.

44. When using criterion-referenced tests, the most important factor in the learning process is
   a. measuring how long it takes each individual to reach the behavioral goal.
   b. that everyone is expected to reach the learning goal eventually.
   c. the length of time learning is retained.
   d. how the individual compares to the group.

45. A test is reliable if
   a. students do better the second time they take it.
   b. the material being tested matches the behavioral goal.
   c. results are comparable to other tests results of the same material.
   d. the grades indicate that all students have reached the behavioral goal.

46. In evaluating the ethics of using behavior modification in the classroom, which of the following considerations does the text suggest should be taken into account?
   a. The fact that it has not yet been proven effective.
   b. The problem of who should decide what behavior should be changed.
   c. The idea that behavior mod is always negative.
   d. The concern that behavior mod will make everyone equal.

47. The withdrawal of an apparently noxious stimulus after a person has made a response which subsequently increases in its occurrence is the definition of a
   a. positive reinforcement.
   b. negative reinforcement.
   c. nonreinforcement.
   d. punishment.

48. In order to extinguish behavior, it should be followed by a
   a. negative reinforcement.
   b. positive reinforcement.
   c. nonreinforcement.
   d. discriminative stimulus.

49. If you wanted to give your students a test to guide further teaching and provide feedback during the learning process, you should give a test that is
   a. summative.
   b. formative.
   c. cumulative.
   d. norm-referenced.

50. If, on two test items both testing knowledge of the same thing, nineteen out of twenty of your students got either both right or both wrong, you could probably conclude that the items were
   a. reliable.
   b. valid.
   c. instructional.
   d. formative.

51. One advantage of using multiple-choice tests instead of essay tests is that
   a. multiple-choice tests are easier to construct.
   b. essay tests are usually more time-consuming both to construct and to grade than multiple-choice tests.
   c. multiple-choice tests can be graded more objectively than essay tests.
   d. essay tests are difficult to use to measure overt behavior while multiple-choice tests are well adapted to this task.

52. Behaviorists believe that education should be based on a psychology which studies
   a. psychic development.
   b. cognition.
   c. love.
   d. behavior.

53. The behaviorists believe that the best way to change behavior is by first
   a. using punishment.
   b. changing the environment.
   c. changing how people feel.
   d. changing how people think.

54. A student's behavior change is a result of operant conditioning if he learns as a result of
   a. the consequences of his behavior.
   b. repeated CS–UCS pairings.
   c. desensitization.
   d. understanding.

55. To cue the behavior of his students effectively, a teacher should
   a. always cue behavior after it occurs and never before.
   b. never use punishment as a cue.
   c. use only nonverbal cues of impending consequences of behavior.
   d. make sure his cues are always reliable indicators of future consequences of behavior.

56. A teacher should use a shaping procedure in the classroom if
   a. punishment is ineffective.
   b. the desired goal behavior occurs infrequently.
   c. students tend to generalize rather than discriminate.
   d. he is using a random reinforcement schedule.

57. A behavioral objective describes
   a. learning but not creativity.
   b. a teacher's goal in terms of behavior.
   c. learning, thinking, and problem solving as mental processes.
   d. an environmental contingency which will lead to learning.

58. The part of an instructional objective that uses an action verb to describe what is to be learned is the
   a. criterion of success.
   b. specification of testing conditions.
   c. informational objective.
   d. learning hierarchy or taxonomy.

59. Among the advantages claimed by behaviorists of using behavioral objectives is that they
   a. are easier to formulate than nonbehavioral goals.
   b. possess flexibility lacking in nonbehavioral goals.
   c. reflect a cognitive understanding of the learning process.
   d. will increase clarity and communication.

60. According to Homme, a contingency contract should always include positive reinforcements which are
   a. frequently administered before behavior occurs as a sign of the teacher's trust in the students.
   b. administered frequently and immediately but only after behavior has actually occurred.
   c. either social and status reinforcers or activity reinforcers.
   d. contingent upon strict obedience to the teacher's rules.

61. The emotionally disturbed student is characterized specifically by

    a. severe retardation.
    b. adjustment problems in relation to social and other academic and nonacademic behaviors.
    c. a striking impatience with tasks requiring memorization.
    d. all of the above.

Directions: Place a check beside those statements which agree with statements made in the text.

_____62. Research indicates that in practice, use of behavioral objectives is not necessarily accompanied by increased student learning.

_____63. One difference between operant and classical conditioning is that the controlling event occurs after the response in operant conditioning.

_____64. The behaviorist position is that since physics deals with inert matter and psychology deals with living human organisms, the principles of a science of physics do not apply to a science of psychology.

_____65. There is research to support the position that some students learn well through programmed instruction and that some students learn better through other methods of instruction.

_____66. Skinner believes that the encouragement of effective cooperative behavior is one of education's primary goals in contemporary society.

_____67. On the whole, culturally different groups score lower on IQ tests than the average population.

Answers to Summative Evaluation

To make it easier to carry out the item analysis provided for you below, it is suggested that you place a check on this page next to the number of those items you answered correctly. Your right answers will then be easily available to use in the item analysis.

Item #	Correct Answer	Item #	Correct Answer	Item #	Correct Answer
1	a	24	d	47	b
2	c	25	c	48	c
3	c	26	b	49	b
4	d	27	a	50	a
5	c	28	b	51	c
6	b	29	d	52	c
7	d	30	c	53	b
8	a	31	a	54	a
9	c	32	a	55	d
10	b	33	d	56	b
11	c	34	d	57	b
12	c	35	d	58	c
13	a	36	b	59	d
14	a	37	c	60	b
15	d	38	a	61	b
16	d	39	c	62	check
17	a	40	d	63	check
18	a	41	c	64	no check
19	b	42	b	65	check
20	a	43	d	66	check
21	c	44	b	67	no check
22	d	45	c		
23	a	46	b		

Item Analysis of Summative Evaluation

Refer to your scores in the answer section above and place a check in the first column of the item analysis next to those items you answered correctly. Then indicate in the last column the total number of items in each chapter which you answered correctly.

Item #	Testing Unit	Total Number of Items	Totals Correct
2	1.1		
18	1.1		
52	1.1		
53	1.2		
64	1.2		
15	1.3		
43	1.3	In Chapter 1: 7	

Item #	Testing Unit:	Total Number of Items	Totals Correct
_____ 47	2.1		
_____ 54	2.1		
_____ 63	2.1		
_____ 19	2.2		
_____ 42	2.2		
_____ 20	2.3		
_____ 35	2.3		
_____ 5	2.4		
_____ 48	2.4		
_____ 17	2.5		
_____ 34	2.5		
_____ 41	2.5		
_____ 12	2.6		
_____ 55	2.6		
_____ 56	2.6	In Chapter 2: 15	_____

Item #	Testing Unit:	Total Number of Items	Totals Correct
_____ 1	3.1		
_____ 66	3.1		
_____ 33	3.2		
_____ 57	3.2		
_____ 26	3.3		
_____ 32	3.3		
_____ 8	3.4		
_____ 58	3.4		
_____ 59	3.5		
_____ 62	3.5	In Chapter 3: 10	_____

Item #	Testing Unit:	Total Number of Items	Totals Correct
_____ 9	4.1		
_____ 24	4.1		
_____ 25	4.1		
_____ 38	4.1		
_____ 30	4.2		
_____ 39	4.2		
_____ 65	4.2		
_____ 3	4.3		
_____ 29	4.3	In Chapter 4: 9	_____

Item #	Testing Unit:	Total Number of Items	Totals Correct
_____ 22	5.1		
_____ 44	5.1		
_____ 49	5.1		
_____ 21	5.2		
_____ 51	5.2		
_____ 14	5.3		
_____ 28	5.3		
_____ 45	5.3		
_____ 7	5.4		
_____ 50	5.4	In Chapter 5: 10	_____

Item #	Testing Unit:	Total Number of Items	Totals Correct
_____ 10	6.1		
_____ 27	6.1		
_____ 31	6.1		
_____ 40	6.1		
_____ 60	6.1		
_____ 4	6.2		
_____ 46	6.2		
_____ 23	6.3		
_____ 31	6.3		
_____ 36	6.3		
_____ 37	6.3	In Chapter 6: 11	_____

Item #	Testing Unit:	Total Number of Items	Totals Correct
_____ 13	7.1		
_____ 67	7.1		
_____ 6	7.2		
_____ 61	7.2		
_____ 16	7.3	In Chapter 7: 5	_____
		Final Total: 67	_____

You can now compare the total number of right answers you gave with the possible number of right answers in the column next to your total to determine how well you answered the items related to each chapter. If you missed more than two items in any chapter, you should reread the relevant learning unit. If you have passed the test, you have learned the basic principles of behaviorism applied to teaching.

REFERENCES

ABRAMSON, THEODORE, AND KAGEN, EDWARD. (1975) Familiarization of content and different response modes in programmed instruction. *Journal of Educational Psychology* 67(1): 83–88.

ANDERSON, R. C. (1967) Educational psychology. *Annual Review of Psychology* 18: 103–146.

ATKINS, J., AND WILLIAMS, R. L. (1972) The utility of self-report in determining reinforcement priorities of primary school children. *Journal of Educational Research* 65: 324–328.

ATKINSON, J. W.; BASTIAN, J. R.; EARLY, R. W.; AND LITWIN, G H. (1960) The achievement motive, goal setting and probability preferences. *Journal of Abnormal and Social Psychology* 60: 26–36.

———, AND O'CONNOR, PATRICIA. (1963) Effects of ability groups in schools related to individual differences in achievement-related motivation. Final report, Office of Education Cooperative Research Program, Project 1283. Available in microfilm from Photoduplication Center, Library of Congress, Washington, D.C.

ATKINSON, R. C. (1971). Computerized instruction and the learning process. In R. E. Ripple, ed, *Readings in learning and human abilities.* New York: Harper and Row, 2nd ed.

BANDURA, A. (1965) Behavioral modification through modeling procedures. In L. Krasner and L. Ullman, eds., *Research in behavior modification.* New York: Holt, Rinehart and Winston.

———; ROSS, D.; AND ROSS, S. (1963) A comparative test of the status envy, social power and secondary reinforcement theories of identificatory learning. *Journal of Abnormal and Social Psychology* 67: 527–534.

BAUERNFEIND, ROBERT H. (1965) 'Goal cards' and future developments in achievement testing. *Proceedings of the 1965 Invitational Conferences on Testing Problems.* University of Illinois.

BENEKE, W. M., AND HARRIS, M. B. (1972) Teaching self-control of study behavior. *Behaviour Research and Therapy* 10: 35–41.

BIGGE, MORRIS L. (1964) *Learning theories for teachers.* New York: Harper and Row.

BLOOM, B. S. (1971) Individual differences in school achievement: A vanishing point. *Education at Chicago* (Winter).

———; ENGELHART, M. B.; FURST, E. J.; HILL, W. H.; AND KRATHWOHL, D. R. (1956) *Taxonomy of educational objectives. The classification of educational goals. Handbook I: Cognitive domain.* New York: Longmans Green.

BORN, D. B. (1971) *Student withdrawals is personalized instruction courses.* Paper presented at the annual meeting of the Rocky Mountain Psychological Association, Denver, Colorado (May).

BRONOWSKI, J. (1964) *Insight.* New York: Harper and Row.

———. (1973) *The ascent of man.* Boston: Little, Brown.

Bugg, C. A. (1972) Systematic desensitization: A technique worth trying. *Personnel and Guidance Journal* 50: 823–828.

Bushell, D., Jr., and Brigham, T. A. (1971) Classroom token systems as technology. *Educational Technology* 11: 14–17.

Campbell, L. M., III (1973) A variation of thought-stopping in a twelve-year-old boy: a case report. *Behavior Therapy and Experimental Psychiatry* 4: 69–70.

Carlson, John G., and Minke, Karl A. (1975) Fixed and ascending criteria for unit mastery learning. *Journal of Educational Psychology* 67 (1): 96–101.

Carpenter, P. W., and Fillmer, H. T. (1965) A comparison of teaching machines and programmed text in teaching of algebra I. *Journal of Educational Research* 58: 218–221.

Clark, C. A., and Wallberg, H. J. (1968) The influence of massive rewards on reading achievement in potential urban school dropouts. *American Educational Research Journal* 5: 305–310.

———, and Wallberg, H. J. (1969) The effects of increased rewards on reading achievement and school attitudes of potential dropouts. In B. Feather and W. S. Olsen, eds., *Children, psychology and the schools*. Glenview, Ill.: Scott Foresman.

Cobb, J. A. (1972) Relationship of discrete classroom behavior to fourth-grade academic achievement. *Journal of Educational Psychology* 63: 74–80.

Coleman, J. S., et al. (1966) *Equality of educational opportunity*. Washington, D.C.: U.S. Government Printing Office.

Cooley, W. W., and Glaser, R. (1969) The computer and individualized instruction. *Science* 166: 574–582.

Cooper, J. M., ed. (1972) *Differentiated staffing*. Philadelphia: W. B. Saunders.

Covington, M. V.; Crutchfield, R. S.; Davies, L. B.; and Olton, R. M. (1974) *The productive thinking program*. Columbus, Ohio: Charles E. Merrill.

Cronbach, Lee J. (1971) Comments on mastery learning and its implications for curriculum development. In Elliot W. Eisner, ed., *Confronting Curriculum reform*. Boston: Little, Brown.

Crowder, N. A. (1963) On the differences between linear and instrinsic programming. *Phi Delta Kappan* 44: 250–254.

Dash, E. F. (1970) Contract for grades. *The Clearing House* 45: 231–235.

Davidson, H. H., and Greenberg, J. (1967) Traits of school achievers from a deprived background. (Cooperative Research Project No. 2805) Washington, D.C.: United States Office of Education.

———, and Lang, G. (1960) Children's perceptions of their teacher's feelings toward them related to self-perception, school achievement, and behavior. *Journal of Experimental Education* 29 (2): 107–118.

deCharms, R. (1968) *Personal causation: The internal affective determinants of behavior*. New York: Academic Press.

Dillard, J. L. (1972) Black English. *Time* (August), p. 46.

DuChastel, P. C., and Merrill, P. F. (1973) The effects of behavioral objectives on learning: A review of empirical studies. *Review of Educational Research* 43: 53–69.

DUELL, O K. (1974) Effect of type of objective, level of test questions, and the judged importance of tested materials upon posttest performance. *Journal of Educational Psychology* 66: 225–232.

DUNKIN, MICHAEL J., AND BIDDLE, BRUCE J. (1974) *The study of teaching.* New York: Holt, Rinehart and Winston.

EBEL, ROBERT L. (1971) Criterion-referenced measurements: Limitations. *School Review* (February) 79 (2): 282–288.

ETS Developments (1974) Field trials start for computer-based guidance systems. (Fall) vol. SSI, (4), pp. 3–4.

FELDMAN, DAVID H., AND SEARS, PAULINE S. (1970) Effects of computer-assisted instruction on children's behavior. *Educational Technology* 10 (3): 11–14.

FERSTER, C. B., AND SKINNER, B. V. (1957) *Schedules of reinforcement.* New York: Appleton-Century-Crofts.

FITZGERALD, H. T. (1962) Teaching machines: A demurer. *School Review* (Autumn) 70: 247–256.

FLANAGAN, J. C. (1971) The PLAN system for individualizing education. *Measurement in Education* 2 (2): 1–8.

FLETCHER, J. D., AND ATKINSON, R. C. (1972) Evaluation of the Stanford CAI Program in initial reading. *Journal of Educational Psychology* 63: 597–602.

FOX, L. (1972) Effecting the use of efficient study habits. *Journal of Mathematics* 1 (1): 75–86.

GAGNE, R. M. (1970) *The conditions of learning,* 2nd ed. New York: Holt, Rinehart and Winston.

GILBERT, T. F. (1962) Mathetics: The technology of education. *Journal of Mathetics* 1: 7–73.

GLASER, R., AND TABER, J. I. (1961) *Investigations of the characteristics of programmed learning sequences.* Pittsburgh, Pa.: Programmed Learning Laboratory.

———, AND NITKO, A. J. (1971) Measurement in learning and instruction. In R. L. Thorndike, ed., *Educational measurement,* 2nd ed. Washington, D.C.: American Council of Education.

GOLDIAMOND, I. (1965) Self-control procedures in personal behavior problems. *Psychological Reports* 17: 851–868.

HILGARD, E. R., AND BOWER, G. H. (1966) *Theories of learning,* 3rd ed. New York: Appleton-Century-Crofts.

HILTS, PHILIP J. (1974) *Behavior mod.* New York: Harper and Row.

HOMME, L. D. (1965) Control of coverants, the operants of the mind. Perspectives in psychology, XX V. *Psychological Record* 15: 501–511.

———. (1966) Human motivation and environment. *Kansas Studies in Education* 16: 30–39.

———; CASANYI, A. P.; GONZALRE, M. A.; AND RECHS, J. R. (1970) *How to use contingency contracting in the classroom.* Champaign, Ill.: Research Press.

———, AND TOTSI, D. T. (1971) *Behavior technology.* San Rafael, Calif.: Individual Learning Systems, Inc.

ISAACS, WAYNE; THOMAS, JAMES; AND GOLDIAMOND, ISRAEL. (1960) Application of operant conditioning to reinstate verbal behavior in psychotics. *Journal of Speech and Hearing Disorders* 25: 8–12.

JOHNSON, W. G. (1971) Some applications of Homme's coverant control therapy: two case reports. *Behavior Therapy* 2: 240–248.

JOHNSTON, J. M., AND PENNYPACKER, H. S. (1971) A behavioral approach to teaching. *American Psychologist* 26: 219–244.

KELLER, F. S. (1967) Neglected rewards in the educational process. *Proceedings of the 23rd American Conference of Academic Deans,* pp. 9–22.

———. (1968) Good-bye teacher! *Journal of Applied Behavioral Analysis* 1: 79–84.

KINKADE, KATHLEEN. (1973) *A walden two experiment.* New York: William Morrow.

KLAUSMEIER, H. J.; MORROW, R.; AND WALTER, J. E. (1968) *Individually guided education in the multiunit elementary school: Guidelines for implementation.* Madison, Wisconsin: Wisconsin Research and Development Center for Cognitive Learning.

KRESS, G. C., JR. (1966) *The effects of pacing on programmed learning under several administrative conditions.* Pittsburgh: American Institute for Research.

KRUMBOLTZ, J. D. (1964) The nature and importance of the required response in programmed instruction. *American Educational Research Journal* 1: 203–209.

LAHADERNE, H. M. (1968) Attitudinal and intellectual correlates of attention: A study of four sixth-grade classrooms. *Journal of Educational Psychology* 59: 320–324.

LAZARUS, ARNOLD A., AND ABRAMOVITZ, ARNOLD. (1962) The use of "emotive imagery" in the treatment of children's phobias. *Journal of Mental Science* 108: 191–195.

LEVINE, D. U. (1971) The culturally different in the institutional setting of the school. *The High School Journal* 54: 368–380.

LUBIN, S. C. (1965) Reinforcement schedules, scholastic aptitude, autonomy need, and achievement in a programmed course. *Journal of Educational Psychology* 56: 295–302.

MAGER, R. F. (1962) *Preparing instructional objectives.* Palo Alto: Fearon Publishers.

———, AND McCANN, J. (1961) *Learner-controlled instruction.* Palo Alto: Varian Associates.

MARKLE, S. M., AND TIEMANN, P. W. (1969) *Really understanding concepts: Or in frumious pursuit of the jabberwock.* Champaign, Ill.: Stipes.

MASLOW, A. H. (1971) *The farther reaches of human nature.* New York: Viking Press.

McKINNEY, JAMES D.; MASON, JEANNE; PERKERSON, KATHI; AND CLIFFORD, MIRIAM. (1975) Relationship between classroom behavior and academic achievement. *Journal of Educational Psychology* 67 (2): 198–203.

McCLELLAND, D. C. (1961) *The achieving society.* Princeton: Van Nostrand.

MEYER, SUSAN R. (1960) A test of the principles of "activity," "immediate reinforcement," and "guidance" as instrumented by Skinner's teaching machine. Ph.D. dissertation, University of Buffalo.

MILES, D. T., AND ROBINSON, R. E. (1971) Behavioral objectives: An even closer look. *Educational Technology* 11: 39–44.

MILGRAM, STANLEY. (1963) A behavioral study of obedience. *Journal of Abnormal and Social Psychology* 67: 371–378.

MILLER, G. W. (1970) Factors in school achievement and social class. *Journal of Educational Psychology* 61 (4): 260–269.

MINKE, K. A., AND CARLSON, J. G. (1972) *Psychology and life unit mastery system instructor's guide.* Glenview, Ill.: Scott, Foresman.

MYERS, K. R. (1972) The self-concept of students in individually prescribed instruction. Paper presented at the meetings of the American Educational Research Association, Chicago, April 3–7.

NAUMANN, T. F. (1965) A laboratory experience in programmed learning for students in educational psychology. *Journal of Programmed Instruction* (March): 9–18.

NOTZ, WILLIAM W. (1975) Work motivation and the negative effects of extrinsic rewards: A review with implications for theory and practice. *American Psychologist* 30 (9): 884–891.

NURNBERGER, J. I. AND ZIMMERMAN, J. (1970) Applied analysis of human behaviors: An alternative to conventional motivational inferences and unconscious determination in therapeutic programming. *Behavior Therapy* 1: 59–69.

OETTINGER, A. G., AND MARKS, SEMA (1969) *Run, computer, run.* Cambridge, Mass.: Harvard University Press.

OLTON, R. M., AND CRUTCHFIELD, R. S. (1969) Developing the skills of productive thinking. In P. Mussen; J Langer; and M. V. Covington, eds., *Trends and Issues in Developmental Psychology.* New York: Holt, Rinehart and Winston.

PAGE, E. B. (1958) Teacher comments and student performance: A seventy-four classroom experiment in school motivation. *Journal of Educational Psychology* 49: 173–181.

PAVLOV, I. P. (1927) *Conditioned reflexes.* London: Oxford University Press.

PEGNATO, C. W., AND BIRCH, J. W. (1959) Locating gifted children in junior high school. *Exceptional Children* 25: 300–304.

POPHAM, W. JAMES (1970) Probing the validity of arguments against behavioral goals. In R. J. Kibler; D. J. Cegala; D. T. Miles; and L. L. Barker, *Behavioral Objectives and Instruction.* Boston: Allyn and Bacon.

———. (1971) Teaching skill under scrutiny? *Phi Delta Kappan* 52: 599–601.

———, AND HUSEK, T. R. (1969) Implications of criterion-referenced measurement. *Journal of Educational Measurement* 6 :1–9.

PREMACK, DAVID (1965) Reinforcement theory. In David Levine, ed., *Nebraska symposium on motivation.* vol. 13. Lincoln: University of Nebraska Press.

RAGOSTA, MARJORIE; SOAR, R. S.; RUTH M.; AND STEBBINS, LINDA B. (1971) Sign versus category: Two instruments for observing level of thinking. Paper presented at the annual meeting of the American Educational Research Association, New York.

RAPPAPORT, A. F., AND HARRELL, J. (1972) A behavioral-exchange model for marital counseling. *Family Coordinator*. (April): 203–212.

RODERICK, M., AND ANDERSON, R. C. (1968) Programmed instruction to psychology versus text-book style summary of the same lesson. *Journal of Educational Psychology* 59: 381–387.

ROGERS, CARL R. (1969) *Freedom to learn*. Columbus, Ohio: Charles E. Merrill.

ROGERS, VIRGINIA M., AND DAVIS, O. L., JR. (1970) Varying the cognitive levels of classroom questions: An analysis of student teachers' questions and pupil achievement in elementary social studies. Paper presented at the annual meeting of the American Educational Research Association, Minneapolis.

ROSEKRANS, M. (1967) Imitation in children as a function of perceived similarity to a social model and vicarious reinforcement. *Journal of Personality and Social Psychology* 5: 424–431.

ROSENTHAL, R., AND JACOBSON, L. (1968) *Pygmalion in the classroom: Teacher expectation and pupils' intellectual development*. New York: Holt, Rinehart and Winston.

ROTH, R. H. (1963) Student reactions to programmed learning: A study in ambiguity. *Phi Delta Kappan* (March): 278–281.

ROTHKOPF, E. Z., AND BISBICOS, E. E. (1967) Selective facilitative effects of interspersed questions on learning from written materials. *Journal of Educational Psychology* 58: 56–61.

ROTTER, J.; SEEMAN, J.; AND LIVERANT, S. (1962) Internal versus external control of reinforcement: A major variable in behavior theory. In N. F. Washburne, ed., *Decisions, Values, and Groups*. vol. 2. London: Pergamon Press.

RUBOVITS, P. C., AND MAEHR, M. L. (1971) Pygmalion analyzed: Toward and explanation of the Rosenthal-Jacobson findings. *Journal of Personality and Social Psychology* 19: 197–203.

RYAN, BRUCE A. (1974) *PSI Keller's personalized system of instruction: An appraisal*. Washington, D.C.: American Psychological Association.

SAMUELS, S. J., AND TURNURE, J. E. (1974) Attention and reading achievement in first-grade boys and girls. *Journal of Educational Psychology* 66: 29–32.

SCANLON, ROBERT; WEINBERGER, JOANN; AND WEILER, JAMES. (1970) IPI as a functioning model for the individualization of instruction. In C. M. Lindvall and R. C. Cox with collaboration of J. O. Bolvin *Evaluation of a tool in curriculum development: The IPI evaluation program*. AERA Monograph Series on *Curriculum Evaluation*, no. 5. Chicago: Rand McNally.

SCHRAG, PETER, AND DIVOKY, DIANE. (1975) *The myth of the hyperactive child*. New York: Random House.

SCHRAMM, W. (1964) *The research on programmed instruction: An annotated bibliography*. Washington, D.C.; United States Government Printing Office.

SKINNER, B. F. (1938) *The behavior of organisms*. New York: Appleton-Century-Crofts.

———. (1948) *Walden two*. New York: Macmillan.

————. (1953) *Science and human behavior.* New York: Macmillan.

————. (1954) The science of learning and the art of teaching. *Harvard Educational Review* 24: 86–97.

————. (1958) Reinforcement today. *American Psychologist,* 13: 94–99.

————. (1968) *The technology of teaching.* New York: Appleton-Century-Crofts.

————. (1971) *Beyond freedom and dignity.* New York: Knopf.

————. (1974) *About behaviorism.* New York: Knopf.

SOBELL, M. B., AND SOBELL, L. C. (1973) Individualized behavior therapy for alcoholics. *Behavior Therapy* 4: 49–72.

SOLOMON, RICHARD L. (1964) Punishment. *American Psychologist* 19: 239–253.

STAKE, R. (1970) Comments on Professor Glaser's paper. In M. C. Wittrock, and D. E. Wiley, eds., *The evaluation of instruction: Issues and Problems.* New York: Holt, Rinehart and Winston.

STOLUROW, L. M. (1962) Implication of current research and future trends. *Journal of Educational Research* 55: 519–527.

STURGES, PERSIS T., AND CRAWFORD, JACK J. (1964) *The relative effectiveness of immediate and delayed reinforcement on learning academic material.* Olympia: Washington State Department of Education.

THORESEN, C. E., AND MAHONEY, M. J. (1974) *Behavioral self-control.* New York: Holt, Rinehart and Winston.

THORNDIKE, E. L. (1911) *Animal intelligence: Experimental studies.* New York: Macmillan.

TOBIAS, S. (1973) A review of the response mode issue. *Review of Educational Research* 43: 193–204.

UPPER, D., AND MEREDITH, L. (1970) A stimulus-control approach to the modification of smoking behavior. *Proceedings of the 78th American Psychological Association Convention* 5: 739–740. Washington, D.C.: American Psychlogical Association.

VINSONHALER, J. F., AND BASS, R. K. (1972) A summary of ten major studies on CAI drill and practice. *Educational Technology* 12: 29–32.

WATSON, J. B. (1930) *Behaviorism,* rev. ed. New York: Norton.

————, AND RAYNOR, R. (1920) Conditioned emotional reactions. *Journal of Experimental Psychology,* 3: 1–14.

WOLPE, J., AND RACHMAN, S. (1960) Psychoanalytic evidence: A critique based on Freud's case of little Hans. *Journal of Nervous and Mental Diseases* 31: 134–147.

ZIGLER, E., AND deLABRY, J. (1962) Concept-switching in middle-class, lower-class, and retarded children. *Journal of Abnormal and Social Psychology* 65: 267–273.

————, AND KANZER, P. (1962) The effectiveness of two classes of verbal reinforcers on the performance of middle- and lower-class children. *Journal of Personality* 3: 157–163.

ZIMMERMAN, ELAINE H., AND ZIMMERMAN, JOSEPH. (1962) The alteration of behavior in a special classroom situation. *Journal of Experimental Analysis of Behavior* 5: 59–60.

Answers
to
Progress Checks

CHAPTER 1

Progress Check 1.1

The following words should be underlined as referring to unobservable rather than observable behavior:

1. inherently destructive (Inherent destructiveness cannot be observed. It looks exactly like destructive behavior that is learned. This is no real explanation or even description of behavior for a behaviorist.)

2. understand (Understanding refers to something supposely going on inside Alfred. All the teacher actually observes is that Alfred carved his initials in the desk, which may have actually increased its property value from Alfred's point of view. In addition, the teacher has not observed how Alfred might respond to other property such as a new car, clothes, or a new drum which he might treat very well.)

3. no words underlined (This explanation refers to observable behavior and so can be tested: Does Susan smile at the carving? Is there very little important reaction to students' papers?)

4. self-expression; deep inner need for love (This explanation uses feelings and needs inside a person that cannot be directly observed

and that, according to the behaviorists, are not the causes of behavior.)

5. no words underlined (Like #3, this explanation can be tested because it refers to observable behaviors. It is possible to observe when a boy is praised and derided on the playground, which boys are included in the group, and which are left out.)

Progress Check 1.2

1. A. Environmental factors of parental attention and praise are given as causes of Francine's hard work.

2. U. Free choice is assumed to be the cause of studying, and since this is inside the person it is not acceptable as a direct cause.

3. U. Unconscious impulses inside Jonathan are identified as the cause of troublemaking. This is unacceptable to the behaviorist for the same reasons that free choice is rejected.

4. U. Self-expression and "the real Barbara" are not environmental causes and so are not acceptable in behaviorism.

5. A. Class snickering, a factor in the environment, is hypothesized as the cause of Harry's behavior.

Progress Check 1.3

1. no check. The behaviorist view is that all of man's behavior including speaking and thinking behaviors follow essentially the same rules as that of all other animals.

2. no check. The behaviorists believe that although the behavior of animals lower than humans on the phylogenetic scale may be simpler, it is controlled by essentially the same but more complexly operating principles.

3. no check. According to the behaviorists, man's "mind" is not a scientific concept as such and it does not make him essentially different from other animals. The concept of mind is supported by Bronowski, not Skinner.

4. check. The behaviorist position is that we can learn a great deal about the laws of human behavior from lower animals because of the great number of similarities among all living organisms.

5. check. The behaviorists believe that underlying the variety of the physical universe is the atom, and underlying the variety of different behaviors is conditioning.

CHAPTER 2

Progress Check 2.1

1. unconditioned response
2. classical conditioning
3. unconditioned stimulus
4. conditioned response
5. operant conditioning
6. operant
7. positive reinforcer
8. positive reinforcer
9. operant conditioning
10. negative reinforcer

Progress Check 2.2

Answers expressing any two of the following ideas may be used to answer 1:

a. can be used more easily to strengthen only the specific desired behavior and no other.

b. could continue to be administered repeatedly no matter how many problems are completed by each student.

c. are more apt to produce positive rather than negative side effects.

Answers expressing any two of the following ideas may be used to answer 2:

a. could strengthen any escape behavior (not coming to school and sitting in any desk at all).

b. could not be indefinitely repeated to students who accomplished more than twenty problems without reinstating the noxious stimulant of two S's.

c. could have undesirable side effects, such as students' increased dislike of school and arithmetic in particular.

Progress Check 2.3

1. no check. Although punishment often does not terminate the specific behavior the punisher may have wanted to terminate, punishment often has strong and long-lasting effects.

2. check. Research has shown that punished behavior often re-emerges when the punishment or its threat is removed.

3. check. Escape behavior is often highly resistent to extinction for long periods of time.

4. check. Side effects include aggression, hostility, and lack of cooperation.

5. no check. Punishment can be used to decrease some behavior, either temporarily or permanently, but does not actually strengthen behavior directly.

Progress Check 2.4

1. a; 2. 1; 3. c; 4. 3; 5. a; 6. 1; 7. d; 8. 2; 9. a; 10. 1; 11. b; 12. 1.

Progress Check 2.5

Example A. infrequent random ratio schedule
Example B. frequent fixed ratio schedule
Example C. fixed interval schedule
Example D. frequent fixed ratio schedule

Progress Check 2.6

1. F (Since Mr. Perles is cueing his class that it is different from Mr. Allen's, he is hoping to teach the students to discriminate between the two classes.)
2. T
3. T
4. F (Mrs. Appleby was not effective because her cues, which threatened punishment, were not reliable indicators of what actually occurred when the students were not quiet.)
5. T
6. F (Since Lucy had pronounced the two words as if they were similar she had inappropriately generalized.)
7. T
8. T
9. F (The reinforcement Miss Richards promised was popcorn.)
10. T (Since popcorn was the reinforcer, students who did not like popcorn would not be reinforced for being quiet.)

CHAPTER 3

Progress Check 3.1

1. no check. Terms such as spiritual transcendence are so nonbehavioral that they can hardly be considered a statement of behaviorist goals.
2. check. Skinner (1953) says that "education is the establishing of behavior which will be of advantage to the individual and to others at some future time."
3. no check. Like self-actualization, "the discovery of identity" is too nonbehavioral to be a behaviorist goal as such.
4. check. Achieving the positive benefits of life would be an expression of freeing oneself from aversive control; sharing these with others is an expression of the second and third kinds of survival behavior.
5. check. A good job is one of the first ways of achieving freedom from aversive control.
6. no check. This goal, offered by Maslow (1971), is not behavioral although it may sound quite lovely.

Progress Check 3.2

1. b; 2. c; 3. b; 4. b.

Progress Check 3.3

For answers to Part I, see Inserts 3.3 and 3.4, and review the text beginning with "Levels of Learning Goals."

Progress Check 3.4

1. a; 2. d; 3. c; 4. a; 5. c; 6. b; 7. d.

If you have answered the questions in this progress check, why don't you try your hand at designing a series of informational goals of your own using Bloom's taxonomy in a field of your choice? Omit the testing and criterion components for the time being since we will be talking about evaluation procedures again in chapter 5.

Overall Educational Goal: _____

Behaviors to be acquired and their products:

1. Knowledge: _____

2. Comprehension: _____

3. Application: _____

4. Analysis: _____

5. Synthesis: _____

6. Evaluation: _____

Progress Check 3.5

The following list includes possible advantages and disadvantages mentioned in the text. You may, however, have listed ideas not covered, and if they are valid, indicate a higher level of learning than the comprehension level asked for here.

A. *Possible Advantages*

1. Behavioral goals can be understood more clearly than nonbehavioral goals.

2. The increased clarity of behavioral goals increases the probability they will be achieved.

3. Behavioral goals make communication of what is to be or has been learned less ambiguous.

4. The improved communication made possible by behavioral goals improves the student's motivation for learning.

5. Behavioral goals make precise measurement of learning possible.

6. Precise measurement of behavioral goals makes it possible to evaluate teachers, teaching techniques, and student learning more objectively.

7. Behavioral goals decrease the trivia taught in the classroom by making it explicit.

B. *Possible Disadvantages*

1. Behavioral goals are based on behaviorist definitions of learning which nonbehaviorists reject as an adequate definition of human learning.

2. Behavioral goals limit what is taught to narrow behavioral specifications.

3. Behavioral goals assume that learning is manifested only in behavior specified by the teacher, while it may be manifested in many other ways ignored by the teacher.

4. Behavioral goals lower the aspirations of teachers and students by focusing on lower levels of learning that can be easily specified.

5. Behavioral goals assume that all learning is manifested in overt behavior, while many important values or feelings may not be directly observable by the teacher.

6. Behavioral goals may actually formalize and increase the trivia taught in the classroom.

CHAPTER 4

Progress Check 4.1

1. mathetics

2. linear programmed instruction

3. The Personalized System of Instruction, PSL, or the Keller Plan

4. CAI or computer-assisted instruction

5–6. linear programs; branching programs

7. mathetics

8. learner-controlled instruction

9–12. Answers which express any four of the following ideas are acceptable: are based on principles of operant conditioning; use positive reinforcement to increase learning; provide for self-pacing; define learning in observable or behavioral terms; divide material to be learned into small units; provide continuous feedback; demand active and continuous responses from the learner.

13. branching

14. CAI or the computer

15. linear programs

16. PSI or the Keller Plan

17. branching programs

Progress Check 4.2

1. no check   (Research has shown that programmed instruction often works very well but we do not know that it is always necessarily better than any other method.)

2. check   (Many students are motivated to learn through programmed instruction when they have been turned off to learning in other educational settings.)

3. no check   (One of the practical limitatitons of programmed instruction is that only a few programs have been developed explicitly to teach problem-solving skills.)

4. check   (Many see this as one of the major benefits of programmed instruction, especially for students who have little access to the teacher in large classes, who are made anxious by the teacher, or who have little confidence in the teacher.)

5. check   (Many feel that the reduction of personal interaction between teacher and students during learning is a great loss to education.)

6. no check   (Some students lag behind more when self-pacing is permitted than when it is limited.)

7. check   (Feedback is a pervasive feature of programmed instruction but some students learn better without it, and some are even confused by it.)

8. no check   (Some students, usually a minority, do not like programmed instruction and much prefer other methods of instruction.)

9. no check   (There are many programs on the market today but it is often a problem to find programs that meet the needs of individual students.)

10. check   (Skinner suggests that it should be 5–10 percent but there is insufficient research to test this hypothesis.)

11. no check   (There is much we do not know yet that is important.)

12. check   (Opponents of behavioral goals question whether they include most important aspects of learning on a human level.)

13. check   (Opponents suggest that programmed instruction is individualized only in terms of the time a student is given to complete the program.)

14. check   (If one is sufficiently convinced of one's position, there will probably always be a way to explain research findings so that a final conclusion is not ever totally provable.)

Progress Check 4.3

You should have listed five steps in the following order:

1. specify behavioral goals;   2. analyze the learning task;   3. assess entry behavior;   4. presentation: provide cues, feedback, reinforcement, and self-pacing;   5. evaluate, record, and adjust.

The characteristics belong to the following steps:

a. 1 (behavioral goals)

b. 4 (presentation)

c. 5 (evaluation)

d. 4 (presentation)

e. 1 (behavioral goals)

f. 2 (task analysis)

g. 2 (task analysis)

h. 3 (entry behavior)

i. 4 (presentation)

j. 1 (behavioral goals)

k. 5 (evaluation)

l. 4 (presentation)

If you have done well on this progress check, why not select one of the behavioral goals you designed after progress check 3.4 in chapter 3 and try to design a lesson plan for it. The following outline is included as a guide, though you may not fill all the spaces in order. Since we will not discuss evaluation until the next chapter, it is suggested that you leave * items blank for the time being.

1. Behavioral Goal:

a. _____
   behavior to be acquired and its product

b.* _____
   testing conditions

c.* _____
   success level

2. Task Analysis: Succeeding behavioral skills in order of acquisition:

a. _____

b. _____

c. _____

d. _____

e. _____

3. Entry Behavior

a. prerequisite behaviors to be tested:

   i. _____

   ii. _____

   iii. _____

   iv. _____

b. intermediate subskills to be tested:

   i. _____

   ii. _____

   iii. _____

   iv. _____

   v. _____

c. final terminal behavior to be tested:

   i. _____

   ii. _____

4. Presentation

a. cues:

   i. _____
      statement of goals to be made to students

   ii. _____
      reinforcer contingent on learning achievements to be announced

   iii. _____
      other cues to be given students

b. feedback:

   i. _____
      method(s) including tests and informal questions of providing feedback during lesson

   ii. questions to be asked after each subunit in task analysis:

      a. _____

      b. _____

      c. _____

      d. _____

      e. _____

c. arrangements made for self-pacing:

   i. _____

   ii. _____

5. Evaluation*

CHAPTER 5

Progress Check 5.1

1. N   (Criterion-referenced grading assumes that with sufficient time and practice, all students can reach the goal.)

2. C   (This statement is not based on comparing students with each other, but the goal of testing is simply to see who has mastered the goal.)

3. C (Again, this statement is not comparing the speed with which different students learn long division but is based on the assumption that all students can and will eventually reach the goal.)

4. N (This statement is norm-referenced because the teacher is assuming that, for better or worse, a certain number of students should pass with high marks, and the lowest 10 percent, no matter how much they have learned, must fail.)

5. N (Norm-referenced because Miss Periwinkle's students have been compared to the national average, rather than to an absolute criterion.)

6. C (Any student who reaches the final criterion, whether it be few or many, will receive an *A*; there is no predetermined number of students who should receive an *A*.)

Progress Check 5.2

Violation	In Item	Violates Rule That
1	a	Negatives should not usually be used. Poor stem.
2	a	The stem should indicate a meaningful problem. (Both violations can be eliminated by changing stem to read "Norm-referenced evaluation is" and the answer to "based on the normal curve.")
3	b	Negatives should not usually be used. (Can be improved by changing stem to ". . . does accurately describe a norm-referenced test?")
4	b	The right answer should be the same length as the foils. (Can be improved by eliminating phrase "showing whether . . . group average" in b.)
5	d	All foils should agree grammatically with the stem. (Can be improved by changing "are" to "is" in c.)
6	d	Right answers should be same length as the foils. (Can be improved by shortening the correct answer, b, or lengthening the foils, a, c, and d.)
7	c	There should be only one right answer in each item. (The problem arises because evaluation takes place before, during, and after instruction; the item can be improved by making the purpose of evaluation explicit.)
8	f	All foils should be plausible answers. (Can be improved by writing a more plausible foil for d.)
9	a-f	All the correct answers should not be put in the first or second position. (Can be improved by putting half the right answers in c and d positions.)
10	g	Essay tests should have **the names of students** where they will not be seen during grading. (Can be improved by directing students to put their names on the back of each answer sheet.)
11	h	There should be only one right answer to com-

plete each fill-in space. (Can be improved by specifying whether a date, a name, or a series of events should be filled in, e.g. "by the man _____".)

| 12 | i | Items in true-false tests should not be ambiguous. (Can be improved by eliminating ambiguity, e.g. "According to the behaviorists, the only point in the instructional process where evaluation should occur is after the lesson.") |

Did you notice that the first six items of this quiz tested the six levels of Bloom's taxonomy? If you did well on this test, you are now ready to try to compose test items yourself. Why not leaf back to the six behavioral goals you developed in relation to Bloom's taxonomy in chapter 3 and construct a multiple choice item for each level?

1. Knowledge:

Stem: _____

a. _____

b. _____

c. _____

d. _____

2. Comprehension:

Stem: _____

a. _____

b. _____

c. _____

d. _____

3. Application:

Stem: _____

a. _____

b. _____

c. _____

d. _____

4. Analysis:

Stem: _____

a. _____

b. _____

c. _____

d. _____

5. Synthesis:

Stem: _____

a. _____

b. _____

c. _____

d. _____

6. Evaluation:

Stem: _____

a. _____

b. _____

c. _____

d. _____

Progress Check 5.3

1. Reliable because retesting would consistently yield comparable results. Invalid because number of books signed out of the library is not a good measure of information actually learned about history.
2. Reliable because repeated tests would continue to rank all students in the same order.

Invalid because weight gain is not a legitimate test of physical fitness in normal healthy children.

3. Unreliable because retesting on another day when students are not ill or tired would probably yield different results. Since the test is unreliable, it is necessarily invalid, but if it were to be given under reliable conditions, would probably be valid since the 100-item test of multiplication problems is legitimately connected with the presumed instructional goal of teaching students how to multiply.

4. Reliable since results probably would remain relatively stable on retesting. They are invalid insofar as what was taught should be connected with the instructional goal, and with what was tested, and in this instance, what was taught and tested were different material.

5. Reliable, since many different ways of testing the learning of geography were used. Valid because the assignments seem to be accurate reflections of the geography learning goals.

Progress Check 5.4

1. d (see step 5)	**5.** d (see step 1)
2. b (see step 3)	**6.** a (see step 6)
3. b (see step 4)	**7.** c (see step 6)
4. a (see step 2)	**8.** c (see step 6)

CHAPTER 6

Progress Check 6.1

1. e; **2.** c; **3.** b; **4.** b; **5.** d; **6.** c.

Progress Check 6.2

You may have listed some of the following objections:

1. The choice of the behavior change fits the teacher's values that social play is desirable but may not be in the student's best interest. Cindy may have a singular ability to concentrate in self-reinforced work which the behavior mod program may be destroying. The use of extrinsic positive reinforcers may deprive Cindy of her appreciation of the intrinsic rewards of scholastic work. The behavioral goal was chosen by the teacher, and apparently imposed on the student without her consent.

2. The desensitization of a deeply-rooted resistence to killing may not be in the best interest of either the individual being desensitized or of society in general.

3. The behavioral goal was chosen without the participation of the student whose behavior was being modified. The effects of the punishment used may be to reduce Jerry's hyperactivity, but it may also result in an aversion for learning.

Progress Check 6.3

1. c is the only fully complete and accurately stated target. Improvements in the other goals are needed as follows:

a. "better" needs to be defined; a definite criterion level should be established; also, is any special kind of reading matter important?

b. "quieter" should be behaviorally defined to make it possible to establish a criterion level.

d. This statement should be stated positively. The teacher would be wise to begin with a very small attainable mathematical goal in light of the student's lack of confidence in his mathematical talents.

e. This goal needs a great deal of work. Do the other students ignore this pupil or is it only his imagination? If he is ignored in reality, why? How can their behavior be modified? How can the behavior of this student be changed to accomplish his goal?

2. c. The sum of total papers is 70 which gives an average of 14 per day.

3. d.

4. b. (Begin using a positive reinforcement wherever possible.)

5. c.

6. d.

7. c.

CHAPTER 7

Progress Check 7.1

1. check (The English spoken in the home may be different in important ways from English expected to be used in school.)

2. no check (Many culturally different students are not disadvantaged.)

3. check (The choice of reinforcers must be adjusted to the individual.)

4. no check (Skinner believes that it is more important to study environmental influences which we can change more easily than genetic ones which are difficult to change.)

5. check (Socioeconomic status in itself does not seem to cause academic failure and many poor students achieve academically.)

6. no check (Behaviorists may believe that initial baselines of disadvantaged students must be taken more realistically into account by teachers but on the whole they reject the solution of lowering final criteria.)

Progress Check 7.2

1. learning disabled
2. retarded
3. gifted
4. retarded
5. gifted
6. learning disabled
7. emotionally disturbed
8. exceptional
9. gifted
10. retarded

Progress Check 7.3

1. no check; 2. check; 3. no check; 4. check.

Index